Lecture Notes in Computer Science   10397

Commenced Publication in 1973
Founding and Former Series Editors:
Gerhard Goos, Juris Hartmanis, and Jan van Leeuwen

More information about this series at http://www.springer.com/series/7407

Takashi Yoshino · Takaya Yuizono
Gustavo Zurita · Julita Vassileva (Eds.)

Collaboration Technologies and Social Computing

9th International Conference, CollabTech 2017
Saskatoon, SK, Canada, August 8–10, 2017
Proceedings

 Springer

Editors
Takashi Yoshino
Wakayama University
Wakayama
Japan

Takaya Yuizono
Japan Advanced Institute of Science
    and Technology
Ishikawa
Japan

Gustavo Zurita (iD)
University of Chile
Santiago
Chile

Julita Vassileva (iD)
University of Saskatchewan
Saskatoon, SK
Canada

ISSN 0302-9743   ISSN 1611-3349   (electronic)
Lecture Notes in Computer Science
ISBN 978-3-319-63087-8   ISBN 978-3-319-63088-5   (eBook)
DOI 10.1007/978-3-319-63088-5

Library of Congress Control Number: 2017946689

LNCS Sublibrary: SL1 – Theoretical Computer Science and General Issues

Printed on acid-free paper

This Springer imprint is published by Springer Nature
The registered company is Springer International Publishing AG
The registered company address is: Gewerbestrasse 11, 6330 Cham, Switzerland

Preface

Message from the General Chairs

CollabTech 2017, the 9th International Conference on Collaboration Technologies, offered a unique forum for academics and practitioners to present and discuss innovative ideas, methods, or implementations related to collaboration technologies, which are greatly needed for various everyday collaboration activities due to recent advances in networking, computing, and interaction technologies.

The previous CollabTech conferences were held in Tokyo in 2005, Tsukuba in 2006, Seoul in 2007, Wakayama in 2008, Sydney in 2009, Sapporo in 2012, Santiago in 2014, and Kanazawa in 2016. Following the success of the joint organization with CRIWG 2014 and CRIWG 2016, CollabTech 2017 was co-located and organized with CRIWG 2017 again, but this time in Saskatoon, Canada. The CRIWG and CollabTech communities had similar research topics and goals, but had been geographically located in different regions. We believed this joint endeavor would provide an interesting opportunity to meet each other.

The success of the conference was largely due to the program co-chairs, the conference committee members, and the reviewers, whose efforts made the conference possible. The success was also due to University of Saskatchewan, the Information Processing Society of Japan (IPSJ), the SIG on Groupware and Network Services of IPSJ, the SIG on Cyberspace of the Virtual Reality Society of Japan, and the SIG on Communication Enhancement of the Human Interface Society.

We are pleased that the conference was fruitful for all participants and played an important role in cultivating the community in this research field.

August 2017

Takaya Yuizono
Takashi Yoshino
Julita Vassileva

Message from the Program Chairs

After eight events in the International Conference on Collaboration Technologies series, we held the ninth edition (CollabTech 2017) in Saskatoon, Canada. The following topics on collaboration technologies were discussed:

- Cross-Cultural Collaboration
- Everyday Computing
- Learning Support System
- Remote Collaboration
- Security, Rescue and Disaster Support
- Social Networking

For this conference, we received 37 submissions (26 full papers, 11 work-in-progress papers) and assigned three reviewers per full paper or two reviewers per work-in-progress paper. As a result, we had ten full papers and six work-in-progress papers. The acceptance rate was 43%. Because of the high quality of the submissions, many excellent papers were not among those accepted. We hope that the detailed technical review comments we provided are helpful.

Without our distinguished Program Committee members, we could not have maintained our high standards. We truly appreciate their devotion. Finally, we hope that these proceedings serve as a reference for future researchers in this rapidly evolving field.

August 2017

Takashi Yoshino
Takaya Yuizono
Gustavo Zurita

Organization

Conference Co-chairs

Takaya Yuizono   Japan Advanced Institute of Science and Technology, Japan
Takashi Yoshino   Wakayama University, Japan
Julita Vassileva   University of Saskatchewan, Canada

Program Co-chairs

Takashi Yoshino   Wakayama University, Japan
Takaya Yuizono   Japan Advanced Institute of Science and Technology, Japan
Gustavo Zurita   Universidad de Chile, Chile

Publication Chair

Junko Ichino   Kagawa University, Japan

IPSJ SIG GN Liaison

Satoshi Ichimura   Otsuma Women's University, Japan

VRSJ SIG CS Liaison

Kazuyuki Iso   NTT, Japan

HIS SIG CE Liaison

Takashi Yoshino   Wakayama University, Japan

Steering Committee

Hideaki Kuzuoka   University of Tsukuba, Japan
Ken-ichi Okada   Keio University, Japan
Jun Munemori   Wakayama University, Japan
Minoru Kobayashi   Meiji University, Japan
Hiroaki Ogata   Kyoto University, Japan
Tomoo Inoue   University of Tsukuba, Japan

Program Committee

Nelson Baloian   Universidad de Chile, Chile
Gwo-Dong Chen   National Central University, Taiwan

Hui-Chun Chu	Soochow University, Taiwan
Hironori Egi	University of Electro-Communications, Japan
Kinya Fujita	Tokyo University of Agriculture and Technology, Japan
Atsuo Hazeyama	Tokyo Gakugei Unversity, Japan
Gwo-Jen Hwang	National Taiwan University of Science and Technology, Taiwan
Satoshi Ichimura	Otsuma Women's University, Japan
Yutaka Ishii	Okayama Prefectural University, Japan
Marc Jansen	University of Applied Sciences Ruhr West, Germany
Jongwon Kim	Gwangju Institute of Science and Technology, Korea
Hyungseok Kim	Konkuk University, Korea
Wim Lamotte	Hasselt University, Belgium
Wolfram Luther	University of Duisburg-Essen, Germany
Hideyuki Nakanishi	Osaka University, Japan
Mamoun Nawahdah	Birzeit University, Palestine
Masayuki Okamoto	Toshiba, Japan
Nobuchika Sakata	Osaka University, Japan
Yoshiaki Seki	Tokyo City University, Japan
Hidekazu Shiozawa	Tamagawa University, Japan
Masahiro Takatsuka	The University of Sydney, Australia

Contents

Anonymity-Preserving Methods for Client-Side Filtering in Position-Based Collaboration Approaches

Henrik Detjen, Stefan Hoffmann$^{(\boxtimes)}$, Gerd Bumiller, Stefan Geisler,
Marc Jansen, and Markus Markard

Computer Science Institute, University of Applied Sciences Ruhr West, Bottrop, Germany
{henrik.detjen,stefan.hoffmann,gerd.bumiller,stefan.geisler,
marc.jansen,markus.markard}@hs-ruhrwest.de

Abstract. This paper describes and evaluates three methods for anonymizing location data in the context of an example of practical relevance. These anonymization methods are designed for a smartphone-based system to integrate voluntary helpers into professional rescue processes, especially in case of time-critical medical emergencies, but can also be used for other collaboration approaches. We analyze the methods with a focus on anonymity of the operation site, precision and filtering.

Keywords: Localization · Anonymity · Privacy · Mobile service

1 Introduction

Let us consider a collaboration scenario where volunteers are integrated into professional rescue processes. For example, in case of a strong or complete capacity utilization of the professional resources due to a large-scale incident at one place, it is possible that a medical emergency that occurs at another place cannot be handled in time.

To acquire and integrate such human resources into professional rescue processes is a main goal of the research project "Automated Allocation of Volunteers in Major Disasters" (German: "Automatisiertes Helferangebot bei Großschadenslagen", abbr.: AHA) [1]. A partial goal is the development of a system that allows for imposing the dynamic states of the voluntary helpers and providing it as additional resources to the dispatchers in the control center. The helpers will be able to install a mobile application on their smartphones, which they can use for configuring their willingness to help, and which will determine the position of the helper before and during an emergency.

In case of a medical emergency, every second might be important to save a life. It is the target of the system not only to find a helper with the required qualification, but also the one which can reach the operation site first. Thus, the spatial distance between operation and person is the first quality criterion and the system has to determine the positions of the potential helpers as fast as possible. Persons who are out of reach should not be considered for help. A security requirement of the system is to keep all sensitive data which is sent during the filtering process private. Sensitive data is not only the name of a victim, but also the operation's location. In many cases, the victim's identity can be deviated from the address and vice versa.

© Springer International Publishing AG 2017
T. Yoshino et al. (Eds.): CollabTech 2017, LNCS 10397, pp. 1–13, 2017.
DOI: 10.1007/978-3-319-63088-5_1

There are basically two ways to filter persons who are in reach for an emergency. The first way is a server-side filtering: The server sends a signal to all users and every user responds with its current position. Next, the server checks which of the received positions lay within a desired area around the operations' location.

The second way is a client-side filtering: The server sends a signal containing the operations' location with an area around it to all users, then the client compares its position to the transmitted one and sends it back only if it is in the desired area.

Both approaches have advantages and disadvantages. If the filtering process is on server-side, the operation's location does not need to be sent to the clients. Therefore, sensitive information of the operation site is protected. But filtering individuals' positions on server-side can become inefficient very fast: as the number of users in the system grows, the amount of position data, which is sent back to the server, also increases at once. This leads to a higher CPU load and potentially slower processing. This is a considerable problem, especially for time-critical processes. Furthermore, if the individuals' positions are sent to the server before a potential operation occurs, privacy protection requirements demand that the locations are anonymized before they are sent from the mobile device.

The client-side filtering is more scalable with the user base, but clearly contradicts the security goal of keeping sensitive data private, given that the position of an operation must be sent to the client for comparison with his own location. Protecting the channel with cryptographic protocols (like TLS) is mandatory but not sufficient for privacy protection in this approach, e.g., a malicious party could have access to the helper's smartphone and read out the sensitive data on the application layer (i.e. from the RAM).

This paper examines methods to deal with this specific problem of client-side filtering by applying privacy-enhancing concepts to the transmitted location. A solution can be abstracted and used in various other position-based filtering contexts.

The paper is organized as follows: After this introduction, Sect. 2 provides an overview on the related work and examines existing anonymity measures, which are suitable for our problem. It also analyses the population distribution properties of a city with mostly urban but also some rural areas. In Sects. 3 and 4, we discuss and evaluate different methods for anonymization that are reasonable for the described scenario. Section 5 provides a summary and an outlook on future work.

2 Spatial Anonymity

Without anonymizing, location data potentially discloses the identity of a certain group (e.g. the families that live in a multi-apartment building) or even of a single person. To avoid this, a position must be transformed in a way that it is indistinguishable from the locations of a certain amount of people. There are several methods to perform such a transformation. The commonality of most of the methods is that locations, which are described by points in coordinate systems, are transformed to areas of a certain size. The size of the area is chosen in a way that a certain number of other individuals are located within the area. In our scenario, however, we only know one position at a time, but we do not know dynamic location data of any other individual at each point in time. To approximate the number of people that stays in a certain area, we use the static population data of a city. In this section, we select a measure for the spatial anonymity, respectively the degree of anonymization, by using population density. Then, we will apply this measure to our spatial-anonymity problem with real data to benchmark the later developed concepts.

2.1 Measuring Spatial Anonymity

In [2] by Sweeney, k-anonymity was published as a framework to anonymize databases in a way that each dataset can be allocated to at least k individuals, even when using external databases for re-identification. Sweeney considered an example of medical data that was published for research purposes, without containing names and addresses. Sweeney successfully linked this database to a publicly available voter list by using the intersecting attributes ZIP code, birthdate and gender. By this means, medical data like diagnosis and procedures could be explicitly linked to individuals.

The k-anonymity framework was further improved in [3, 4]. Another approach is *differential privacy* [5] which ensures that changing a database by adding or deleting datasets has no significant influence on a database request result [6].

In [7], a notion called *location k-anonymity* was introduced. An individual's location is called k-anonymous, if it is indistinguishable from the locations of k - 1 other individuals. Formally, the spatial anonymity can be described as follows [8]: A location-time tuple $([x_1, x_2], [y_1, y_2], [t_1, t_2])$, where $[x_1, x_2]$ and $[y_1, y_2]$ describe a two-dimensional area and $[t_1, t_2]$ a period, is k-anonymous for a subject, when it also describes k - 1 other subjects in the same period and area. The greater k is, the greater is the degree of anonymization. In a database, a typical way to achieve anonymization is to replace exact locations with areas of a size that is large enough to include the locations of $k - 1$ other individuals.

The scenario described in this paper is different; our goal is not to anonymize databases of positions. Instead, we must anonymize a single position of a single individual at one time. It is obviously not possible to make a single dataset indistinguishable from k - 1 others. To evaluate the degree of anonymity, we have to use a different measure. In our case of an individual at one spot it is reasonable to consider the number of people that is currently staying within a certain area around the position that we want to anonymize. The greater the amount of people, the greater is the value k. The greater k is, the larger an area theoretically has to be. To have a real foundation to estimate k for this reference area, we use the static population density of the city where our scenario is located. We describe and evaluate methods to perform anonymization for the described scenario.

2.2 Spatial Anonymity of a City

We examine a real-world population distribution for our approach to estimate the potential spatial anonymity. Hence, we use the population distribution of Dortmund with an overall area of 280,4 km^2, where our approach will be tested later, as an example and set the measure of location k-anonymity in relation to the data collected in the 2011

European Union census [9]. Because there is no dynamic population data, the time aspect of the measure cannot be considered in the following.

First, the minimal area that is needed to cover an amount of k people is analyzed. The given census data provides a grid map (100 m x 100 m squares) with the population count for each of them (see Fig. 1).

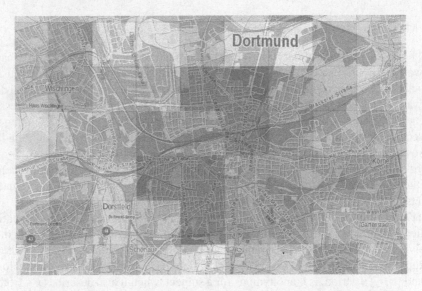

Fig. 1. Grid layout of the census data (darker means higher population density)

To examine the degree k of anonymity over the map, we iterate from grid center to grid center. From each grid center, we increase the area until the target amount of k is reached. This procedure is repeated for different values of k and provides a distribution of minimal areas to reach a certain anonymity. We assume a uniform distribution of people within each grid and a uniform distribution of buildings (addresses) they live in, which can be true in a best case scenario. But we keep the following problem in mind: In a worst-case scenario, all subjects within a grid could share one address (i.e. skyscraper), which would result in high k for a small radius and the operation site would be revealed with a very high probability through the address (at the skyscraper). Even if it is not possible to derivate the victim directly from the address, the address is still sensitive data, because a possible threat is e.g. that a reporter might be at the operation's site before the professional forces arrive. Therefore, for an improvement of our uniform-distribution-assumption, a map of buildings with corresponding residents would be necessary.

Figure 2 shows the cumulative distribution function of the minimal area to cover k people with $k = 10$, $k = 50$, $k = 100$, $k = 500$ and $k = 1000$.

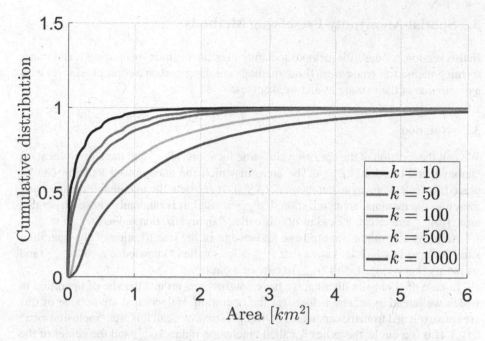

Fig. 2. Cumulative distribution function of the minimal anonymization area

The result tells us for example that in more than 50% of all locations in the city an area of 1 km² leads to a covered number of at least 1000 persons. To cover $k = 100$, an anonymization area of around 5 km² (a circle with radius $r = 1280$ m) is sufficient in all cases. For the same k, $A = 0.2$ km² ($r = 250$ m) reaches the anonymity target in 55% of all cases, while $A = 1.77$ km² ($r = 750$ m) covers it in 94% of all cases. Table 1 summarizes the coverage ratios (percentage of iterated locations) for different radiuses and different values for k.

Table 1. Coverage of k-values

	$k = 10$	$k = 20$	$k = 50$	$k = 100$	$k = 200$	$k = 500$	$k = 1000$
$r = 50$ m	31.7	26.9	14.1	4.4	0.7	0	0
$r = 100$ m	52	46.1	37.1	27.6	13	1.6	0
$r = 200$ m	72.5	66.5	57.9	50.4	41.5	23.8	6.5
$r = 300$ m	85.6	80.6	72.7	65.7	57.8	43.1	26.6
$r = 500$ m	96.9	95.2	90.9	86.4	80.7	69.4	56.1
$r = 750$ m	99.7	99.3	98.4	96.8	94.6	89.3	81.3
$r = 1000$ m	100	100	99.9	99.6	98.9	97.6	93.5
$r = 1250$ m	100	100	100	100	99.7	99.1	98.2
$r = 1500$ m	100	100	100	100	100	99.7	99.2

3   Spatial-Anonymity-Preserving Methods

In this section, we describe methods to anonymize the position by blurring it and transforming them to a certain area. Those methods are described on a conceptual level with a discussion of their strengths and weaknesses.

3.1   Notation

We call the location of the operation site "true location" (P_{true}) and the blurred location "anonymized location" (P_{anon}). The area, in which the anonymized location can be placed, is called "anonymization area" (A_{anon}). It restricts the maximal blurriness and therefore the maximal anonymization. If P_{anon} is used, it is randomly chosen from this area. If A_{anon} is a circle, the radius of it is called "anonymization radius" (r_{anon}).

An adversary might want to have knowledge of the true location of the operation site. The area in which he knows that P_{true} is in is called "knowledge area" A_{know} (and its radius "knowledge radius" r_{know} in case of a circle).

In case of client-site filtering, we have another area around the site of operation in which we intend to acquire helpers for the operation. Helpers that are outside of this area are excluded from the candidates of the operation. We call this area "inclusion area" (A_{inc}). If it is a circle, the radius is called "inclusion radius" (r_{inc}) and the center of the inclusion area is (usually) the true location. Furthermore, we use N to describe the set of people covered by a certain area A.

The consequence of anonymizing the position is a certain loss of information. The true location of the operation site is not known to the mobile app; therefore we need to consider a larger area than the inclusion area when sending a blurred position to acquire all helpers from the actual inclusion area. We call this area "extended inclusion area" ($A_{inc-ext}$) and the difference between inclusion area and extended inclusion area is the "overhead" area A_{over} with $A_{over} = A_{inc-ext} - A_{inc}$ (see Fig. 3).

This method guarantees that no relevant helpers get lost as candidates for the operation. The drawback however is that the server also receives answers from helpers that are in the extended inclusion area but not in the (actual) inclusion area. The server must filter out those helper profiles.

3.2   Anonymization Methods

An established method to blur the position is based on using randomness. In our approach, we choose P_{anon} uniformly random from the area A_{anon} which is described by the radius r_{anon}. The coordinates of P_{anon} and the radius r_{anon} are sent to the mobile apps of the helpers. In this approach, the center of the knowledge area is P_{anon}, and $r_{anon} = r_{know}$. The extended inclusion area $A_{inc-ext}$ is a circle with the center P_{anon} and the radius $r_{inc-ext} = r_{anon} + r_{inc}$.

The anonymization area must be defined in a way that in all situations the area covers the desired amount of k people. The choice of the size of A_{anon} can happen by different means, from which we describe three in the following.

P_{true} = true position
P_{anon} = anonymized position
r_{anon} = anonymization radius
r_{inc} = inclusion radius
$r_{inc\text{-}ext}$ = extended inclusion radius
A_{anon} = anonymization area
A_{inc} = inclusion area
$A_{inc\text{-}ext}$ = extended inclusion area
A_{know} = knowledge area

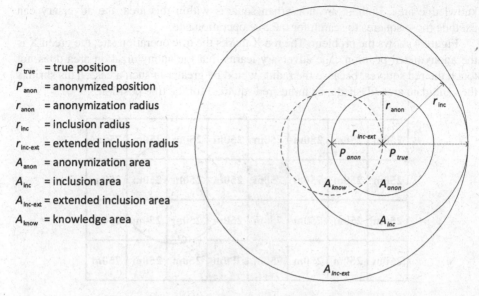

Fig. 3. Notation overview

Method 1: constant anonymization area

The first method always uses a constant r_{anon}, no matter where the operation site is located. To guarantee anonymity, we need to take the radius that guarantees the desired value k for all locations. For $k = 100$, a radius of 1280 m (see Sect. 2.2, Spatial Anonymity of a City) provides sufficient anonymity in all possible locations, so a radius $r_{anon} = 1280$ m should be chosen.

The value of r_{anon} is determined by the most sparsely populated region in the city and thus is unnecessarily large in urban regions like the city center. The amount k is overfilled there, which is a drawback of this approach.

Method 2: adaptive anonymization area

To further optimize the needed radius, an alternative method is to adaptively choose the anonymization area dependent from the population density at the actual operation site's location. We define three different radius classes *urban*, *suburban*, and *rural*. For $k = 100$, the rural anonymization radius should be $r_{anon} = 1280$ m, because it covers 100 people at every place all over the city, it is equivalent to the constant anonymization area. From Sect. 2.2, we know that $r = 250$ m covers $k = 100$ in (more than) 50% of all cases, so $r_{anon} = 250$ m is a reasonable value for the urban radius. The threshold of 95% for example could provide a value for the suburban radius, namely $r_{anon} = 750$ m.

This approach has still a security lack. Let us consider the following example: The operation site is in an "urban" 100 m-square, the radius hence is $r = 250$ m. All squares touched by the circle with radius of 250 m are also classified as urban, so the final anonymization radius is 250 m. Assume that the randomly chosen pseudo position is on the border of this circle. An adversary knows that the operation site must be within the knowledge area. If there are non-urban squares within this area, the adversary can exclude those squares to search for the true operation site.

Figure 4 shows the problem. The red X marks the true operation site, the green X is the anonymized position. The adversary learns that the anonymization area does not touch the red squares, because the radius would be greater in such a case. This shrinks the candidate area (dashed area minus red squares) for the true position.

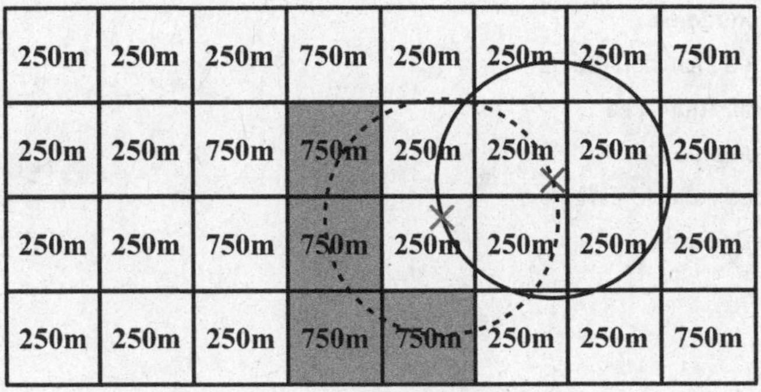

250m	250m	250m	750m	250m	250m	250m	750m
250m	250m	750m	750m	250m	250m	250m	250m
250m	250m	750m	750m	250m	250m	250m	250m
250m	250m	250m	750m	750m	250m	250m	750m

Fig. 4. Adaptive approach with different radius class for each of the squares (Color figure online)

We solve this problem by the following means. After choosing the final anonymization radius, we check if there are differently classified squares that are located within a circle with *twice* the anonymization radius. The population number of those squares is subtracted from the total population number covered by the circle. If the resulting number is still greater than k, the anonymization radius can be used. If not, the next higher radius class is used.

Method 3: minimal radiuses
The basic idea of this approach is to construct a pre-computed map with areas such that each area covers at least k individuals. Beforehand, we overlay the map with a fixed-distance grid (e.g. the census map). Every intersection point in the grid represents a center of a circle. In the first step, the radius of each circle is computed as the minimal radius such that the circle area covers at least k people. Step one of creating the map is described in Fig. 5, where the numbers represent the population in each grid.

It must be assured that each point in the map is covered by at least one circle. I the second step, we iterate over all squares that are not completely covered and increase the radiuses of the square's corner until the area is fully covered. This finishes the map computation.

When an operation occurs, the identifier of the circle that covers the operation site location is published. If the operation site is covered by more than one circle (overlapping), the published circle is chosen uniformly random from the set of available circles. Always choosing the e.g. smallest circle would lead to a security problem similar to the one described for method 2.

The pre-computed map can be represented (and thus stored) by a table with the columns "identifier", "latitude", "longitude" and "radius", sorted by latitude and

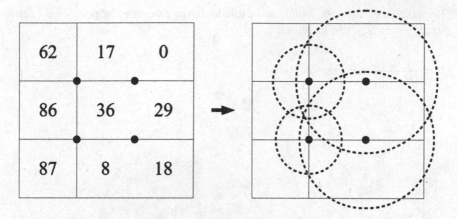

Fig. 5. Static map with circle areas that include exactly 100 individuals

longitude. Each table entry represents a grid intersection anonymization area. To anonymize a location, the anonymization areas with the closest four corner midpoints can be easily tested for their coverage of the location. The identifier is published instead of the location.

4   Evaluation

In this chapter, we compare the different approaches. Therefore, we define measures to benchmark them and show their strengths and weaknesses in a brief overview table.

4.1   Evaluation Measures

To rate the filtering ratio F of an approach, we divide the number of helpers in the extended inclusion area by the total number of helpers in Dortmund $\left| N_{city} \right|$ and, to have a more intuitive measure, invert the scale by subtracting the ratio from 1.

$$F = 1 - \frac{\left| N_{inc-ext} \right|}{\left| N_{city} \right|}$$

To rate the precision of an approach, we compare the population N_{inc} covered by the inclusion area with the coverage $N_{inc-ext}$ of the extended inclusion area. For simplicity, we assume that the helper distribution corresponds to the overall population distribution by a constant factor. The precision P, which is known from the context of information retrieval, is calculated as follows.

$$P = \frac{\left| N_{inc} \cap N_{inc-ext} \right|}{\left| N_{inc-ext} \right|}$$

Because we do not want to exclude any relevant helpers, we define $N_{inc} \cap N_{inc-ext} = N_{inc}$, and therefore:

$$P = \frac{|N_{inc}|}{|N_{inc-ext}|} \text{ (see Fig. 6),}$$

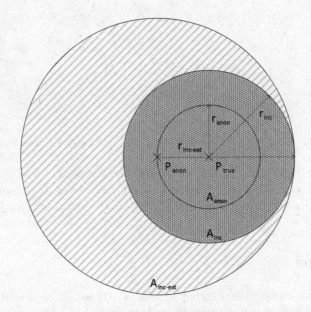

Fig. 6. Precision: Inclusion area in relation to the extended inclusion area. Hatched: the overhead of the extended inclusion area.

Through the constraint of keeping all relevant helpers in $A_{inc-ext}$, we have a correlation between the two measures. The filtering ratio shows how strong a method relieves the server from potential responses or the other way around: how much computational work is done on the client-side. The precision on the other hand, shows how many of these responses are relevant (efficiency). A good precision means that less of the remaining responses have to be filtered out on server-side (optimal: 0 at $P = 1$, $F \rightarrow 1$).

We clearly have a trade-off between the precision and the strength of the anonymization of the operation site. The smaller the anonymization area, the higher is the precision, but the weaker is the privacy protection, and vice versa. The maximum reasonable anonymization area (through maximal blur factor) is the total area of the city, in which the system is used. In this case, we have the strongest anonymization, but no filtering advantage at all. The other extremum, in case that the anonymization area is 0 (no blur factor), we will have several cases of $k = 1$ (in case of people living alone in a building), and thus proper anonymity is not achieved. The goal must always be to maximize the filter ratio in a way that in all cases sufficient anonymity is guaranteed. In the context of information retrieval, in addition to the precision we have the attribute "recall". In our scenario, the value of recall is always 1, because we want to avoid that any relevant helper is filtered out from the operation. If we would relax this condition and decrease the recall value, it would be possible to increase the precision value while keeping the degree of anonymity constant.

Single operation site anonymizations can be evaluated by using both described measures P and F. To evaluate a complete anonymization method, we need to compute the average values of both measures. Therefore, we generated many random operation site locations and calculated their measures. We assume that operations are not uniformly distributed over the city, and thus, we generate more operations in areas with higher population density. We know that the operation site density does not exactly correlate to the population density, as one expects a slightly higher amount of operation e.g. in industrial areas or on highways. To cover this expectation, we use a distribution weighted by the population density with an additional uniform offset. This offset causes random operations even in sparsely populated areas.

As constants over all methods we choose an anonymity target of $k = 100$ and an inclusion area of $A_{inc} = 0.79\,\text{km}^2$ ($r_{inc} = 500\,\text{m}$). The inclusion radius is motivated by the distance that a helper can cover by foot in a few minutes.

4.2 Comparison of the Approaches

Based on the European census [9], Dortmund has 586.181 inhabitants in 2015. If we assume that 1% of them participate in our system, the estimated number of helpers is around 6000. For each for the following methods, we use this as a reference to compute numerical benchmarks. To determine average values for each method, we iterate over all grids of the map and compute the numbers for each grid, weighted by the number of people living in each grid. Thus we implicitly assume that more operations occur in areas with a higher density.

Method 1: non-deterministic with constant radius
We use the same (large) anonymization area all over the city, namely $A_{anon} \approx 5\,\text{km}^2$, which corresponds to a radius $r_{anon} = 1280\,\text{m}$. The extended inclusion radius thus is $r_{inc-ext} = (1280\,\text{m} + 500\,\text{m}) = 1780\,\text{m}$, which leads to a static extended inclusion area of $A_{inc-ext} = 10\,\text{km}^2$. We obtain an average filter ratio of $F = 94.8\%$ (313 responses instead of 6000) and an average precision of $P = 17.8\%$ (from 313 responses, 55 are relevant).

Method 2: non-deterministic with adaptive radius
This approach uses three different anonymization radiuses. In our simulation, the smallest radius of $r_{anon} = 250\,\text{m}$ occurred in 67.5% of all cases. $r_{anon} = 750\,\text{m}$ was necessary in 29.4% cases. In the remaining cases, $r_{anon} = 1280\,\text{m}$ was used. This leads to an average filter ratio of $F = 97.6\%$ (144 responses instead of 6000) and an average precision of $P = 40.4\%$ (from 144 responses, 58 are relevant).

Method 3: deterministic with precomputed map
This approach uses an individual anonymization area for each point of the census grid. The computed average filter ratio is $F = 98.9\%$ (68 responses instead of 6000). The precision is $P = 74.6\%$ (from 68 responses, 51 are relevant).

Comparison

For a better overview, the approaches are listed in Table 2 with their individual strengths and weaknesses, as well as their benchmarks. Method 1 already provides a strong filtering; Method 2 and 3 even optimize the filtering at the price of a more complex implementation. For all three approaches, the filtering means a huge benefit for the computational work on server-side.

Table 2. Different anonymization approaches

Approach	Pro	Contra	Precision	Filtering
(1) Constant anonymization area	Very simple	Low precision	17.4%	94.8%
(2) Adaptive anonymization area	High precision	Complex implementation	40.4%	97.6%
(3) Minimal radius	Higher precision	More complex implementation	74.6%	98.9%

Simulating the case of using no filtering at all yields a precision of $P = 0.9\%$ with a filtering ratio of $F = 0$.

5 Conclusion

We have seen that spatial k-anonymity is a sufficient measure for our scenario: The higher we choose our k, the higher is our anonymization of the operation site. However, in a city, there is no uniform distribution of citizens. This aspect has been considered in our approach. For different values of k, the radius of the area needed to cover that amount was computed. Next, we added a blur factor to the position of the operations, which lead to an extended acquiring radius. In other words: there is a trade-off between security and filter benefit.

We evaluated three methods to anonymize single positions for a privacy-protected client-site filtering approach. All three methods guarantee that a pre-defined anonymization target is reached in all cases. In terms of precision, we observed that method 3 (deterministic) delivers the highest precision and the best filtering ratio. A drawback is a rather complex implementation. A pre-computed map must be delivered to the client device, on base of which the client must decide in which area it is located in. In terms of complexity, the best approach is method 1. In this approach, a position must be chosen uniformly from an area that is based on a fixed radius around the client position. Although the precision is low, the filtering ratio of 94.8% tells us that this approach still has a strong advantage in comparison to a method where no client-site filtering is performed at all.

We achieve the goals in context of our scenario by using the constant anonymization area approach: First, because it provides sufficient anonymity in all cases. Second, the filtering ratio is high enough and thus improves the communication between volunteers and professional helpers by guaranteeing the minimal system processing time in our time critical scenario.

References

1. Detjen, H., Hoffmann, S., Rösner, L., Winter, S., Geisler, S., Krämer, N., Bumiller, G.: Integrating volunteers into rescue processes: analysis of user requirements and mobile app conception. Int. J. Inf. Syst. Crisis Response Manag. 7, 1–18 (2015)
2. Sweeney, L.: K-anonymity: a model for protecting privacy. Int. J. Uncertainty Fuzziness Knowl. Based Syst. 10, 557–570 (2002)
3. Machanavajjhala, A., Kifer, D., Gehrke, J., Venkitasubramaniam, M.: L-diversity: privacy beyond K-anonymity. ACM Trans. Knowl. Discov. Data 1, 3 (2007)
4. Li, N., Li, T., Venkatasubramanian, S.: t-Closeness: privacy beyond k-anonymity and l-diversity. In: 2007 IEEE 23rd International Conference on Data Engineering (2007)
5. Dwork, C.: Differential privacy. In: Bugliesi, M., Preneel, B., Sassone, V., Wegener, I. (eds.) ICALP 2006. LNCS, vol. 4052, pp. 1–12. Springer, Heidelberg (2006). doi: 10.1007/11787006_1
6. Vagts, H.-H.: Privatheit und Datenschutz in der intelligenten Überwachung. KIT Scientific Publishing, Karlsruhe (2013)
7. Gruteser, M., Grunwald, D.: Anonymous Usage of Location-Based Services Through Spatial and Temporal Cloaking. In: Proceedings of the 1st International Conference on Mobile Systems, Applications and Services, San Francisco, California (2003)
8. Masoumzadeh, A., Joshi, J., Karimi, H.A.: LBS (K, T)-anonymity: a spatio-temporal approach to anonymity for location-based service users. In: Proceedings of the 17th ACM SIGSPATIAL International Conference on Advances in Geographic Information Systems, Seattle, Washington (2009)
9. European Commission, "europa.eu". http://ec.europa.eu/eurostat/de/web/population-and-housing-census/census-data/2011-census. Accessed May 10 2016
10. Kim, J.: A method for limiting disclosure in microdata based on random noise and transformation. In: Proceedings of the Section on Survey Research Methods of the American (1986)

What Do Remote Music Performances Lack?

Hiroyuki Tarumi[✉] [iD], Tomoki Nakai, Kei Miyazaki,
Daiki Yamashita, and Yuya Takasaki

Kagawa University, Takamatsu, Kagawa, Japan
tarumi@eng.kagawa-u.ac.jp

Abstract. Our research interest is in supporting live music performances for remote audiences. Using the Evaluation Grid Method (EGM), we have analyzed why music audiences prefer live shows to recorded media and have found that a sense of unity is one of the important factors. It can be at least partly reproduced at the remote site by sharing information on audiences' reactions.

Keywords: Evaluation grid method · Internet streaming · Live music performance · Nonverbal communication · Entertainment · Remote interaction

1 Introduction

Live music performances can be considered as a kind of social interaction. Performers (musicians) play their music tunes and audiences respond to the music. Especially, in cases of rock and popular music performances, audiences often move their hands, sing, or clap. These responses are considered to be nonverbal communication between the audience and musicians. Hence, we are interested in live music performances as a field of social communication.

With the background of CSCW, it is interesting to design a remote communication environment that is similar to a local communication field. In the case of live music, using an internet streaming service is a simple solution to watch and listen to the performance remotely. However, it is obviously impossible for remote audiences to send responses back to musicians through this simple design. We have been trying to solve this problem [1, 2]. In these studies, we have designed and implemented a system that enabled remote audiences to send their reactions to musicians (e.g., waving a hand, pushing up a fist, or rhythmically shaking a hand) by showing them animations of hand avatars. However, we did not provide enough reasons to show that this design helped remote audiences enjoy the live performance.

When we design such kinds of remote communication systems, we should analyze the essential aspects of communication because remote communication always suffers from the limit of bandwidth. Especially in the case of our research domain, multi-point communication with many audiences should be supposed so that the limit of bandwidth would be more severe. As a result, we should select some essential elements of communication to be exchanged between the both ends of communication, and discard other aspects to save the bandwidth resource.

© Springer International Publishing AG 2017
T. Yoshino et al. (Eds.): CollabTech 2017, LNCS 10397, pp. 14–21, 2017.
DOI: 10.1007/978-3-319-63088-5_2

We then have an important but simple question: What are the essential communication elements in cases of live music performances for remote audiences? To find the answer, we raised another question: Why do people prefer joining live music performances to watching them remotely or watching a recorded video?

In this paper, we will describe our analysis of this issue. We have adopted the Evaluation Grid Method (EGM) for the analysis. We will also discuss the results of analysis to design appropriate functions that can be supported by remote watching systems for live music performances.

We have also focused on the key idea of a "sense of unity." The *sense of unity* (in Japanese, *ittaikan*) is a kind of buzzword often used by both musicians and audiences to represent good experiences in live music performances. However, it is not clear in what aspects of their experiences they felt this sense of unity. We used EGM to analyze the sense of unity as well. The result will help us design what we can call *a remote sense of unity* and enable us to support it with relevant technology.

2 Evaluation Grid Method

EGM is a semi-structured interview method [3, 4]. Through this method, an interviewer recurrently asks a participant, why one thing (called *element*) is more preferable than others. By repeating this question, each participant's requirements are elicited structurally with explicit descriptions of reasons. By integrating each participant's requirement structure, an extensive structure of the requirements of the group of participants is produced.

EGM consists of the following steps:

(Step 1) An interviewer prepares a set of *elements*. An element is an object to be analyzed and compared with other elements. Usually a card with a picture or an illustration of the object is used as an icon of the element.

(Step 2) The interviewer shows the set of elements to a participant. The participant is then asked to sort the elements in the order of his/her preference.

(Step 3) The interviewer asks the participant to provide a reason as to why one element is preferable to others. The described reason is recorded as an *evaluation item*.

(Step 4) The elicited evaluation items are further analyzed by *laddering*. Laddering is performed by recurrent questions from the interviewer to the participant. Two kinds of laddering are performed: *laddering up* and *laddering down*.

The process of *laddering up* is performed by recurrent questions of "why do you think it is preferable?" This kind of questioning helps the interviewer discover more abstract reasons for the preference.

On the other hand, the process of *laddering down* is performed by recurrent questions of "can you give any concrete conditions to realize the preference?" This way, the interviewer will discover more physical or quantitative requirements.

The final output is an (or a set of) integrated graph structure(s) of evaluation items with arcs that represent laddering. We call the obtained graph an *evaluation structure*.

These steps are shown in Fig. 1.

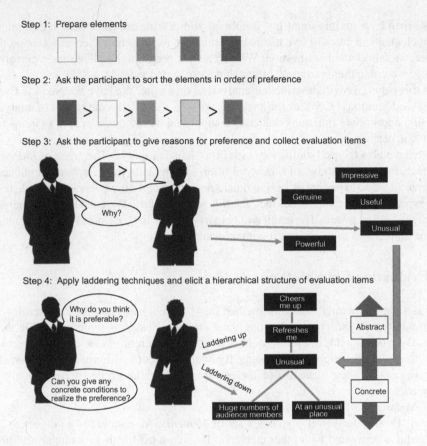

Fig. 1. The process of EGM

3 Survey

3.1 Outline

We conducted a survey using EGM from December 2016 to March 2017. We recruited 14 participants between the ages of 19 and 23. Two of them were females; the rest were males.[1] Four of the participants were student band members. Before the interview, we confirmed that all participants had had several experiences and strong interest in live shows of rock and popular music. Participants were paid for their time and cooperation. We took approximately one hour for the EGM interview of each participant.

We prepared five *elements* to compare different listening-to-music situations: (1) outdoor live festivals, (2) live shows in concert halls, (3) live shows in live houses, (4) recorded DVDs or Blu-ray Disks (BD), and (5) recorded CDs or downloaded audio files without motion pictures. Watching live shows using internet streaming

---

[1] We did not find any gender differences in their evaluation, at least in this group of participants.

services was not included as an *element*, because few participants had such experiences. However, watching music performances on one-way internet streaming services can be regarded as the same kind of experience as watching recorded music videos.

The survey was basically conducted in the standard EGM method (Fig. 1). However, because our research interest had a special focus on the *sense of unity*, we inserted an additional step to include the phrase "sense of unity" to the evaluation items elucidated in step 3. The inserted step was as follows:

(Step 3 +) If the phrase "sense of unity" was not included in the evaluation items, we asked the participant, "Did you have any experiences that made you feel a sense of unity during live shows?" If the answer was "yes," we further asked him/her, "Do you think that the sense of unity is one of the good reasons why you prefer live shows?" If the answer was "yes" again, we appended the phrase "sense of unity" to the list of evaluation items.

Our research interest is in supporting remote communication *during* music performances. However, collected evaluation items often included something the participants felt or experienced when music was not playing. For example, they felt something when musicians spoke, or before or after the shows. In some cases we did not apply the laddering technique to such kinds of evaluation items at step 4.

3.2 Result

Evaluation structures for the preference of live shows

We have integrated the common evaluation structures of evaluation items for three types of live shows: outdoor festivals, concert halls, and live houses (Fig. 2). The below diagram represents the value of live shows as compared with recorded music (DVDs, BDs, CDs, or audio files). In other words, it enumerates the reasons why people go to live music shows instead of listening to recorded music.

By analyzing the diagram, we suggest that the following key values are found in live show experiences.

Unusual experiences. Being at the same place as popular music players is an unusual experience in itself. Directly listening to live music with powerful sound is also an important aspect of *unusualness*.

Sense of unity. Two "senses of unity" are found: with musicians and with other audiences. A *sense of unity with musicians* is aroused by responses from musicians when audiences take reactions during the music. A s*ense of unity with other audiences* is aroused by taking reactions, cheering, or shouting with other audiences. These experiences also arouse so-called *fellow feelings* with others. With both senses of unity, audiences feel excitement owing to the synergic effect with other people's excitement.

Viewpoint. Audiences at live shows can look anywhere they want; they can watch particular musicians, see the instruments used, or observe other audiences.

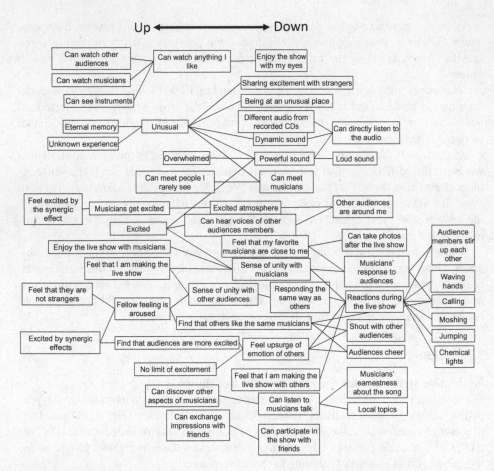

Fig. 2. Common evaluation structure for live music shows (translated from participants' casual representation in Japanese)

Tired feeling. By taking reactions, shouting, or dancing, audiences are physically tired. They feel a sense of fulfillment with this tired feeling.

Evaluation structures for three types of live shows

We drew diagrams for three evaluation structures for each type of live music performance: outdoor festivals, concert halls, and live houses. The analyzed values of each type of live shows are described below. Owing to the lack of space, diagrams have been omitted from this paper.

Outdoor live festivals. Outdoor live festivals are often held in the summer season, at places far from metropolitan areas. Many groups of musicians usually appear on the stage one by one. Survey participants enjoy outdoor festivals because they share the feeling of excitement with *huge* numbers of audience members. Some of them often swarm the stage. By watching them, audiences feel a kind of *unusualness*.

Listening to music under the sky in an open space is another example of *unusualness*.

Concert halls. In the case of concert halls, *stage effects* are highly valued. For example, audiences become overwhelmed with elevating stages, wire work, and lighting effects. These effects also arouse the sense of *unusualness*.

As with outdoor live festivals, huge numbers of audience members have been mentioned as the value of experiences at concert halls. Some participants highly valued their experience in overlooking the audiences.

Each audience member has an assigned seat, which gives him/her enough personal space. Concert halls are better than live houses because audience members do not have to worry about others and can take reactions (e.g., hand waving) more easily.

Live houses. Live houses are generally smaller than concert halls; they typically have capacities of a few hundred audience members. In many cases seats are not provided. The audience remains standing to listen to the music and members are able to move about within the live house. It is easier to dance in live houses than in concert halls, but usually too crowded to dance in the front of the stage.

In the case of live houses, proximity to the music players has been identified as one of the most important aspects. Audiences feel a stronger *sense of unity with musicians* and *unusualness* when they are close to their favorite musicians. Physical proximity allows audiences to feel mental proximity as well. When audience members take reactions, they are more likely to be recognized by the musicians.

Sound is generally louder in live houses than in concert halls or at outdoor festivals. Some participants enjoy feeling the vibration of bass tones produced in live houses.

4   Discussion

4.1   What to Support

In this section, we discuss how we can support remote audiences of live music shows by providing technical assistance to share experiences.

Let us review the values of the three types of live shows. Values of experiences at outdoor festivals are mainly found in factors related to huge numbers of audience numbers and the open-air environment. In order to share this with remote audiences, we probably need some devices to send and receive a very wide view. Such devices are costly and not popular among usual audiences. Another problem is that interactive social communication between musicians and their audiences is a less important factor in the case of outdoor festivals.

In the case of concert halls, stage effects are considered as important factors of experience. However, it is not easy to share this experience with remote audiences. Interactivity between musicians and audiences is also less important than in live houses.

Finally, in the case of live houses, physical proximity to musicians is an important factor of experiences. However, it is impossible to share remotely. Another important factor is interactive social communication — reactions of the audience and responses from musicians. From the viewpoint of CSCW, it is worth supporting. Our participants added another value to live houses — loud sound. However, this is not easy to reproduce for remote audiences because of the sheer variety of their audio devices.

In the first half of Sect. 3.2, we have mentioned other values of live performances. One of them is the audience's viewpoint. To support multiple viewpoints, a lot of cameras must be set up at the live venue. However, it is impossible to support arbitrary viewpoints for each audience. Another value we have mentioned is the tired feeling, which is not easy to reproduce technically.

Consequently, we should focus on interactive social communication between musicians and their audiences. We then need to consider how we can share it remotely. According to our analysis (Fig. 2), a *sense of unity* is aroused when musicians respond to the reactions of audiences and when an audience is taking reactions with other audiences. If we can design a low-cost system that supports the *remote sense of unity* by providing functions that appropriately transmit reaction information between remote places, it will enhance the video streaming systems for live music shows.

4.2 Support for Minor Musicians and the Cost Problem

We have another reason to focus on live houses, which are the most popular places of live music performances. Major musicians can appear at concert halls or outdoor festivals, but most minor or amateur musicians can only use live houses, owing to the cost problem. It is not easy for them to plan a concert tour, either, for the same reason. They need a low-cost method to access listeners who live far from them. Social communication with individual fans is more important for minor musicians than for major musicians.

In introducing the viewpoint of cost, possibilities of support functions for remote audiences are described as follows:

- *Impossible or unrequired support*: the "tired feeling" of the audience; open-air atmospheres at outdoor festivals; physical proximity to musicians or other audiences; arbitrary viewpoints for individual remote audience.
- *Higher cost*: very wide view to overlook huge numbers of audience members; powerful sound.
- *Lower cost*: audience's reactions (e.g., [1, 2]); multiple (but a small number of) views.

The *sense of unity* can be (at least partly) extended to the remote site by sharing information on the audience's reactions. *Unusualness* is another important value of live performances, but it is not easy to reproduce at the remote site through technological support. It has many aspects.

5 Conclusion

We have analyzed the values of live music performance using EGM. We have elicited some important evaluation items including *unusualness*, *sense of unity*, and others.

However, it is impossible to reproduce all the values of a live music performance at a remote site. For example, physical proximity to musicians can never be reproduced.

Even if advanced virtual reality technology is used, it is less satisfactory to fans than physical proximity. *Unusualness* involves many factors including physical proximity. Hence, it is impossible to reproduce proper *unusualness* at the remote site.

Some other values could be extended to remote sites, but they are not cost-effective. Providing several views for remote audiences is one such example.

Through our analysis, we have found how a *sense of unity* is aroused by the experiences at live music shows. The reactions of the audience and the responses of the musicians are important factors. It is (at least partly) possible to remotely share this information [1, 2]. These sharing systems are expected to enhance remote experiences in live music shows.

We can discuss business models for remote live music shows. As long as the values of live shows remain at the local site, the current style of business of live music shows will survive even if some advanced remote live systems are introduced. Systems that support *the remote sense of unity*, for example, by sharing information on audiences' reactions, will provide better experiences for remote audiences. Pay services for remote live shows can be supposed. Such systems will enable even minor musicians to have social communication with remote fans at a lower cost.

Acknowledgments. This work was supported by KAKENHI (15K00274).

References

1. Morino, Y., Miyazaki, K., Tarumi, H., Ichino, J.: Comparison of input methods for remote audiences of live music performances. In: Yoshino, T., Chen, G.-D., Zurita, G., Yuizono, T., Inoue, T., Baloian, N. (eds.) CollabTech 2016. CCIS, vol. 647, pp. 58–64. Springer, Singapore (2016). doi:10.1007/978-981-10-2618-8_5
2. Tarumi, H., Akazawa, K., Ono, M., Kagawa, E., Hayashi, T., Yaegashi, R.: Awareness support for remote music performance. In: Nijholt, A., Romão, T., Reidsma, D. (eds.) ACE 2012. LNCS, vol. 7624, pp. 573–576. Springer, Heidelberg (2012). doi:10.1007/978-3-642-34292-9_62
3. Sanui, J.: Visualization of user's requirements: introduction of the evaluation grid method, design & decision support systems in architecture. DDSS. Spa, Belgium (1996)
4. Sanui, J., Maruyama, G.: Revealing of preference structure by the Evaluation Grid Method. In: Proceedings of the 7th International Conference on Human-Computer Interaction, pp. 471–474. San Francisco, CA, USA (1997)

A Method for Estimating Worker States Using a Combination of Ambient Sensors for Remote Collaboration

Kazuyuki Iso[1](✉), Minoru Kobayashi[2], and Takaya Yuizono[1]

[1] Japan Advanced Institute of Science and Technology,
1-1 Asahidai, Nomi, Ishikawa, Japan
{iso.kazuyuki,yuizono}@jaist.ac.jp
[2] Meiji University, 4-21-1 Nakano, Nakano-ku, Tokyo, Japan
minoru@acm.org

Abstract. Estimation methods that check worker states for remote collaboration have been used in research via wearable sensors, cameras, and microphones, but these methods have some drawbacks. An estimation method that uses both vibration sensors and distance sensors is presented in this research. A prototype module with two sensors is tested to estimate the four states of a user by creating a self-organizing map (SOM) using the sensor data. Tests show that the prototype module estimates the user state by classifying it into one of three clusters, including "key typing" and "leaving a seat," and others.

Keywords: Remote collaboration · Workers state · Vibration sensor · Distance sensor · Self-organizing maps

1 Introduction

The recent diffusion of broadband networks and social network services has made it easy for workers to collaborate with each other remotely by using video, audio, and document sharing with a multipoint video conferencing system. On the other hand, workers who collaborate at the same location often use physical assets such as paper and whiteboards. Therefore, using these physical assets and sharing physical user states are assumed to be desirable for collaboration between remote workers.

An improved method for sharing physical states is needed to enhance remote collaboration when users are located in various physical spaces, as depicted in Fig. 1. In this example of remote collaboration, several people undertake a task in the conference room in space X, while a worker in space Y participates in the task remotely. In this situation, workers in space X may focus only on the discussion with workers in the same space. This situation may cause problems if the worker in space X forgets to share the discussion with the remote worker in space Y. To resolve this problem, a remote collaboration system needs to ensure that the workers in space X naturally share their working states with the remote

© Springer International Publishing AG 2017
T. Yoshino et al. (Eds.): CollabTech 2017, LNCS 10397, pp. 22–28, 2017.
DOI: 10.1007/978-3-319-63088-5_3

Fig. 1. Concept of remote collaboration.

worker in space Y. If the workers in space X are aware of the presence of the remote worker, then the collaboration will proceed more smoothly.

To support remote collaboration, a realistic method that represents face and gaze direction with a 3D display [3, 7, 8] was proposed. This method is expected to effectively support the awareness of remote workers. However, this expression method has two issues: first, it requires a very large capacity network for video transmission, and second, it requires many input devices, which are not easy to set up for video generation. Therefore, an alternative method that does not use video is also considered.

In this research, a vibration sensor and a distance sensor are proposed, prototyped, and tested. The vibration sensor detects signals associated with worker behavior. The distance sensor detects the area in which the worker is present. Each sensor is extremely compact and easy to integrate in the environment, and can detect various kinds of information about the worker. The combination of sensors creates an ambient environment, which is expected to further develop with the Internet of Things (IoT).

2   Related Research

Recognition of a remote worker's state is an important factor in remote collaboration. Research related to this factor has focused on awareness support [2, 4, 5, 11]. Various methods to estimate worker states have been investigated, but each method has some drawbacks.

The first method uses the operational log of a personal computer (PC) to estimate a user state. Hashimoto et al. [6] obtained useful information from workers using this method, but the method did not differentiate between each user's state and the log in the shared workspace.

The second method uses wearable sensors that are attached to a worker to estimate worker states. Olguin et al. [1] attached various sensors to workers to measure worker conditions. The workers wore microphones, acceleration sensors, infrared sensors, etc. This direct measurement of a worker captured detailed information, but attaching the sensor to users could be a major hindrance in remote collaboration.

The third method uses a microphone or a camera to estimate worker states. Kennedy et al. [9] installed a microphone in the environment to estimate worker states during a conference. The microphone method encountered difficulty in estimating the participants who weren't speaking. Otsuka [10] reconstructed the state of the speaker and that of the listener from a video image. The camera method could estimate various kinds of information but encountered difficulty in adjusting to various conditions, and it did not work in instances of physical occlusion.

In this research, a method using a combination of vibration sensor data and distance sensor data to estimate worker states is investigated by prototyping and testing. This method is not an alternative method, but may become supplemental to other methods in the new IoT environment.

3   Estimation Method and Prototype Module

A prototype module with a combination of vibration and distance sensors was developed. The module is used simply by placing it on a desk (Fig. 2). This module has one vibration sensor and one distance sensor, and receives data from both sensors synchronously using an Arduino microcontroller. The data are transmitted to and stored in a PC.

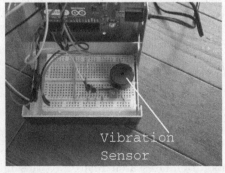

Fig. 2. Prototype module with Arduino.

In order to classify the worker state, the relationship between the sensor data and the state of the worker is analyzed with self-organizing maps (SOM). A Fourier transform is applied to the vibration sensor data, and distance sensor data is averaged over a short time in the data analysis.

4   Test of Prototype Module

4.1   Test Method

The prototype module was tested on its ability to infer four states: "writing on a desk," "key typing," "viewing a PC monitor," and "leaving a seat." The first three states are shown in Fig. 3. These four states were selected from usual works using PC and physical assets.

writing on a desk   key typing   Viewing a PC monitor

Fig. 3. Worker state in test of prototype module.

During the 20-minute test, a user works at a desk, and at times may leave the desk. The user is video recorded at a sampling rate of 1 [kHz] in order to label the sensor data with user states. The window size of the Fourier transform on the vibration sensor data is 5 [s], and the average interval for the distance sensor is the same length of time.

4.2   Result and Discussion

The graphs of the data from both sensors are shown in Fig. 4. The vibration data labeled with the worker states is shown in Fig. 4. The results of the short-time Fourier transform of the vibration sensor are shown in Fig. 5. The result of the SOM is shown in Fig. 6. The rate of correct worker status included in each cluster was 63 [%].

The SOM classified the sensor data into three areas, as shown in Fig. 6. Area 1 included the state "key typing," area 2 included the two states "writing on a desk" and "viewing a PC monitor," and area 3 included the state "leaving a seat." By comparing Fig. 4 with Fig. 5, it is evident that the vibration data was related to the state "key typing." Therefore, the difference in vibration properties impacts the classification of area 1 and area 2. Figure 4 shows that the distance data was related to the state "leaving a seat." Therefore, the distance sensor

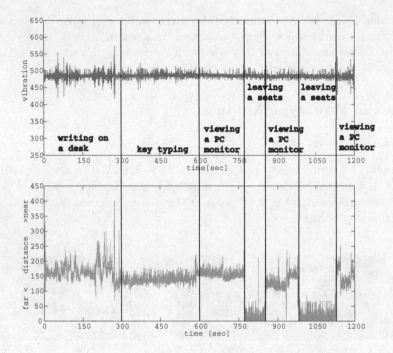

Fig. 4. Data Results from both sensors and vibration data labeled with worker states. Y-axis is 10-bit value of A/D converter with Arduino.

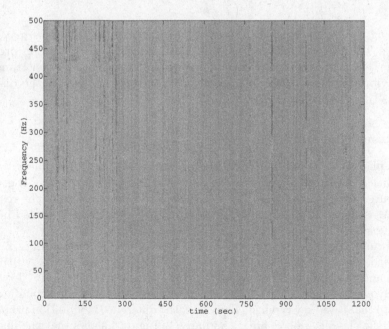

Fig. 5. Results of short-time Fourier transform of vibration sensor.

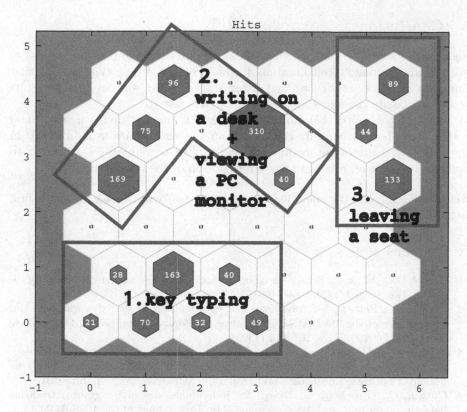

Fig. 6. SOM resulting from analysis.

influenced the classification to area 3. These effects suggest that the two sensors could be useful in estimating worker states.

In this test, area 2 contained two states, thus illustrating that the data from both sensors cannot easily distinguish between the two states "writing on a desk" and "viewing a PC monitor." The vibration level corresponding to the state "writing on a desk" was small owing to frequent stops in writing motion, and the vibration level corresponding to the state "viewing a PC monitor" was also low. In order to distinguish between the two states, we will consider the time length of low-vibration activities, especially the intermittent motion of writing.

The data of the vibration sensor varies depending on the material that transmits the vibration, and the data of the distance sensor also changes according to the position of the worker's seat and the distance sensor. The relationship between the sensor data and the state of the worker will be investigated, including the state of the working environment. To estimate the more detailed states of the worker, this method will be investigated using combinations with other methods with cameras, microphones, PC logs, etc.

5   Conclusion

Recognizing a worker state at a remote site is necessary to develop a sense of work sharing in remote collaboration. In this research, a prototype module that combines vibration sensor data and distance sensor data was developed, and its ability to classify the four states of a worker was tested.

The test confirmed that three states ("key typing," "leaving a seat," and "other") can be mechanically classified from the sensor data using a SOM. In the future, the prototype module will be applied to remote collaboration to evaluate its effect on a local worker's recognition of the remote worker.

Acknowledgments. We would like to thank Editage (www.editage.jp) for English language editing.

References

1. Daniel, O.O., Alex, P.: Sensor-based organisational design and engineering. Int. J. Organ. Des. Eng. **1**(1/2), 69–97 (2010)
2. Dourish, P., Bellotti, V.: Awareness and coordination in shared workspaces. In: Proceedings of the 1992 ACM Conference on Computer-Supported Cooperative Work (CSCW 1992), pp. 107–114 (1992)
3. Feldmann, I., Waizenegger, W., Atzpadin, N., Schreer, O.: Real-time depth estimation for immersive 3D videoconferencing. In: 2010 3DTV-Conference: The True Vision - Capture, Transmission and Display of 3D Video, pp. 1–4, June 2010
4. Gutwin, C., Greenberg, S.: Design for individuals, design for groups: tradeoffs between power and workspace awareness. In: Proceedings of the 1998 ACM Conference on Computer Supported Cooperative Work (CSCW 1998), pp. 207–216 (1998)
5. Gutwin, C., Greenberg, S.: A descriptive framework of workspace awareness for real-time groupware. Comput. Support. Coop. Work **11**(3), 411–446 (2002)
6. Hashimoto, S., Tanaka, T., Aoki, K., Fujita, K.: Improvement of interruptibility estimation during PC work by reflecting conversation status. IEICE Trans. Inf. Syst. **E97.D**(12), 3171–3180 (2014)
7. Iso, K., Ozawa, S., Date, M., Takada, H., Andoh, Y., Matsuura, N.: Video conference 3D display that fuses images to replicate gaze direction. J. Disp. Technol. **8**(9), 511–520 (2012)
8. Jones, A., Lang, M., Fyffe, G., Yu, X., Busch, J., McDowall, I., Bolas, M., Debevec, P.: Achieving eye contact in a one-to-many 3D video teleconferencing system. ACM Trans. Graph. **28**(3), 64:1–64:8 (2009)
9. Kennedy, L.S., Ellis, D.P.W.: Pitch-based emphasis detection for characterization of meeting recordings. In: 2003 IEEE Workshop on Automatic Speech Recognition and Understanding (IEEE Cat. No.03EX721), pp. 243–248, November 2003
10. Otsuka, K.: Multimodal conversation scene analysis for understanding people's communicative behaviors in face-to-face meetings. In: Salvendy, G., Smith, M.J. (eds.) Human Interface 2011. LNCS, vol. 6772, pp. 171–179. Springer, Heidelberg (2011). doi:10.1007/978-3-642-21669-5_21
11. Rodden, T.: Populating the application: a model of awareness for cooperative applications. In: Proceedings of the 1996 ACM Conference on Computer Supported Cooperative Work (CSCW 1996), pp. 87–96 (1996)

Tag Chat: A Tag-Based Past Topics Recollection Support System

Junko Itou[1]([✉]), Rina Tanaka[2], Jun Munemori[1], and Noboru Babaguchi[3]

[1] Faculty of Systems Engineering, Wakayama University,
930, Sakaedani, Wakayama 640-8510, Japan
itou@sys.wakayama-u.ac.jp
[2] Graduate School of Systems Engineering, Wakayama University,
930, Sakaedani, Wakayama 640-8510, Japan
[3] Graduate School of Engineering, Osaka University, Suita, Japan

Abstract. In this article, we propose a chat system that uses tags to help users resume past conversations. In online chat, it is often difficult to continue conversations regarding issues that were discussed in the past because the relevant parties may have forgotten the contents of the conversation. Our proposed chat system, called "Tag chat," helps users to remember past conversations by focusing on the words in each topic to provide information on the past topic. The results of three experiments using the proposed system and a comparison system indicate that viewing tags helps users to recall topics more specifically than re-reading chat logs and does not impose a burden on users.

Keywords: Online chat · Tag · Topic · Recollection · Morphological analysis

1 Introduction

In this paper, we propose a chat system called "Tag chat" that uses tags to help users remember past conversations and topics. In computer-mediated synchronous communication, the contents of conversations are often mixed because users typically discuss several topics in the same session. Users are also apt to forget what they were discussing as they are frequently compelled to interrupt their conversations. Therefore, it is often difficult to continue conversations regarding issues that were being discussed in the past. In order to recall the topics that they may have forgotten, users need information regarding the contents of the conversation. However, in order to resume and continue online conversations, users have to try to recall the nuanced transitions between topics by re-reading whole chat logs.

To solve this problem, we have developed a topics recollection support system that uses tags extracted from ongoing chat logs to help users resume past conversations. The developed system is targeted at informal chats rather than official conference talks. The system shows users words associated with an ongoing chat topic on the screen at any given time. Users can select multiple words as

© Springer International Publishing AG 2017
T. Yoshino et al. (Eds.): CollabTech 2017, LNCS 10397, pp. 29–36, 2017.
DOI: 10.1007/978-3-319-63088-5_4

tags that represent the topic, and help remind them of the content of a relevant conversation at a later date.

2 Related Work on Communication Focusing on Conversational Topics

2.1 Existing Communication Support Systems

Skype[1], LINE[2], and ICQ[3] allows users to register their icons, usernames. A chat history is shown once the user logs in. In these services, users need all conversation logs while relying on their memory to determine where the relevant conversation was interrupted, or what they were talking about at the time.

Some systems can glean the topic of ongoing conversations by analyzing chat logs [1,2], but cannot help users remember past conversation topics. Kawabata et al. [3] proposed a system that extracts chat topics from a chat room using a history of messages. The system extracts nouns from chat logs and classifies the conversation theme at the time based on the nouns. Users' intentions are not reflected in this classification because the results of analysis in this system are only used to classify conversations into broad topics such as food, hobbies, and economy. Moreover, the system does not help to remind users of past chat topics.

Collective Kairos Chat [4] is a chat support system in which users can determine the degree of importance of each message. This system allows users to delete chat messages from the log at different speeds. The chat screen in the system has three columns, and messages are divided in accordance with their degree of importance as determined by all users. Users obtains chat logs as the collective memory of the discussion reflecting the preferences of all participants. The criterion for the importance of a message is whether it is associated with a given theme. Hence, Collective Kairos Chat does not cater to situations where multiple conversation topics are spanned in a short time.

2.2 Existing Support Systems for Making Meeting Minutes

Various systems focusing on automatic text summarization or extract of key sentences have been proposed. Hirashima et al. [5] proposed a system that automatically produces text minutes by collecting and editing meeting data, so as to easily understand the sequence of meetings. A major drawback of the system is that recording the discussion remarks and tags is labor-intensive.

In the other meeting summarization systems [6,7], key sentences are automatically extracted and presented so that users can understand the contents, structure, and purpose of meetings in a short time. However, users are not be involved in the summarization and annotation task.

---

[1] Skype: https://www.skype.com/en/.
[2] LINE: https://line.me/en.
[3] ICQ: https://icq.com/.

3 Proposed Chat Support System "Tag chat"

3.1 Goal

Our goal is to implement a chat system that supports the recommencement of past chat topics by tagging chat logs. It is assumed that the proposed system will be used in frank conversation for about 10–30 min. The scenarios include simple meetings or talks held several times a month, rather than formal meetings such as taking of the minutes. The design policy of our system is as follows:

1. **A mechanism to help users easily grasp the contents of past chat**
   In order for users to continue discussion on a past chat topic, information regarding the topic, such as the relevant conversation log, is needed. Time and effort is needed to keep track of all logs; hence, our system registers nouns from chat conversation as tags.
2. **Recording key phrases and transitions between topics from user's viewpoint**
   The proposed system only presents candidate tags to the user, who ultimately decides which tags to assign to a given conversation. If there is another phrase to be recorded as a tag, the user can input an arbitrary word.

3.2 System Overview

The proposed system consists of a server and multiple clients connected to a network. Figure 1 gives an overview of the chat screen of a client. A text input form is located at the bottom of the screen. The user enters text here, and clicks the submit button or presses the Enter key to send a message to the server. Chat logs are displayed in the chat log field at the center of each client screen.

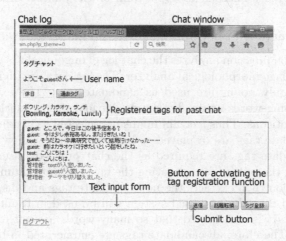

Fig. 1. Overview of a client screen.

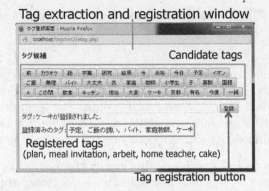

Fig. 2. The tag extraction and registration window.

Each client has three functions: a candidate tag extraction function, a tag registration function, and a tag display function. These three functions are described below.

3.3 Tag Registration Function

Users click the button at the bottom of the screen to simultaneously activate the tag registration function and launch the tag extraction and registration window, Fig. 2. The system then shows candidate tags to users as buttons. On clicking a candidate tag button, a message is presented indicating that the candidate has been recorded as a tag for the conversation. In addition, users can register free words other than candidate tags as tags.

A list of registered tags is also displayed on the window. In Fig. 2, the tags "meal invitation" and "home teacher" are free word tags as they are not in the list of candidate tags. There is no upper limit on the number of tags.

3.4 Tag Extraction Function

The tag extraction function analyzes the chat log of ongoing chats using MeCab[4], a Japanese language morphological analyzer. The log data are divided into parts of speech, and only nouns are used as candidate tags. The extracted nouns include overlapping words or words that do not make sense, such as pronouns, suffixes, and emoticons. Thus, certain nouns are selected as candidate tags. The extracted candidate tags are displayed as buttons on the window.

If new candidate tags are required as the chat proceeds, users can register them by clicking the button for activating the tag registration function. The tag extraction function then extracts the new candidate tags and displays them.

It is assumed that the proposed system will be used in frank conversations for a short time. It is anticipated that so many words are not extracted to be candidate tags. Therefore, all candidate tags are enumerated in button format.

---

[4] MeCab: http://taku910.github.io/mecab/.

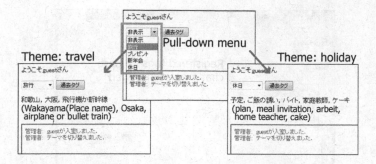

Fig. 3. List of themes and tags registered with a selected theme.

3.5 Tag Display Function

The tag display function displays the tags registered using the tag registration function in past chats. The proposed system displays the registered tags respectively for each chat topic or theme. Figure 3 shows the theme selection screen. The themes are displayed in a list. The screen after selecting the theme is shown on the bottom of Fig. 3.

4 Evaluation Experiments

4.1 Experiment Outline

We performed comparison experiments to investigate whether displaying tags in our system helps users to easily recall past conversation topics. The participants in our experiment were sixteen college students, divided into eight pairs.

The participants used two types of systems, a comparison system and the proposed system. The comparison system was based on the proposed system without the display of tags on the last topic. Other related functions and the interface in the system were similar to those of the proposed system. The chat screen of the comparison system is shown in Fig. 4. No restrictions were imposed on the participants in using these systems.

We conducted three experiments at intervals of six days. The experimental procedure is as follows.

1. We explained the operation of the system to the participants.
2. We proposed one theme for the conversations.
3. We instructed each pair to chat for 10 min using the system, and to register tags during the chat. The tags were selected according to whether they would be useful to remember the topic of conversation later.
4. The participants took a break for several minutes.
5. We repeated Steps 2, 3, and 4 for all four themes.

The conversation topics of the participants were on the following four themes: "Travel," "Birthday present," "New Year's party," and "Holiday." At the conclusion of each experiment, we asked the participants to answer a few questions.

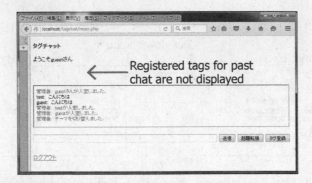

Fig. 4. The comparison system.

Experiment 1. The first chat experiment was performed to collect data regarding the last topic to use in subsequent experiments. As there was no log for previous chats with respect to the first chat, it was not possible to display tags from previous conversations for the first chat. For this reason, the participants used the comparison system only.

Experiments 2 and 3. In the second experiment, four pairs of participants used the proposed system while the other four pairs used the comparison system considering the influence of order effects. In the third experiment, the participants used the other system in the second experiment.

We asked the participants to recall the topic of their conversation from the last experiment before they started chatting. After completion of the third experiment, we presented the chat log of the theme with the most remarks in all the chat logs obtained in the first experiment to the participants. We then asked them to read the full sentence of the chat log and answer a questionnaire.

4.2   Experimental Results

We denote experiments in which used the proposed system was used by exp_p and those in which the used the comparison system was used by exp_c. A summary of questionnaire results is given in Table 1. Each number signifies the total number of persons who selected that particular evaluation value.

As shown in Table 1, participants' assignment of scores for item (iii) for our system was about the same as those for the comparison system. Item (iv) had a median of 4.0 and a norm of four for both systems. A significant difference in neither item was obtained between the comparison system and our proposed system from a Wilcoxon signed rank test. Hence, we can conclude that the difference in the system did not affect the restart and concreteness of conversations.

Comparing the results for item (ii) to those for item (v), it can be seen that the values for both experimental conditions were similar, whereas items (i) had lower grades, for the theme "Travel" and "New year's party." There was a

Table 1. Summary of questionnaire results obtained in the three experiments.

Questionnaire item	Theme	System	Value				
			1	2	3	4	5
(i) I was able to recall the contents of the last topics from my memory alone	Travel		2	4	4	6	0
	Party		1	5	3	5	2
	Present		0	1	2	11	2
	Holiday		1	0	2	12	1
(ii) I was able to recall the contents of the last topics by reading the registered tags	Travel		0	0	1	9	6
	Party		0	0	1	7	8
	Present		0	0	1	5	10
	Holiday		0	1	0	4	11
(iii) I was able to start chatting about the last topics smoothly		exp_p	0	2	4	7	3
		exp_c	0	0	5	10	1
(iv) I was able to chat about the theme concretely		exp_p	0	2	2	8	4
		exp_c	0	1	5	7	3
(v) I was able to recall the contents of the last topics by reading the chat logs			0	0	0	5	11
(vi) Reading the chat logs was tiresome			2	0	3	10	1

Evaluation value: 1: strongly disagree, 2: disagree, 3: neither, 4: agree, 5: strongly agree.

significant difference between item (i) and item (ii) in the Wilcoxon signed rank test. Moreover, it can also be seen from the results for item (vi) that participants felt that reading all of the previous chat logs was tiresome. Thus, it is possible that tags are less burdensome for users to recall previous chat contents.

We summarize the specificity of topic recollection and the degree of burden. Re-reading the whole chat logs is effective for recalling topics, however, it is burdensome for the user. On the other hand, it is difficult to remember the content specifically only with user's memory. We conclude that the method of browsing tags helps users remember and resume past conversations specifically with a small burden.

The tag extraction function displayed 45.5 candidate tags per chat on the screen. Some participants reported that tag registrations was inconvenient because of inaccuracies in the separation of some words. Some participants also needed a function to delete or edit registered tags. From these results, we need to implement a function that does not merely extract nouns but edits tags. In addition, it is necessary to incorporate multiple dictionaries to improve accuracy, and incorporate indices such as word significance and degree of relevance.

5 Conclusion

In this paper, we proposed a chat support system that helps users restart conversation topics from past chats. In the proposed system, users check the contents of past conversations by tagging.

We performed three comparative experiments using our proposed system, which displays tags associated with past topics, and a chat system that does not display tags. The experimental results show that the proposed system helps to remind users of the topics of past conversations and that showing tags is less burdensome than checking entire logs.

In future work, we plan to improve the interface and implement a tag edit and delete function other than simply extracting nouns. We also perform long-term and continuous experiments to confirm the proposed system's effectiveness.

Acknowledgments. This work was supported by JSPS KAKENHI Grant Number 16K00371.

References

1. Adams, P., Martel, C.: Conversational Thread Extraction and Topic Detection in Text-Based Chat. Semantic Computing, Wiley-IEEE Press (2010)
2. Matsumoto, M., Matsuura, S., Mitsuhashi, K., Muarkami, H.: Supporting human recollection of the impressive events, using the number of photos. In: Proceedings of the 6th International Conference on Agents and Artificial Intelligence, vol. 1, pp. 538–543 (2014)
3. Kawabata, T., Satou, T., Murayama, T., Tada, Y.: Construction of a topic extraction system based on statement history in the chat room. In: Proceedings of the 77th National Convention of the Information Processing Society of Japan, vol. 72, no. 1, pp. 385–386 (2010). (in Japanese)
4. Ogura, K., Matsumoto, Y., Yamauchi, Y., Nishimoto, K.: Kairos Chat: A novel text-based chat system that has multiple streams of time. In: Proceedings of CHI 2010, Extended Abstracts on Human Factors in Computing Systems, pp. 3721–3726 (2010)
5. Hirashima, D., Tanaka, M., Teshigawara, Y.: Development and evaluation of a minutes system focusing on importance in a meeting. In: Proceedings of the 18th International Conference on Advanced Information Networking and Application, vol. 2, pp. 293–298 (2004)
6. Lee, J., Song, H., Park, S.: Two-step sentence extraction for summarization of meeting minutes. In: Proceedings of the 2011 8th International Conference on Information Technology: New Generations, pp. 614–619 (2011)
7. Nagao, K., Inoue, K., Morita, N., Matsubara, S.: Automatic extraction of task statements from structured meeting content. In: Proceedings of the 7th International Joint Conference on Knowledge Discovery, Knowledge Engineering and Knowledge Management, pp. 307–315 (2015)

Availability of Disaster Preparedness Awareness Improvement for Supplying Knowledge Using Microblog and Comic Expression

Sojo Enokida[1]([✉]), Taku Fukushima[2], Takashi Yoshino[1], Tomoki Motozuka[3], and Nobuyuki Egusa[1]

[1] Wakayama University, Sakaedani 930, Wakayama, Japan
enokida.sojo@g.wakayama-u.ac.jp, yoshino@sys.wakayama-u.ac.jp
[2] Osaka Institute of Technology, Osaka 573-0196, Japan
[3] Disaster Reduction and Human Renovation Institution, Hyogo 651-0073, Japan

Abstract. The Great East Japan earthquake that occurred in March, 2011 caused large-scale damage in the Tohoku area. Japan has frequently been geographically and economically damaged by natural disasters, such as the 2014 Mount Ontake eruption, 2015 Kanto and Tohoku heavy rain, and 2016 Kumamoto earthquake. In general, disaster preparedness awareness (DPA) increases immediately following a disaster; however, this preparedness diminishes over time. Therefore, the continuation and improvement of disaster preparedness of people is essential. To address this critical issue, we have distributed a "disaster preparedness four-frame comic (DPFFC)" to provide knowledge pertaining to disaster preparedness by using comic expressions via online social network Twitter. The DPFFC aims to improve the DPA by helping users to acquire related knowledge in their daily lives via Twitter. In this study, we considered the possibility that the DPFFC may continue and improve DPA by combining Twitter, which is used in daily life, with a comic, which provides a significant learning effect, and our results confirmed this. In addition, we found that the DPFFC has the potential bridge the gap between DPA and action.

Keywords: Disaster preparedness awareness · Disaster preparedness knowledge · Comic expression · Twitter · Disaster information

1 Introduction

The Great East Japan earthquake was a large-scale disaster caused by an earthquake off the Pacific coast of Tohoku in March 2011, along with the accompanying tsunami and aftershocks. People's disaster preparedness awareness (DPA) had increased after the Great East Japan earthquake. In an DPA survey (WEB

© Springer International Publishing AG 2017
T. Yoshino et al. (Eds.): CollabTech 2017, LNCS 10397, pp. 37–52, 2017.
DOI: 10.1007/978-3-319-63088-5_5

survey) conducted in 2013[1], approximately half of the respondents answered that a "large-scale earthquake disaster will occur soon;" however, they also answered that "Although consciousness increased after the Great East Japan earthquake, it has faded slowly." In general, DPA increases immediately following the occurrence of a disaster; however, preparedness diminishes over time. Moreover, there exists the possibility of a Tokyo Inland earthquake and Nankai Trough earthquake occurring in the future.

Following the Great East Japan earthquake, it became clear that "the limit of public help" by administration itself was affected, and we recognized that, if self-help, mutual help, and public help do not mesh well, disaster control measures are not effective after a large-scale disaster. In the results of the "consciousness of self-help, mutual help and public help measures" of the Public Opinion Survey on Disaster Preparedness (Cabinet Office of Japan), the rate of "we should correspond to placing emphasis on public help" decreased from 24.9% (N = 2155) to 8.3% (N = 3110) in 2002, that of "we should correspond to placing emphasis on self-help" increased from 18.6% to 21.7%, and that of "we should correspond to balancing self-help, mutual help, and public help" increased from 37.4% to 56.3%[2]. Civilians can only practice self-help and mutual help, because public help is carried out by administration. Studies on DPA have been conducted for a long time, and have confirmed that it is improved through traditions and school education [1]. Many studies on DPA have placed emphasis on mutual help, with school education on disaster preparedness and disaster prevention drills in the community being mutual help targets.

In terms of self-help, many people believe it is possible that a large-scale disaster will occur; however, people who do not make preparations for a disaster are in the majority, according to the survey on awareness of and activities related to disaster management in daily activities (May 2016)[3]. Regarding reasons for lack of disaster management, the survey results show that "lack of time," "lack of opportunities," and "lack of information" were frequently referred to. From the survey results, it was considered that management may be effective in the case of those who referred to a lack of time, in the form of contacting people during activities on which they are already spending time as an effective measure to raise awareness. In the case of those who referred to a lack of information, providing information in an easier-to-understand way could be beneficial, while in the case of those who referred to a lack of opportunities, the Internet may be an effective measure (see Footnote 3).

---

[1] Panasonic conducts an DPA survey - one in two people answered "After the Great East Japan earthquake, I have faded from DPA" and over 70% people answered "There are not preparation enough for disaster" — Panasonic Newsroom Japan [Japanese], http://news.panasonic.com/jp/topics/2013/38104.html.

[2] Result of Public Opinion survey on Disaster Preparedness, etc. - Cabinet Office of Japan (2013 survey) [Japanese], http://www.disasterpreparedness.go.jp/kaigirep/kentokai/hisaishashien2/pdf/dai5kai/siryo2.pdf.

[3] White Paper on Disaster Management in Japan 2016, 2–3 Awareness of and Activities Related to Disaster Management, http://www.disasterpreparedness.go.jp/kyoiku/panf/pdf/WP2016_DM_Full_Version.pdf.

Twitter was used as a medium for obtaining disaster information when the Great East Japan earthquake occurred [2], and the Special Committee for New Strategy Promotion reported on issues and objectives for effectively utilizing Twitter and other social network services (SNSs) for disaster preparedness and reduction[4]. Based on the case in which Twitter was used for disaster preparedness and reduction, many local governments and organizations have opened Twitter accounts for sending disaster information, and conducted disaster drills using Twitter[5]. Younger age groups show a higher tendency not to prepare for disasters; however, the usage rate of Twitter is 31.0% (N = 2000), and in particular that of people in their 20s is 52.8% (N = 400), so the usage of young people is higher[6]. Twitter is an SNS that people use daily, and not only for transmitting information at the time of a disaster, but it may aid in disaster preparedness and reduction, and therefore may be a motive for continuing and improving DPA among younger age groups.

It is clear that the continuation and improvement of disaster preparedness is essential. Therefore, we have distributed the "disaster preparedness four-frame comic (DPFFC)" to provide knowledge pertaining to disaster preparedness by using comic expressions via Twitter. The DPFFC aims to continue and improve DPA by helping users to acquire disaster preparedness knowledge in daily life via Twitter, and may aid with self-help during disaster response.

In this study, we consider the possibility of continuing and improving disaster awareness by combining Twitter, which is used in normal time, with comic expressions that have a significant learning effect. We analyzed Tweet activity for 30 episodes (approximately 3 months) in terms of whether DPFFC was likely viewed and obtained user responses. In addition, by providing disaster preparedness knowledge to users, we conducted a questionnaire survey on whether the DPFFC continues and improves their DPA.

2   Related Work

2.1   Relationship Between Twitter and Disaster

Many studies have analyzed the use trend of Twitter, and propagation and spread of Tweets [2,4–6]. Sakaki et al. [4] and Miyabe et al. [5] compared Tweets at the time of a disaster between regions. Liza et al. gathered examples when the

---

[4] Report of the investigation committee to utilize civil information such as SNS for disaster preparedness and reduction (Disaster Preparedness and Reduction Working Group on September 4, 2014), http://www.kantei.go.jp/jp/singi/it2/senmon_bunka/disasterpreparedness/dai6/houkokusyo.pdf.

[5] Toward information transmission and collection in local government at time of disaster (Twitter Japan) [Japanese], http://www.kantei.go.jp/jp/singi/it2/senmon_bunka/disasterpreparedness_SNS_kentoukai/dai2/shiryo_3_5.pdf.

[6] White Paper on Information and Communications in Japan 2015, Part 2 Future Society Spearheaded by ICT, Chap. 4 ICT and Future Lifestyles, Sect. 2 Transformations Resulting from Social Media Growth [Japanese] http://www.soumu.go.jp/johotsusintokei/whitepaper/ja/h27/pdf/n4200000.pdf.

Canterbury earthquake struck the South Island of New Zealand with a moment magnitude of 7.1 on September 4 2010, as well as when the Great East Japan earthquake occurred, and analyzed Tweets by means of hashtags. Adam et al. [2] analyzed Tweet spreads at the time of the Great East Japan earthquake and raised the problematic point of the authenticity of retweeted information.

We carried out analysis using Tweet activity, rather than hashtags, retweets or networks that are generally used in Twitter analysis. These studies show how the Twitter usage pattern changes at various points during a disaster's occurrence. Since the 2016 Kumamoto earthquake occurred while distributing the DPFFC, we analyze differences in usage between before and after the earthquake by using the Tweet activity.

2.2 Comic Learning Effect

Matt et al. described the learning effects of comic expression [3]. Comics can promote reader understanding through interaction between text and illustration, and is often used for education. Furthermore, a comic is expected to have the effect of added attraction. Jay et al. investigated the learning effects of comics in the science field, and found that they are effective as a medium for communicating information to students [7], especially non-science students.

These studies placed importance on the learning difference between comics and text, and applied the experimental procedure of performing a test after learning by means of using a comic at educational sites. Since the DPFFC is distributed via Twitter, we did not use it at educational sites; however, its aim is to continue and improve DPA by helping users to acquire disaster preparedness knowledge in daily life through Twitter. Tweets are displayed on the timeline by following the relative account or being retweeted by other users; however, whether they are read depends on user decision. The same applies to other SNSs, such as Facebook. Matt et al. and Jay et al. investigated comic effects in the environment using experimental and education situations; however, they did not study services in daily use, such as SNSs.

3 Disaster Preparedness Four-Frame Comic

3.1 Disaster Preparedness Four-Frame Comic

The DPFFC is a four-frame comic for learning about disaster preparedness and reduction. It is aims to continue and improve DPA by sharing this knowledge with many users, and helping people to acquire disaster preparedness knowledge in their daily lives via Twitter. According to Matt et al. [3] and Jay et al. [7], the DPFFC may promote users' understanding and add attraction by using comic expression to distribute disaster preparedness knowledge. The contents are created by referring to high-certainty information distributed by the government or

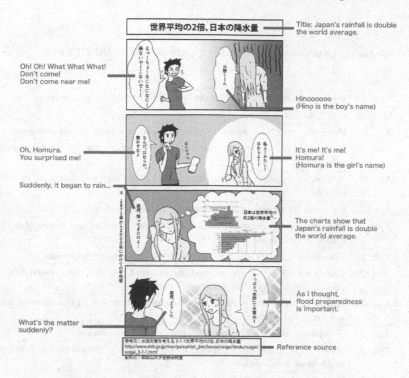

Fig. 1. Episode 29, "Japan's rainfall is double the world average."

universities, such as Disaster Management, Cabinet Office of Japan.[7]. Distribution is adjusted adjusting to seasonal trends, and news on disasters or disaster preparedness, among others.

Table 1 shows the distribution days and contents of the DPFFC up to June 23, 2016. Since episode 3, we had distributed the contents every third day. We adjusted the contents from damage overview to the 2016 Kumamoto earthquake from episode 8, and that of flood damage to the approaching rainy season from episode 22. Figure 1 shows an example of the DPFFC for episode 29, "Japan's rainfall is double the world average."

3.2 AkariMapBot

To distribute the DPFFC, we developed AkariMapBot (@AkariMapBot)[8], which is a Twitter bot that detects users moving and provides disaster preparedness information, such as shelter and AED[9]. The number of AkariMapBot followers

---

[7] Disaster Management, Cabinet Office of Japan, http://www.disasterpreparedness. go.jp/kyoiku/panf/report_brochure_etc.html.

[8] AkariMapBot — Twitter, https://twitter.com/akarimapbot.

[9] Automatic External Defibrillator.

Table 1. Distribution date and contents of distributed DPFFCs.

Episode	Date	Contents
1	Mar. 22	Feeling quake of an earthquake like other disasters or accidents
2	Mar. 28	Confirming the origin of fire before evacuation
3	Apr. 3	Possibility of block fences blocking due to the quake of an earthquake
4	Apr. 6	In the case of tsunami evacuation, "not to return home" is an inviolable rule
5	Apr. 9	A wooden building increases flow rate when the flood depth exceeds 2 meters
6	Apr. 12	Example of returning from the high place moved to
7	Apr. 15	Example of returning from the high place moved to and overconfidence in a tide embankment
8	Apr. 18	Recognition that local government staff are the same victims
9	Apr. 21	Goods cannot be delivered to disaster areas that are not reported by the press immediately after disaster occurrence
10	Apr. 24	A lack of relief and personnel during reconstruction in the disaster area not reported by press
11	Apr. 27	Securing a good living environment for the evacuation
12	Apr. 30	Atopic dermatitis develops due to experiences of disaster and changes in residential environment
13	May 3	Bronchial asthma of affected children increases
14	May 6	Types of volunteers
15	May 9	Details of types of volunteers
16	May 12	Kumamoto City released a picture book for affected children
17	May 15	Kumamoto City released a picture book for affected children
18	May 18	Assistance you can provide without going to a disaster area
19	May 21	Assistance you can provide without going to a disaster area
20	May 24	Recognizing pregnant women as weak people in a disaster
21	May 27	Kumamoto earthquake Victim Support Guidebook
22	May 30	Increasing floods and sediment disasters during rainy season
23	Jun. 2	Intermittent rain from June 2 to July 26, 2015
24	Jun. 5	Acceptance of donation by the Headquarters for the Relief of Animals in Emergencies
25	Jun. 8	The flood damage summit held on June 7
26	Jun. 11	National Seismic Hazard Maps for Japan of The Headquarters for Earthquake Research Promotion
27	Jun. 14	What is "flood preparedness"?
28	Jun. 17	Risk of sediment disaster due to occurrence of earthquake and intermittent rain during rainy season
29	Jun. 20	Japan's rainfall is double the world average
30	Jun. 23	Self-help, mutual help and public help

was 112 at the distribution time of episode 1 (March 22), and 135 at that of episode 30 (June 23).

4   Analysis of Tweet Activity

We analyzed how the DPFFC was shared by means of Tweet activity provided by Twitter[10].

4.1   Tweet Activity

In Tweet activity, impressions and engagements are provided along with the number of retweets and likes. Impressions are the amount of times a user receives a Tweet in the timeline or search results, while engagements are the total number of times a user interacts with a Tweet, and include retweets, replies, follows, likes, links, cards, hashtags, embedded media, username, profile photo, or Tweet expansion.

Twitter analysis often makes use of retweets or networks [4,5]; however, these do not show private user responses. Since impressions are the number of displayed Tweets and are counted without a distinction being made between public and private accounts, they can be used as an indicator that a Tweet has been viewed. Engagements are the total count of user responses, without distinction made between public and private accounts, including not only retweets, but also likes and click counts of hashtags, among others; therefore, we can analyze user response details. However, it is possible that Tweets may be skipped by certain users, as impressions provide only the number of displayed Tweets. In addition, we can only refer to the Tweet activity of our own account, and not other accounts.

4.2   DPFFC Tweet Activity

We analyzed whether the DPFFC was possibly browsed and received user responses. Figure 2 shows the impressions transition of the DPFFC, while Fig. 3 shows its engagements transition. We could not acquire data on April 16 and 17 in Figs. 2 and 3. There were cases where the acquired Tweet activity decreased from the previous day, and greatly increased compared to the next day. The value of them never decreased, because the impressions were the number of displayed Tweets, and the engagements were the total user response count. We removed the data from the results in this case.

The impressions and engagements of episode 7 were lower than those of episodes 4 to 6, considering that episode 7 was distributed on April 15, after the 2016 Kumamoto earthquake that occurred on April 14. Important information communications were overloaded with other Tweets due to the large mass information regarding unrelated disaster areas being posted when the Great East Japan

---

[10] Tweet activity dashboard — Twitter Help Center, https://support.twitter.com/articles/20171990.

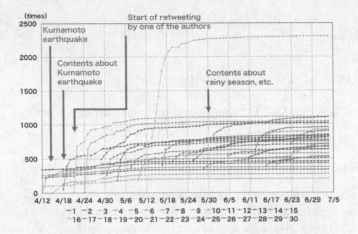

Fig. 2. The impressions transition of each DPFFC

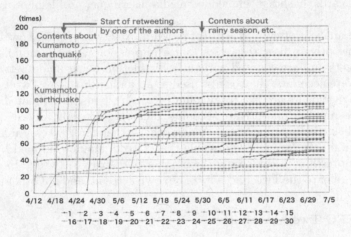

Fig. 3. The engagements transition of each DPFFC

earthquake occurred[11]. Because of this, it is possible that users may have selected information related to the disaster area of the 2016 Kumamoto earthquake. Episode 7 covered a shift to high elevation and tide embankment at the time of tsunami reconstruction, and its contents were not related to the 2016 Kumamoto earthquake. Therefore, it may not have been assessed as important information, and it is possible that impressions and engagements were low. Furthermore, Twitter Japan reported that Tweets related to the 2016 Kumamoto earthquake numbered approximately 26.1 million within one week, which is approximately 23 times the number of Tweets within a week immediately following the Great East

---

[11] Difficulty in emergency communication has discovered by the Great East Japan Earthquake - the Great East Japan Earthquake, information, Internet, and Google [Japanese], http://www.google.org/crisisresponse/kiroku311/chapter_18.html.

Japan earthquake[12]. Therefore, it is possible that, due to overloading of other Tweets, those of DPFFC were not seen.

After episode 8, the contents of the DPFFC were adjusted according to the disaster damage situation of the 2016 Kumamoto earthquake. In addition, one of the authors (with approximately 1,000 Twitter followers) retweeted the DPFFC Tweets. AkariMapBot, which distributed the DPFFC, has only around 100 followers. We decided that AkariMapBot alone could not distribute disaster-related information to a sufficient number of users in disaster situations; thus, the author retweeted the Tweets.

From episode 8, the impressions and engagements of episodes were higher than those of other episodes, and were increasing even after several days. A great deal of user reactions were obtained, because people had an increased interest in disaster immediately following the occurrence of the 2016 Kumamoto earthquake. We distributed the contents according to the earthquake situation phase, such as episode 8, "Recognition that a local government staff are the same victims," and episode 11, "Securing a good living environment for the evacuation life." However, the impressions and engagements the episodes decreased since episode 11. Therefore, it is possible that users' interest in disaster increased more than usual immediately following the 2016 Kumamoto earthquake, but this has gradually faded.

Episode 16 had higher impressions than other episodes; however, engagements were roughly the same as those of episode 9. Although both episodes 9 and 16 were retweeted 8 times, 3 were from private accounts in episode 8, and 2 from private accounts in episode 16. Many more private accounts retweeted episode 9 than episode 16, which appears to have influenced episode 16. Since episode 16 had 5 likes, compared to episode 9 with 0 likes, it is possible that episode 16 had a great deal of interest.

The contents of the DPFFC changed to flood disaster-related during the rainy season, from episode 22. From episode 11, the impressions and engagements decreased; however, these values increased when we changed the contents for the rainy season. Therefore, we can conclude that users' interest may be increased by adjusting to seasonal trends. Although the extent of the damage was local to the Kumamoto and Oita Prefectures, disasters during the rainy season may cause damage throughout Japan; in other words, many users may suffer from such disasters and therefore take it more seriously.

Although episodes 24, 26, and 30 were not related to rainy season disasters, their impressions were relatively high, which indicates that decreased user interest may be prevented by distributing contents other than seasonal trends.

---

[12] The 2016 Kumamoto earthquake: Twitter are posted about 26.1 million in one week - The Mainichi Newspapers [Japanese], http://mainichi.jp/articles/20160519/k00/00m/040/059000c.

4.3   Tweet Activity of Scenarios

We compared the DPFFC with its scenarios to investigate the extent to which the impressions and engagements of the DPFFC were viewed and responded to by users.

The scenarios correspond to each episode of DPFFC, and they were distributed from episode 7. In addition, one of the authors retweeted since episode 15, in order to verify the influence of their retweet on the DPFFC. The scenarios have a distributed image format, because the number of characters per Tweet is limited to 140.

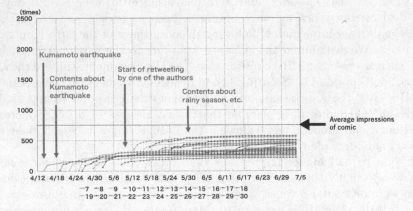

Fig. 4. The impressions transition of each scenario

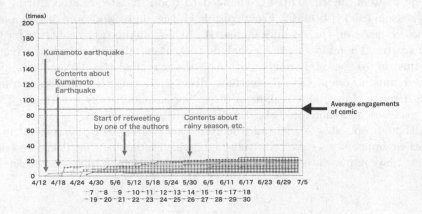

Fig. 5. The engagements transition of each scenario

Figure 4 shows the scenario's impressions transition, while Fig. 5 shows its engagements transition. There were cases in which the acquired Tweet activity decreased from the previous day, and greatly increasing the following day. As with the comic, we removed the data from the results in this case. We could not acquire data on April 16 and 17 in Figs. 4 and 5.

The comic in Fig. 2 has higher impressions than the scenario in Fig. 4. Similarly, the comic in Fig. 3 has higher engagements than the scenario in Fig. 4. The impressions were increased as a result of the retweeting by one of authors after the scenario of episode 15; however, the engagements in Fig. 5 increased less than those in Fig. 3. As a result of the author's retweets, the scenario Tweets were displayed to many users; however, many did not respond.

Because the scenario was distributed since episode 7, and retweeted since episode 15 by one author, it includes situation differences, such as distribution and retweeting time. However, we believe that the changes in Figs. 2 and 3 were influenced more by many users having interests in the comic than by one author's retweets.

From the results, we found that the impressions and engagements values of the comics were higher by comparing between the comic and scenario during the Tweet activity collection period from April 12 to July 3.

4.4   Tweet Activity of Regular Posted Tweets

We compared the DPFFC and regular posted Tweets of AkariMapBot, in order to investigate the degree to which the impressions and engagements of the DPFFC were viewed and responded to by users.

Figure 6 shows the impressions of the regular posted Tweets, while Fig. 7 shows their engagements. The regular posted tweets were Tweets posted by AkariMapBot on a regular basis. For example, "Introduction of the functions: If you post such as "I'm at Wakayama University" or "I came to Tokyo Skytree," this bot provides disaster preparedness information in your area." Every point of Figs. 6 and 7 plots the impressions and engagements for each Tweet acquired on July 3 in the order of date of posting, without plotting the same Tweet data.

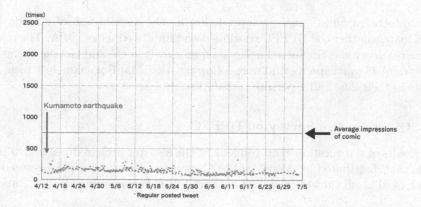

Fig. 6. The impressions of regular posted tweets

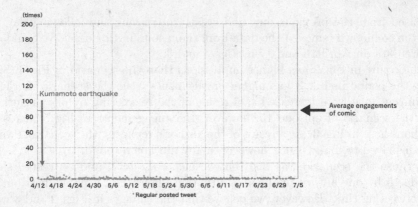

Fig. 7. The engagements of regular posted tweets

There are cases that increasing impressions in Fig. 6, and engagements in Fig. 7. This is because there are tweets that were retweeted on regular posted tweets. The comic in Fig. 2 has higher have impressions than the regular posted tweets in Fig. 6. The comic in Fig. 3 has higher have engagements than the regular posted tweets in Fig. 7. As these results, we found that the impressions and engagements values of the comics were higher by comparing between the comic and the regular posted tweets during the Tweet Activity collection period from April 12 to July 3.

According to the Tweet activity of the regular posted tweets and those of the scenario in Sect. 4.3, we expect the DPFFC to be capable of adding attraction on Twitter, as with the results of Jay et al. [7] and Matt et al. [3]. Therefore, there exists the potential to incorporate learning into daily life by combining SNSs that are used daily, such as Twitter, with comic expression.

5   Questionnaire Survey

We conducted a questionnaire survey following the distribution of episode 10, to evaluate whether the DPFFC continued and improved users' DPA. The questionnaire survey was conducted using a paper answer sheet and Google Forms[13]. There were 28 participants who were following AkariMapBot, namely 1 teen, 26 people in their 20s, and 1 person in their 30s.

5.1   Questionnaire Survey on DPFFC

The results of the question "Did you look at the disaster preparedness four-frame comic that distributed by AkariMapBot?" were as follows: 3 people answered "I have looked at all the episodes," 23 answered "I have sometimes looked," and 2

---

[13] Google Forms, https://www.google.com/intl/en/forms/about/.

answered "I have never looked." The two answers of "I have never looked" were removed from the questionnaire results, due to their lack of reliability.

Table 2 shows the results of the DPFFC questionnaire. We used a five-point Likert scale for evaluation, in which the individual responses were 1: Strongly disagree, 2: Disagree, 3: Neutral, 4: Agree, and 5: Strongly agree.

Table 2. Results of questionnaire about DPFFC

Question items	Evaluations					Median	Mode
	1	2	3	4	5		
(1) You acquired disaster preparedness knowledge by looking at disaster preparedness four-frame comics	2	4	4	12	4	4	4
(2) You got a starting point for disaster preparedness awareness by looking at disaster preparedness four-frame comics	2	3	9	10	2	3	4

– Evaluation: 1: Strongly disagree, 2: Disagree, 3: Neutral, 4: Agree, 5: Strongly agree.
– "Evaluation" is the number of people who answered the evaluation.

Table 2 (1) indicates that for the question: "You acquired disaster preparedness knowledge by looking at disaster preparedness four-frame comics," the median and mode scores were both 4. In the free description field of the questionnaire, many participants commented, "Disaster preparedness knowledge is included." The following comments pertain to the provision of disaster preparedness knowledge using comic expression.

- "Because it is easier to see than text with only typographical characters, the frequency of touching information increased."
- "It is easy to understand, because it can be learned on a communication basis."
- "I do not think of reading text that is written redundantly about disaster preparedness; however, I was able to read it with interest through comic expression. It is easy to understand."

Furthermore, one participant commented regarding the provision of disaster preparedness knowledge via Twitter: "It is helpful that information is provided on Twitter, which I am frequently watching." However, in the free descriptions of participants who answered "Disagree," there were the following comments: "There are many contents that I already know," and "The amount of information and sentences were big."

Table 2 (2) shows that for the question: "You got a starting point for disaster preparedness awareness by looking at the disaster preparedness four-frame comics," the median score was 3 and the mode score was 4. In the free description of participants who answered "Agree," there were the following comments: "My consciousness worked because there are contents that take up timely topics, such as the 2016 Kumamoto earthquake," and "Because I thought that it is not easy to notice when I suffer a disaster and think myself into a state of panic." In addition, participants who evaluated the ease of using comic expression made the comment: "The comic was easy to watch." However, in the free description of participants who answered "Disagree," there were the following comments: "If it is measures and knowledge that can be used immediately after reading, the consciousness may change. However, the contents were knowledge at the time of disaster, therefore it was not triggered watching the comic." Even in the free description of participants who answered "Neutral," there were the following comments: "Because there are no contents that apply to myself, it is hard to have a sense of danger."

As a result of these two questions, we concluded that it is possible for DPFFC to continue and improve DPA, because it may be capable of adding attraction to users and promoting understanding of disaster preparedness knowledge by using comic expression. Although using knowledge of the Great East Japan earthquake in the DPFFC may enhance user awareness, certain users remained unaware because they were not affected by the disaster. Therefore, it is necessary to be careful about which information is handled as the subject of the DPFFC.

5.2 Questionnaire Survey About DPA and Action

We investigated whether DPA and actual action are linked. We provided a free description field for the question "Have you taken any disaster preparedness measures by watching the disaster preparedness four-frame comic?" There were 22 people who answered "I have never taken anything" or left the description blank. The free descriptions of the people who took some disaster preparedness measures were as follows.

– "I began to check evacuations at travel destinations."
– "It gave me a chance to see various websites, because I felt that I wanted to study anything I do not understand in the comic, and know about actions, etc. at the time of disaster."
– "I examined some evacuations near my house."
– "I tried to know the state of the 2016 Kumamoto earthquake, and confirm the truth of disaster information that was posted at the time of the earthquake."

The motivation for confirming the shelter is providing shelter information as disaster preparedness information by AkariMapBot that distributed the DPFFC.

In the questionnaire, we could not determine decreasing DPA, because it was conducted only one month after the distribution of episode 1, and the period was short. However, it is possible that the DPFFC can continue and improve DPA, because there were several participants who took certain disaster preparedness measures.

"Awareness of and Activities Related to Disaster Management" is summarized in the White Paper on Disaster Management in Japan 2016 (Cabinet Office of Japan) (see Footnote 3). Even among people who recognize a high possibility of disaster, approximately 54% do not prepare for disasters, according to the White Paper on "Recognition of the importance of disaster preparedness by awareness of disaster possibility."

"The gap between disaster preparedness awareness and action" was referred to in the White Paper on Disaster Management in Japan 2008 (Cabinet Office of Japan)[14]. The citizens of Japan are highly interested in disasters, because Japan is prone to disasters including earthquakes, tsunamis and floods. However, it was pointed out that DPA does not necessarily lead to action, and there is a situation known as "A gap between consciousness and action on disaster preparedness." It is important that citizens' interest in disaster lead to actual disaster preparedness actions. By providing the DPFFC, a few people actually take disaster preparedness actions; therefore, the DPFFC has the potential to bridge the gap between DPA and action.

6   Tweet Activity and Questionnaire Survey

According the Tweet activity analysis results in Sect. 4, the comic has higher impressions and engagements than the scenario format text. Since both the impressions and engagements were high, we found not only that the Tweets of the DPFFC were displayed on users' timelines, but that they were watched and responded to by users.

According the questionnaire survey results in Sect. 5.1, we found that the DPFFC can be expected to have effects such as promoting users' understanding and adding attraction by using comic expression to distribute disaster preparedness knowledge, as in Matt et al. [3] and Jay et al. [7]. Since we found that it is possible to include learning into daily life by combining Twitter and comic expression, we can expect a daily learning effect by providing educational material using comics on other SNSs.

It is possible that the DPFFC can address the reasons provided on Twitter using daily life for the lack of disaster management: "lack of time" and "lack of opportunities." Furthermore, the DPFFC may succeed in using comic expression as an effective measure for providing information in an easier-to-understand manner than a white paper. Moreover, as a result of the questionnaire on DPA and action in Sect. 5.2, we found that the DPFFC has the potential to bridge the gap between DPA and action, because with the provision of the DPFFC, a few people actually took disaster preparedness actions. Finally, we found that the DPFFC can continue and improve DPA by combining Twitter, which is used in daily life, with comics, which have a high learning effect.

7   Conclusions

In this study, we distributed a DPFFC to provide DPA using Twitter and comic expression. We analyzed Tweet activity to determine whether the DPFFC was

---

[14] White Paper on Disaster Management in Japan 2016, Introduction, DPA of citizens to action, http://www.disasterpreparedness.go.jp/kaigirep/hakusho/h20/disaster-preparedness2008/html/honbun/1b_0josho_01.htm.

likely viewed and obtained user responses. In order to evaluate whether the DPFFC can continue and improve DPA, we analyzed the Tweet activity and conducted a questionnaire survey. Based on the results, we found that the DPFFC can continue and improve DPA by combining Twitter, used in daily life, with comics, which have a high learning effect. In addition, we found that the DPFFC has the potential to bridge the gap between DPA and action.

In the future, we will quantitatively evaluate how learning can be adopted into daily life by combining Twitter and comics by means of a DPFFC.

References

1. Katada, T., Kanai, M.: Implementation of tsunami disaster education for children and their parents at elementary school, Solutions to Coastal Disaster 2008, Tsunamis, pp. 39–48 (2008)
2. Acar, A., Muraki, Y.: Twitter for crisis communication: lessons learned from Japan's tsunami disaster. Int. J. Web Based Communities **7**(3), 392–402 (2011)
3. sUpson, M., Hall, C.M.: Comic book guy in the classroom: the educational power and potential of graphic storytelling in library instruction. In: Kansas Library Association College and University Libraries Section Proceedings, vol. 3, No. 1, pp. 26–38 (2013)
4. Takeshi, S., Toriumi, F., Matsuo, Y.: Tweet trend analysis in an emergency situation. In: Proceedings of the Special Workshop on Internet and Disasters, pp. 3:1–3:8 (2011)
5. Miyabe, M., Miura, A., Aramaki, E.: Use trend analysis of twitter after the great east Japan earthquake. In: Proceedings of the ACM 2012 Conference on Computer Supported Cooperative Work Companion, pp. 175–178 (2012)
6. Potts, L., Seitzinger, J., Jone, D., Harrison, A.: Tweeting disaster: hashtag constructions and collisions. In: Proceedings of the 29th ACM International Conference on Design of Communication, pp. 235–240 (2011)
7. Hosler, J., Boomer, K.B.: Are comic books an effective way to engage nonmajors in learning and appreciating science? In: CBE-Life Sciences. Education, vol. 10, pp. 309–317 (2011)

Technological Feasibility
of a Smartphone-Based System to Integrate
Volunteers into Professional Rescue Processes

Stefan Hoffmann(✉), Markus Markard, Marc Jansen, Gerd Bumiller,
Henrik Detjen, and Stefan Geisler

Computer Science Institute,
University of Applied Sciences Ruhr West, Bottrop, Germany
{stefan.hoffmann,markus.markard,marc.jansen,
gerd.bumiller,henrik.detjen,
stefan.geisler}@hs-ruhrwest.de

Abstract. We evaluate the technological feasibility of a system that allows to contact a mobile device over the internet and to determine its position. We apply this system to a scenario where voluntary human resources are semi-automatically integrated into professional rescue processes. The latency of two different location APIs on the Android OS when using different localization technologies (GPS, WiFi, and mobile network) are examined. We also describe an architecture that allows for contacting mobile devices, receive their positions and evaluate the round-trip time of this approach. We describe the influences and consequences for our scenario. Results from this work can be used for other collaboration approaches based on mobile services.

Keywords: Mobile service · Localization · Round-trip time · Accuracy

1 Introduction

In case of large-scale catastrophic events, it is a common situation that the number of available professional helpers outnumbers their capacity. At the same time, there might be human resources with adequate medical or technical qualification among the population. Efficiently integrating these resources into the processes of professional rescue resources would be desirable by potentially compensating the impact of overloaded emergency teams.

To achieve this, the research project "Automated Allocation of Volunteers in Major Disasters" (German: "Automatisiertes Helferangebot bei Großschadenslagen", abbr.: AHA) [1] was initiated. One of its goals is the development of a system that allows for imposing the dynamic willingness and location of potential voluntary helpers. The fact that modern smartphones became very widespread in the last decade allows for offering such a system to the helpers on a low-cost basis. Each potential helper will install a mobile application on his/her smartphone, which will determine the position of the helper in case of an emergency. A central server (AHA server) collects the dynamic

© Springer International Publishing AG 2017
T. Yoshino et al. (Eds.): CollabTech 2017, LNCS 10397, pp. 53–67, 2017.
DOI: 10.1007/978-3-319-63088-5_6

helper information; afterwards it rates and offers it as an additional resource to the dispatcher in the control center.

This paper studies the feasibility of such a system from a technological point-of-view. The focus lies on the process of contacting several mobile devices at once and locating their positions. Some tasks for the volunteers, for example helping in medical emergencies, are highly time-critical. The best choice in such a case is a qualified helper that is as close as possible to the operation site. Therefore, the position of the helper must be determined and transmitted as fast as possible. Furthermore, the position must be accurate to allow for a reliable decision on the available helper.

This paper is organized as follows. Section 2 provides an overview on the related work. In Sect. 3, we describe the scenario that is in the focus of the research project AHA and the research questions that we derive from the requirements. Section 4 provides an overview on the technologies for localization and contacting which are provided by Android. In Sect. 5, we describe the experiments that we performed in detail and provide results. Section 6 discusses the results and their consequences to the scenario in detail. In Sect. 7, we give a conclusion and describe some of our future work.

2 Related Work

Accuracies of different localization technologies have been evaluated in detail in the past. Modern state-of-the-art smartphones use the Global Positioning System (GPS), information of WiFi access points and cell tower positioning to detect their positions.

In case of cell tower positioning, the localization method and quality depends on the mobile network standard that is used. In case of GSM (2. Generation, 2G), accuracies of 450 m in urban areas and 2825 m in rural areas with a precision of 50% each were reported [2]. With improved methods, accuracies of 200 m (urban) and 430 m (suburban) were reached [3]. For UMTS (3. Generation, 3G), an accuracy of up to 70 m (precision 67%) in urban areas [4] and an accuracy of 87 m (precision 67%) in rural areas [5] are the best results. For positioning methods based on WiFi, accuracy values of up to 2.4 m (precision 67%) were reported [6]. The GPS standard [7] claims an accuracy of 7.8 m with a precision of 95%. A drawback is its very constrained indoor availability.

A detailed overview of non-GPS location technology studies is given in [8]. An overview on indoor localization techniques is provided in [9]. Even localization technologies with low accuracy can be helpful for our collaboration approach, because they still provide enough information to e.g. exclude potential helpers from an operation, in case that they are too far away from the operation site. Furthermore, the evaluation of indoor localization techniques is important for our approach, because during the day most helpers are expected to be located indoors at their apartments or workplaces.

In our system, a central server needs to determine the position of mobile devices on demand. The mobile device thus has to implement a service that can be used remotely over the internet. In [10], an architecture that allows for offering mobile services while overcoming certain limitation was introduced. This approach was further improved in terms of energy consumption in [11]. In this work, we do not evaluate the energy consumption, but we address it implicitly by using the results to develop communication concepts of which we expect to have minimal energy consumption while fulfilling primary requirements given by the scenario.

3   Scenario

The main goal of the research project is to develop a system that allows for a smooth, reliable and fast integration of voluntary resources from the population into the existing professional helping processes in case of major catastrophic events. The dispatcher in the control center shall be able to utilize and dispose these helpers for medical and technical operations in the case that professional resources are bound in other operations. Ideally, the disposition of the voluntary helpers is as easy as the disposition of professional resources.

One of the application scenarios is help in medical emergencies. A volunteer with certain medical qualifications (like emergency doctor, nurse, first aid course) can be alarmed to help in a rescue operation, if the volunteer is able to be at the operation site (much) earlier than the professional resource. Before being able to alarm the helper, his/her eligibility for the operation must be rated and provided to the dispatcher. The rating is mainly based on the current position of the helper.

This is a strongly time-critical process. Every second can decide on somebody's life. To dispose a voluntary resource in such a case, the current information of the helper must be available for the dispatcher as early as possible.

3.1   Technological Requirements

For reasons of privacy protection, it is highly important to impose and transmit the helper's position only in case that a concrete purpose for the use of the data exists. Thus, the ideal approach is to determine the helper's position only after a concrete operation arises, in which a voluntary resource might be disposed. If the technologies are not able to fulfill the high demands of this approach, an alternative is to collect helper's position before an operation arises. In such a case, it is recommended to pseudonymize the positions for privacy reasons (e.g. by blurring the coordinates).

Figure 1 shows a sequence diagram for the described ideal communication. When the dispatcher receives an emergency call, he/she opens the file for the operation in the control center software. Right after that, the AHA system can be informed to start collecting positions of all helpers. Because at this point no current positions of the helpers are known, the server must contact the mobile devices of all helpers that are willing to help in order to get their positions.

From the moment at which the operation file is opened until the point when the resources need to be available to the dispatcher in the control center, a time of at least 20 s will pass. It is hence necessary to consider this time slot as an upper bound to collect as much precise helper locations as possible. In the remaining time, the received positions must be interpreted and rated relating to the operation, which consumes

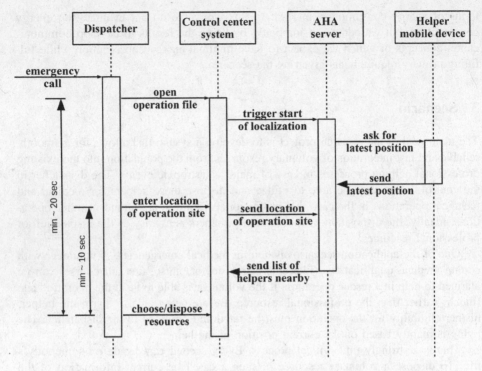

Fig. 1. Communication concept that is ideal in terms of privacy protection

additional time. In this paper, we only address the process of contacting the mobile devices and receiving a response.

Another requirement is the accuracy of the position. To reliably rate if a helper is in walking distance (say 500 m) to the operation site, a low accuracy such as reported for 2G is not enough. In case that we have to collect positions before the operation occurs, non-accurate positions can still be helpful e.g. to filter helpers that are too far away from the operation site.

3.2 Research Questions

To verify the feasibility of the desired concepts, it is necessary to evaluate the following research questions.

- Localization process (dependent on the localization technique)
  - How large is the duration of this process?
  - How accurate and precise is the determined location?
  - How reliable is the determined precision value?
- Process of contacting mobile devices (dependent on different network techniques)
  - How large is the round-trip time of the complete process to contact the mobile device, request the position, and to receive a response?

4 Technological Background

To run experiments to evaluate the described research questions, we developed different mobile applications for Android. In this section, we want to provide an overview on the different technologies and APIs that we used.

4.1 Android Location APIs

Google provides two APIs to determine the position of an Android device. The older Platform Location API[1] is available since Android API Level 1 (version 1.0 and higher) and part of the Android API. The Fused Location Provider API[2] is part of the Google Location Services API integrated in Google Play Services and available since API Level 17 (version 4.2 and higher). Both APIs use cell tower positioning, WiFi and GPS localization to detect the current geographic position, but the ways in which they perform this task are different.

With the Platform Location API, only one location provider can be used at a time. The decision on which of these two fits best for a certain situation is up to the developer. There are two location providers that are relevant for our scenario, the network location provider and the GPS location provider. In contrast to the GPS location provider that only delivers locations obtained by GPS, the network location provider uses cell tower positioning and WiFi to detect locations. It is the responsibility of the developer to keep track of previously obtained locations and to implement a strategy that delivers the most accurate location.

The Fused Location Provider API is recommended by Google due to its energy efficiency and accuracy and has, in contrast to the Platform Location API, the ability to automatically take care for the accuracy of the requested locations. Based on parameters specifying the priority of accuracy and energy consumption it is able to automatically choose the appropriate location source. If on the one hand, the priority is given to energy efficiency ("balanced mode"), it is more likely that the location service uses cell tower positioning and WiFi and if on the other hand the priority is given to accuracy ("high accuracy mode") it is more likely that the location service uses GPS. It is not possible to tell if a location was determined by cell tower positioning, WiFi or GPS when all sources were enabled on the device during the request.

4.2 Push Notification Concept for an Experimental Test Setup

Mobile devices establish their connection to the internet through various networks, indoors the network of choice is commonly a WiFi network, and outdoors the devices are typically connected via mobile networks based on 2G, 3G or 4G. When a device changes its location, it often changes the network and the IP address provided by this network as well. In addition, the provided IP addresses are usually private and therefore

---

[1] http://developer.android.com/guide/topics/location/strategies.html.

[2] http://developer.android.com/reference/android/location/LocationManager.html.

not directly accessible from the internet. As described in [10], one can overcome the problem of changing IP addresses by using a Push Notification Service. In case of Android, Google Cloud Messaging (GCM) is the native service for that purpose and is used in the experimental architecture as shown in Fig. 2.

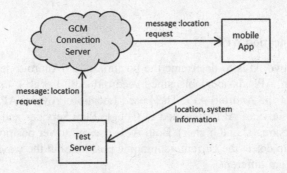

Fig. 2. Testing architecture to contact mobile devices by means of GCM

The test server sends a GCM message to the GCM Connection Server, by which it is broadcasted immediately afterwards to all instances of our test app that are currently connected to the GCM Connection Server. The message informs each app to run a certain service with optional parameters delivered by the message. The result of the service is sent to the test server. With this architecture, it is possible to address an unbounded number of devices with just one request to GCM, so that it can be elegantly used to contact a high number of devices at the same time, a fact that is clearly useful for the described scenario.

5   Experimental Evaluation

This section describes how we evaluate the given research questions by experimental means. Section 5.1 describes how the localization techniques were evaluated for the available positioning technologies. In Sect. 5.2 we describe how we tested the reliability of the accuracy value that is delivered by the localization method. Section 5.3 describes the experiments to examine the round-trip time of the process of contacting the mobile devices and to receive responses. Section 5.4 consolidates the results of Sects. 5.1, 5.2 and 5.3 to provide results for the complete process of contacting and localizing.

5.1   Localization Quality

In these experiments, the localization duration and accuracy of both the Fused Location API and the Platform Location API are evaluated. The goal is to decide which of the APIs is the most suitable for our scenario. Beforehand, we developed a mobile application that can be used to start the localization process repeatedly in a desired frequency. The app takes time stamps immediately before and after the localization; the difference of both is the duration of a single localization process on the mobile device. We ran the experiments from this section on five mobile devices on which only our experimental app was installed after a hard reset.

Duration of the localization using Fused Location API. As described, the developer has no control over the localization technology when he/she is using the Fused Location API. To be able to examine a certain technology anyway, we forced the test devices to use a certain technology by disabling all other. Table 1 shows which techniques we evaluated and describes how to force Fused Location API to use them.

Table 1. Settings to force Android (version 6.0) to use certain localization techniques

GPS	• Choose "Device only" under "Settings", "Location", "Mode"
3G	• Choose "Battery saving" or "WiFi and mobile networks" under "Settings", "Location" and "Mode" • Choose "3G" under "Settings", "Mobile network" and "Preferred network type" • Deactivate "WiFi" under "Settings" • Deactivate "Scanning always available" under "Settings", "Wi-Fi", "Advanced"
2G	• Analogous to 3G above, choose "2G" instead of "3G"
WiFi	• Activate "Airplane mode" under settings • Choose "Battery saving" or "WiFi and mobile networks" under "Settings", "Location" and "Mode" • Activate "Wi-Fi" under "Settings"

To ensure a typical dynamic change of the device's position, we ran the experiments while passing predefined routes through an urban area such that WiFi access points are available at most points. The same route was used for the different parameters to achieve comparable results. For each technology, we passed the route repeatedly for one hour with a localization frequency of 10 s, which leads to a number of 360 data sets for each technology.

The following tables shows the duration (Table 2) and accuracy (Table 3) results for the different localization methods.

Table 2. Duration of localization techniques with Fused Location API

	GPS [ms]	WiFi [ms]	3G [ms]	2G [ms]
Min	213.7	22.5	58.3	47
L. Quartile	662.7	1270	67.3	94.7
Median	**2748**	**1394**	**94.7**	**108.5**
U. Quartile	3147	1629	176.1	148.6
Max	5021	4943	5413	5713
Mean	**2206**	**1453**	**478.2**	**539.5**
StD	1507	1006	989.1	1035.4

Table 3. Accuracy of localization techniques

	GPS [m]	WiFi [m]	3G [m]	2G [m]
Min	4	17.3	600	724
L. Quartile	8	27	810	999.5
Median	**12**	**36**	**980**	**1133**
U. Quartile	32	45.5	1410	1355.5
Max	64	109.6	1610	1985
Mean	**20.5**	**39.8**	**957.5**	**1198.3**
StD	16.6	20.6	212.2	285.7

Localization with mobile network techniques (2G, 3G) is the fastest, but provides the weakest accuracy values. On the other hand, GPS localization is very accurate but is the slowest method on average. The accuracy of WiFi localization is weaker than GPS by only a factor of around three, but it is twice as fast. The range of the accuracy numbers is as expected from the literature, except for the 3G-based method, which was much less accurate in our experiments.

Duration of the localization using Platform Location API. The same experiments were performed for the Platform Location API. Table 4 (duration) and Table 5 (accuracy) show the results.

Table 4. Duration of localization techniques with Platform Location API

	GPS [ms]	WiFi [ms]	3G [ms]	2G [ms]
Min	26	215.7	46	46.6
L. Quartile	232	1739	104.9	104
Median	**410.5**	**13237**	**14444**	**10240**
U. Quartile	713.6	15992	17958	18295
Max	5354.9	22433	27670	19813
Mean	**516.7**	**10679**	**11034**	**8507**
StD	602.2	7247	8106	8890

Table 5. Accuracy of localization techniques with Platform Location API

	GPS [m]	WiFi [m]	3G [m]	2G [m]
Min	4	23.9	100	955
L. Quartile	8	36.9	800	1128
Median	**8**	**40.5**	**900**	**1929**
U. Quartile	12	47.3	1200	1985
Max	24	198	1600	1986
Mean	**10.5**	**47.8**	**939**	**1651**
StD	3.6	25.7	270	451.8

The duration of the localization when using network-based techniques was very low in most cases on all our test devices, the median in all three cases is greater than 10 s. The accuracy numbers are in the same range as for the Fused Location API.

Influence of the accuracy parameter to the localization technique. In this experiment, we evaluated the influence of the accuracy parameter ("balanced mode" and "high accuracy mode") to the choice of the localization method. We use the same devices on the same route, but this time we allowed the Fused Location API the free choice of the localization technology; all methods (GPS, WiFi, mobile network) in the device were activated.

Table 6 shows the latencies and accuracies that we achieved.

Table 6. Duration and accuracy for "balanced mode" and "high accuracy mode" (urban)

	"Balanced mode"		"High acc. mode"	
	Lat [ms]	Acc [m]	Lat [ms]	Acc [m]
Min	12.6	10	25.2	6
L. Quart.	801.6	17.4	297.3	18.2
Median	**1090.9**	**27.9**	**1027.7**	**29.8**
U. Quart.	1700.6	37.5	1128.7	45.2
Max	5705.5	154.7	2602.7	135.7
Mean	**1391.6**	**32.3**	**872.8**	**37.7**
StD	1125.3	22.9	543	28.1

We see no essential differences between both accuracy parameters, both for latencies and accuracies. We expected such a result because of the characteristics of the urban track, where WiFi is available at most points and thus GPS is not necessary, because WiFi localization is both fast and accurate. This probably leads Fused Location API not to work without GPS in case that a WiFi-based localization is possible. To validate this assumption, we repeated the test on a different track in a rural area with only a small density of access points. Table 7 shows the results.

Table 7. Duration and accuracy for "balanced mode" and "high accuracy mode" (rural)

	"Balanced Mode"		"High Acc. Mode"	
	Lat [ms]	Acc [m]	Lat [ms]	Acc [m]
Min	37.5	12	23.7	4
L. Quart.	189.2	265	257.3	16.7
Median	**215**	**487**	**1079.3**	**27.8**
U. Quart.	871.2	719	1158.7	42.1
Max	2137	1200	2652.7	168.1
Mean	**1391.6**	**32.3**	**837.8**	**35.7**
StD	1125.3	22.9	513	26.1

The results now are essentially different between both accuracy parameters. The balanced method has a much smaller accuracy, whereof we derive that GPS was not used (often). This corresponds to Google's claim that the probability for using GPS is smaller for that parameter[3]. In consequence, the localization duration of the balanced method is smaller, but the accuracy is weaker.

In our scenario, we are clearly not able to force the helper's device to use a certain localization technique, so we need to evaluate the influence of this parameter. In case that a high accuracy is necessary, we can influence the Fused Location API to use an accurate localization method by using the accuracy parameter by a sufficient means.

The conclusion of Sect. 5.1 is to use the newer Fused Location API for our approach because of its better performance: the accuracy has the same quality while the duration is smaller. For example, the mean duration of the WiFi localization with Fused Location API is 1.45 s, whereas Platform Location API needs 10.6 s on average.

5.2   Reliability of the Localization Accuracy Value

For both APIs, it is stated that the real position in 68% of all cases is located within the area of the circle that is described by the radius (=returned accuracy) around the returned position. This number corresponds to the standard deviation of a Gaussian distribution function.

In the following experiment, we evaluate the correctness of this statement for both APIs. We run the experiment on the same route as in the previous experiments. Additionally, we use a high-precision GPS tracker to get a reference position trajectory with a high accuracy. We performed tests for all different localization technologies for both APIs. We compared each position value with the corresponding reference value. Table 8 shows the ratio of positions with a higher deviation for all technologies and both APIs, and the real accuracy value according to a Gaussian distribution.

Table 8. Comparison of delivered and measured accuracy

	API accuracy	Experimental accuracy	Exp. acc. < API acc.
	Mean [m]	Mean [m]	[%]
FLA: GPS	10.3	8.9	57.3
FLA: WiFi	41.2	39.3	71.3
FLA: 3G	912	987	68.3
FLA: 2G	1198	1077	65.8
PLA: GPS	12.7	11.7	57.1
PLA: WiFi	52.6	69.1	67.2
PLA: 3G	1035	1062	71.2
PLA: 2G	1517	1629	65.3

---

[3] https://developers.google.com/android/reference/com/google/android/gms/location/LocationRequest.

The result of this show that the accuracy values provided by the API are reliable. This is an important result for our scenario, because we can use this value to rate the quality of a position reliably and independently of which API and which technology was used.

5.3   Round-Trip Time

To analyze the feasibility of possible communication concepts for our scenario, it is essential to evaluate the round-trip time. This is the duration of the complete process of contacting the mobile devices, including the approach to contact the mobile devices by using the GCM services (request time) and the time needed for the transmission from the mobile app to our server (response time). To analyze the round-trip time is the goal of the experiments in this section. The time for performing the localization is not included, because it was evaluated independently in the previous section.

In contrast to the experiments in Sects. 5.1 and 5.2, the tests in this section were not performed on the five testing devices only. Instead, we installed the mobile application that was developed for this experiment on the personal smartphones of more than 50 test persons. In the experiment, the test server contacts all mobile devices every ten minutes by using the architecture described in Sect. 4.2. The mobile application takes some time stamps, collects system information that allows for a detailed analysis and sends a response to the server.

The data sets on which the results are based were extracted from the whole set of collected data by the following means. We only considered data sets where the server received a response and thus achieved a number of data sets of around 110,000. The devices are not always online, e.g. because they are turned off intentionally by their users at night or because they are located in a region with no network connection or a couple of other reasons. However, a few devices achieved a response ratio of more than 95% over several weeks. Under experimental conditions, we were able to reach response ratios of up to 99%.

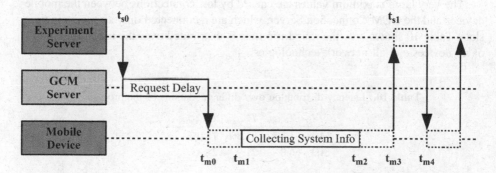

Fig. 3. Timestamps on chronological stations of a request

Figure 3 shows on which steps of the process we take time stamps on which devices.

Using those time stamps, we calculate the following durations.

- $T_{system} = t_{m2} - t_{m1}$ is the time that is consumed by collecting system information to support our analysis. In our scenario, we will not collect such information, so this time must be subtracted from the round-trip time.
- $T_{rtt} = t_{s1} - t_{s0} - T_{system}$ is the round-trip time cleaned by T_{system}.
- $T_{response}$ is the time from the point when the mobile device sends its response until the server receives it. We cannot compute it as the difference between t_{s1} and t_{m3}, as the clocks of server and mobile devices are not synchronous. Instead, we estimate it as $T_{response} = \frac{t_{m4} - t_{m3}}{2}$ according to Cristian's algorithm [12], because we expect that an immediate response of the server to the mobile device will take roughly the same time.
- $T_{mobile} = t_{m3} - t_{m0} - T_{system}$ is the time consumed by processing the request and preparing the response on the mobile device.
- $T_{request} = T_{rtt} - T_{mobile} - T_{response}$ is the time needed for contacting the device via GCM.

Table 9 shows the results of T_{rtt} for different communication technologies over all mobile devices.

Table 9. Durations for different network technologies (without localization time)

	WiFi [ms]	4G [ms]	3G [ms]	2G [ms]	All [ms]
Min	43	211	793	1259	43
L. Quart.	1426	1582	3062	5029	1561
Median	1802	1960	3957	7066	2195
U. Quart.	2556	2397	5476	12862	3942
Max	21268951	21269098	21336926	1703608	21336926

The very large maximum values are caused by lost connections between the mobile devices and the GCM Connection Server, which are reconnected only after certain time slots. Table 10 shows how the round-trip time is distributed over the measuring points of all devices and all network technologies.

Table 10. Latency distribution over different stations of the process

	T_{mobile}	$T_{request}$	$T_{response}$
Mean	1.3%	83.8%	15.0%
StD	6.0	21.9	21.3

The process to contact the mobile device via the GCM service consumes the largest part of the round-trip time.

5.4 Combining the Results

We combine the results from Sects. 5.2 and 5.3 by including the results for the duration of the localization process into the results for the round-trip time. Therefore, we add the median values of the localization durations to the median values of the round-trip time. Table 11 shows the results for the localization techniques combined by the network technologies.

Table 11. Round-trip times including localization for all positioning and network technologies

	Network: All	Network: WiFi	Network: 4G	Network: 3G	Network: 2G
Localization: GPS (12 m)	4943 ms	4550 ms	4708 ms	6705 ms	9814 ms
Localization: WiFi (36 m)	3589 ms	3196 ms	3354 ms	5351 ms	8460 ms
Localization: 3G (980 m)	2290 ms	1897 ms	2055 ms	4052 ms	7161 ms
Localization: 2G (1133 m)	2304 ms	1911 ms	2069 ms	4066 ms	7175 ms

For example, when using WiFi connection and positioning, in more than 50% of all cases the server receives a response in less than 3.5 s after it sent the request. Localization based on mobile networks is even faster, but provides a rather low accuracy.

Figure 4 shows the percentage of responses that the server received after each second up to 10 s (excluding location). The number of devices that responded successfully after 20 s is at 91%.

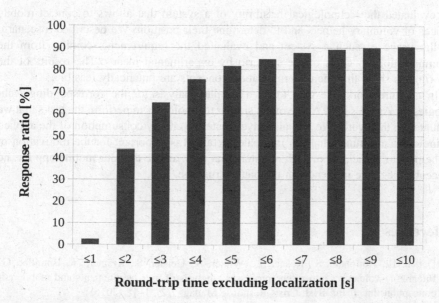

Fig. 4. Response ratios in certain time slots after starting the request from the server

6 Implications for the Collaboration Scenario

In this section, we want to collect and discuss the main implications of the experimental results for our scenario and thus answer the research questions that we posed in Sect. 3. The most important facts that resulted from our experiments are the following.

- We receive the positions of more than 80% of the helpers that are online and willing to help within less than 6 s after contacting all devices.
- Localization based on WiFi is faster than GPS-based positioning, provides much better accuracy than cell tower positioning and works indoors.
- The precision values that are delivered together with the position are reliable.

We can derive that when we use the ideal communication concept which starts collecting positions only after an operation arises, we have reliable positions of more than 80–90% of all helpers after around one third of the upper bound of 20 s, so that there is still time for the system to interpret the delivered values. Even when helpers are indoors, they can be reliably located by using WiFi. However, under the remaining non-covered 10–20% of the helpers could be the one which would be the best suitable helper for the operation. Thus, we recommend to collect positions already before a certain operation occurs. In this case, even non-accurate positioning methods can be used to strongly delimitate the set of candidates for a certain operation beforehand. When an operation is opened, not all helpers have to be contacted, but only the ones which are roughly located in the region of the operation, the others are filtered out.

Furthermore, positions of high accuracy can be reliably used for rating the helpers.

7 Conclusion and Future Work

We evaluated the technological feasibility of a system that allows to contact mobile devices of voluntary helpers and to determine their position. We described a scenario for the usage of such a system and evaluated the requirements coming from the communication concepts of the scenario by experimental means. The results of the experiments show that the communication concepts are practically feasible.

In a future work, we plan to do a similar analysis for the corresponding technologies for Apple's iOS. Apple offers similar technologies to perform the tasks that we evaluated in this work. We will also investigate the energy consumption of the applied technologies and functionalities in greater detail. It is important for the motivation of the helpers to participate in such a system that they realize that our mobile app has no noticeable negative influence on the battery runtime.

References

1. Detjen, H., Hoffmann, S., Rösner, L., Winter, S., Geisler, S., Krämer, N., Bumiller, G.: Integrating volunteers into rescue processes: analysis of user requirements and mobile app conception. Int. J. Inf. Syst. Crisis Response Manag. 7(2), 1–18 (2015)

2. Pettersen, M., Eckhoff, R., Lehne, P.H., Worren, T.A., Melby, E.: An experimental evaluation of network-based methods for mobile station positioning. In: 13th IEEE International Symposium on Personal, Indoor and Mobile Radio Communications (2002)
3. Murray, E.D., Performance of network based mobile location techniques within the 3GPP UTRA TDD standards. In: 3G Mobile Communication (2002)
4. Borkowski, J.L.J.: Pilot correlation positioning method for urban UMTS networks. In: European Wireless Conference (2005)
5. Porcino, D.: Performance of a OTDOA-IPDL positioning receiver for 3GPP-FDD mode. In: Second International Conference on 3G Mobile Communication (2001)
6. Yamasaki, R., Ogino, A., Tamaki, T., Uta, T., Matsuzawa, N., Kato, T.: TDOA location system for IEEE 802.11b WLAN. In: Proceeding of Wireless Communications (2005)
7. U. government, GPS Standard Positioning Service (SPS) Performance Standard. 4th edn. (2008)
8. Laoudias, C. http://www2.ucy.ac.cy/~laoudias/pages/penek/deliverables/D3.pdf. Zugriff am 10 May 2016
9. Currana, K., Fureya, E., Lunneya, T., Santosa, J., Woodsa, D., McCaugheya, A.: An evaluation of indoor location determination technologies. J. Location Based Serv. 5(2), 61–78 (2011)
10. Jansen, M.: About an architecture that allows to become a mobile web service provider. In: Proceedings of the 7th International Conference on Internet and Web Applications and Services (ICIW 2012) (2012)
11. Analysis and improvement of energy consumption for providing mobile web services. Int. J. Soft Comput. Softw. Eng
12. Cristian, F.: Probabilistic clock synchronization. Distrib. Comput. 3, 146–158 (1989)

A Triage Training System Considering Cooperation and Proficiency of Multiple Trainees

Kento Izumida[1]([⊠]), Ryuga Kato[1], and Hiroshi Shigeno[2]

[1] Graduate School of Science and Technology,
Keio University, 3-14-1, Hiyoshi, Kohoku-ku, Yokohama, Kanagawa, Japan
{izumida,kato}@mos.ics.keio.ac.jp
[2] Faculty of Science and Technology, Keio University,
3-14-1, Hiyoshi, Kohoku-ku, Yokohama, Kanagawa, Japan
shigeno@mos.ics.keio.ac.jp

Abstract. In large-scale disasters, an activity which determines the priority of treatment based on the severity of the injured person, called triage, is important. In recent years, collaboration between medical institutions and people working in disaster sites is much emphasized. However, the triage training that takes each trainee's proficient and cooperative level into consideration has not been implemented. Based on this background, we propose a triage training system in which the expression of information changes according to the skill level of each trainee. We use beacons instead of real victims in this training. A couple of trainees actually move around to search for beacons, and cooperate to respond to each event. While scenario in the training is not changed, we will change an method of presenting the biometric information of victims according to the skill level of trainees. This enables trainees with different levels of proficiency to collaborate and perform triage exercises. We conducted experimental evaluation of this system. The results revealed the system was effective to implement triage quickly and accurately. In addition, we found the proposal was good for awareness of sharing important information in cooperative activities.

Keywords: Triage · Training · User proficiency · Cooperative work support · Wearable device

1   Introduction

In the case of large-scale disasters, There are supposed to be a lot of injured people and lack of medical resources. Under these circumstances, we need to save a lot of human lives by utilizing limited resources. The priority of treatment is important to be determined based on the severity and urgency of the injured. This decision-making process is called a triage. After the triage has done, the victims with high priority to medical treatment are transported to the medical rescue facility, and receive appropriate medical treatment.

© Springer International Publishing AG 2017
T. Yoshino et al. (Eds.): CollabTech 2017, LNCS 10397, pp. 68–83, 2017.
DOI: 10.1007/978-3-319-63088-5_7

In recent years, because doctors should devote themselves to medical activities in disasters, someone other than doctors tend to triage the injured. In Japan, various efforts related to the triage, such as nurturing triage nurses and teaching the triage to ordinary citizens, are made nationwide. In order to quickly and accurately implement triage at the time of a disaster, it is necessary to train and acquire knowledge and skill from day to day. Also, cooperation among medical institutions and people working in disaster sites is more important than ever. However, the current trainings do not take it into consideration that each trainee's proficiency level because a couple of people are trained in the same environment at the same time. As a result, training is not conducted in line with the skill level of the trainees. Such training will not only diminish the effectiveness of the training, but reduce the motivation of the trainees. Furthermore, it is difficult to create a scenario according to the proficiency level of each trainee. It is also not easy to arrange an instructor that evaluates the achievement of the trainees, adjusts difficulty level, and feedbacks the result to the trainees.

In this paper, we propose a triage training system in which the expression of information changes according to the skill level of each trainee. First, we change the information of the injured according to the distance between the injured person and the trainees, using beacons. This reproduces the state of the actual disaster site. Also, the presentation method of biometric information of the victims is changed according to the proficiency level of the trainees. By using the same scenario and dynamically changing the information presentation according to the skill level of each trainee, it is possible to save time and effort to create training scenario for each degree of difficulty. In addition, it enables to train cooperative triage exercises even among trainees with different levels of proficiency.

In the following, Sect. 2 gives a general overview of disaster relief based on the present situation and related research. In Sect. 3, we describe the triage training system which considers cooperation by multiple people and their proficiency level. Section 4 provides the implementation of the proposed system. In Sect. 5, we describe the evaluation experiments, results and discussions. Finally, we will conclude this paper in Sect. 6.

2   Triage Training

In this section, we describe matters related to triage training. In particular, we will explain three points based on related research, including overview about triage, current triage trainings, and using IT for training.

2.1   Triage

If a large-scale disaster such as an earthquake occurs and a large number of injured people come out at the same time, the ability of the afflicted area to respond to the medical system may reach a limit. In that case, it is necessary to efficiently use medical resources of limited people and things to save as many people as possible. For this purpose, triage in which you determine the priority of treatment according to the severity and urgency of the victims is conducted. The first triage for diagnosing the injured person adopts the START method (Simple Triage And Rapid Treatment) [1].

Victims by triage are classified into four categories: black, red, yellow and green. The highest priority of category is red, next yellow, then green, and the lowest is black. The medical staff reflects the determined treatment priority on cards with markers of four colors called triage tags shown in Fig. 1 and attaches victims to the wrist of them.

2.2 Disaster Relief Activities

In Japan the Great Hanshin-Awaji Earthquake, occurred on January 17, 1995, highlighted many issues such as delays in the initial medical system and emergency medical care levels for disaster medical care. Japan Disaster Medical Assistance Team (Japan DMAT) was established by the Ministry of Health, Labor and Welfare, in recognition of the need for doctors to do medical treatment at disaster sites in cooperation with administrative agencies and fire departments [2]. DMAT is composed of doctors, nurses, work coordinators (non-doctor or non-nurse medical administrative staff). DMAT provides a wide range of medical assistance making full use of mobility and expertise (e.g. hospital support and wide-area medical transport for conducting on-site medical treatment and maintaining hospital functions at disaster sites). In the event of a disaster, residents must deal with each situation among limited resources, so local governments across the country have the opportunity to learn about disaster countermeasures that they can make through disaster prevention drills and evacuation drills on a daily basis. Also, when the road is cut off by collapsing buildings or sediment disasters, it is not always possible for emergency services to arrive at the site. There is no possibility that doctors, nurses and emergency life saving persons are present, in situations where there are only citizens on the disaster site, they do life saving activities [3]. At that time, if the citizens knows the triage, they will know whether to bring the injured to the emergency tents or directly to the hospital and who should be carried preferentially, so they can take appropriate cooperation with the medical institution. Citizen triage rewrites the triage into an easy-to-understand judgment procedure without using a technical term by a doctor and an emergency life-saving person, and there are parts taken into disaster drill in Japan in some places [4,5]. Citizen triage is almost the same procedure as the START method used in triage performed by a doctor, but it is added to a method of identifying crash syndrome which is various symptoms occurring after compressing and releasing the body of victims.

2.3 Using IT for Training

In recent years, there is a trend to apply ICT technology to disaster relief training and disaster prevention drills in the world, like education making use of evolving IT technology. MoLE (Mobile Learning Environment) project is an international

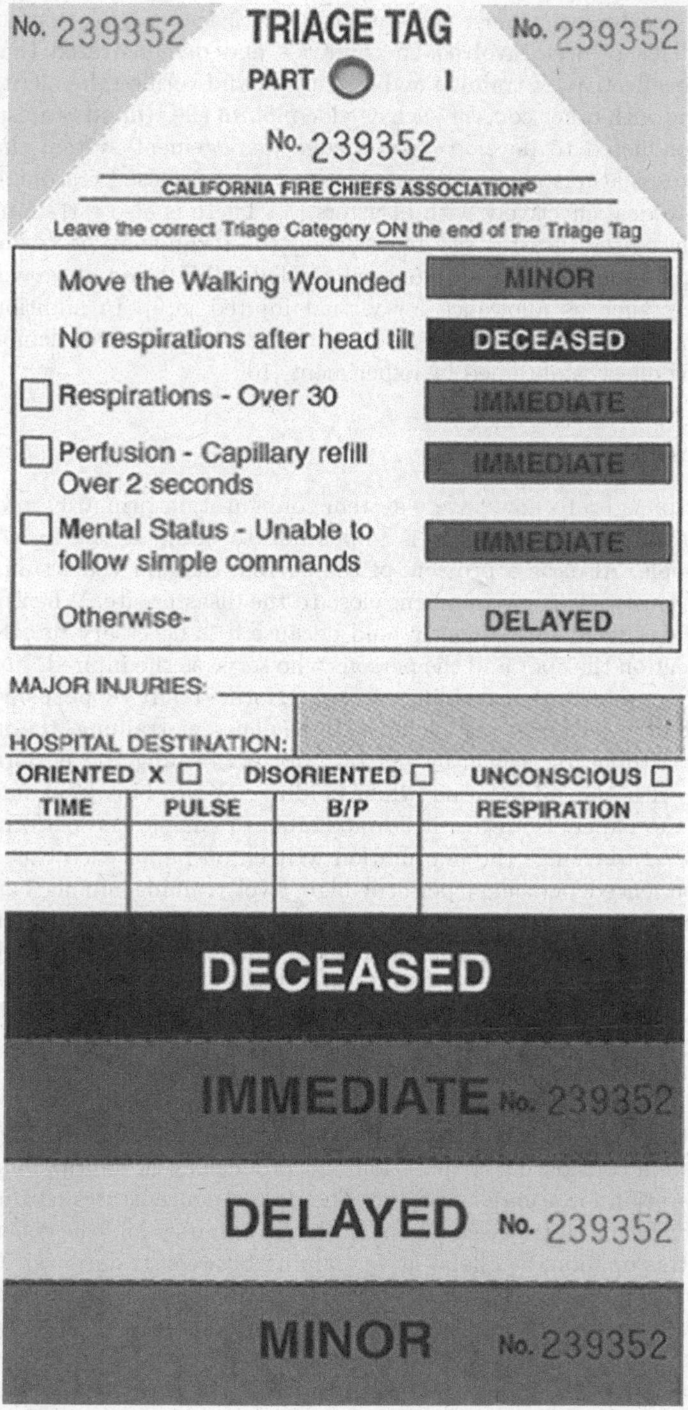

No. 239352   **TRIAGE TAG**   **No.** 239352

PART ◯   I

No. 239352

CALIFORNIA FIRE CHIEFS ASSOCIATION©

Leave the correct Triage Category ON the end of the Triage Tag

Move the Walking Wounded	MINOR
No respirations after head tilt	DECEASED
☐ Respirations - Over 30	IMMEDIATE
☐ Perfusion - Capillary refill Over 2 seconds	IMMEDIATE
☐ Mental Status - Unable to follow simple commands	IMMEDIATE
Otherwise-	DELAYED

MAJOR INJURIES: _____

HOSPITAL DESTINATION: _____

ORIENTED X ☐   DISORIENTED ☐   UNCONSCIOUS ☐

TIME	PULSE	B/P	RESPIRATION

DECEASED

IMMEDIATE No. 239352

DELAYED No. 239352

MINOR No. 239352

Fig. 1. Triage tag

project on disaster occurrence and provision of learning tools for emergency situations. This project involved 25 countries and demonstrated that mobile terminals are effective for training and education, and verified the merits created by combining with other content such as video [6]. In the United States, research has been conducted to develop a knowledge management system that learns about countermeasures against disasters based on case-based reasoning, and to learn skills to deal effectively with disasters [7]. There is also a training system that reproduces the disaster site by utilizing the technology of virtual reality (VR), and puts immersive head-mounted display (HMD) and glove with sensor and practices such as allowance for virtual injured [8,9]. In addition, in the serious game field, a system for disaster training was proposed, demonstrating that learning effect is obtained by experiment [10].

2.4 Issues

Training systems up to now have a system configuration primarily intended for individual training. Therefore, it is impossible to train at the same time by multiple people. Also, as a problem of the current disaster relief training, it is not easy to construct an environment close to the disaster site. When practicing training, it is difficult to frequently hold because it is necessary to actually use the equipment on the spot and the persons who serve as the injured. In addition, there is also a problem that training can be performed only by people with close technical ability and knowledge volume. In the current training, the injured or injured role is done by a healthy person, and performing the performance in accordance with the information while holding up the biological information written on the paper. However, it is impossible to change the performance for each trainee or to change the information written on paper each time. For this reason, experienced personnel perform high level training among experienced people, and beginners must carry out easy training at the level of beginners. As a result, scenarios that match the level of the trainees must be created for each level, and the burden on holding the training has increased.

3   Requirements for Triage Training System

In this section, we describe the requirements to be met in creating a triage training system considering cooperation and proficiency of multiple people.

In preparation for a major disaster, The doctor concentrates on the medical practice and the initial triage should be in charge of nurses and the general public [11]. From this opinion, a collaborative training between trainees with different training level is necessary. However, the current trainings are carried out only by the same technical skill or knowledge level group. Therefore, the collaborative training system is required to easily construct situations close to the disaster site, and to change the difficulty level of training according to the skill level of each trainee.

In the following, we will describe details of the requirement for the system.

3.1 Presenting Information According to Distance to Victims

In order to quickly gather information on victims and injuries at the actual site, even in training it is necessary to reproduce the same environment as the harm site and to train under that environment. When there are two or more victims of injuries, they grasp the information on which area the victims are concentrated and how many people are present and act with judgment as appropriate. Therefore, even in training, it is necessary to have an environment that can simultaneously detect the presence of multiple people.

Furthermore, the amount of information obtained varies depending on the distance to the victim at the actual site. For example, when the victim is far away, recognition of the position or existence, when the person is in front of the eyes, can know detailed features such as presence or absence of consciousness, breathing rate, pulse rate, injury location.

3.2 Presentation of Information According to Proficiency Level for Each Trainee

In order to obtain a high training effect among people with different technological skills and knowledge amounts in a limited time, training with varying degrees of difficulty according to the level of each trainee is performed rather than unifying the level of training. For example, even if exercises with a low level of difficulty are performed for people with sufficient knowledge about triage, the correct answer rate naturally becomes high and does not make sense as training. On the contrary, under circumstances where triage beginners have no hint at all or under circumstances where they must act in accordance with experienced people, beginners rely on the experienced too much so they cannot train with thinking by themselves.

When learning some skills, people can understand features of skills more efficiently by practicing combined things (e.g. items, methods, or ideas). In cognitive psychology, that is called interleaving, and is taken into practice of music and training of sports. So, we think that even in triage, learning effectiveness will be increased by training combined items or methods. This interleaving are necessary for creating collaboration regardless of proficiency level. At that time, while using the same training scenario, it is necessary to change the presentation contents depending on the skill level of each trainee. By appropriately changing the presentation of information according to the level of the trainees, high quality training can realize.

4   Proposal and Implementation

We describe the proposal system in this section. This system offers the training in which the trainees learn how to cooperate at disaster sites and triage the injured.

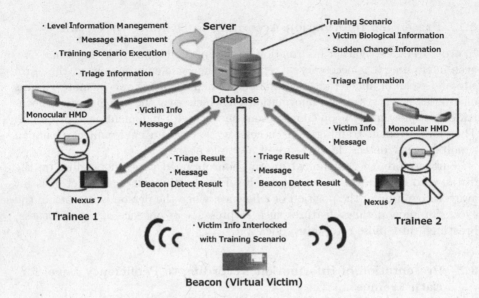

Fig. 2. System Configuration

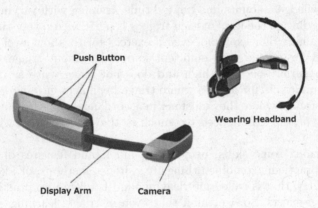

Fig. 3. Monocular HMD

4.1 System Configuration

The overall configuration of this system is shown at Fig. 2. This training system is used by two trainees basically. Each trainee holds one Nexus 7, the tablet-type device, so as to detect the radio signals from beacon terminals while wearing the monocular HMD (Fig. 3). Biometric information of one virtual injured person is transmitted in conjunction with one beacon terminal. We place beacon terminals for the number of victims at training environment instead of people who act as the injured. When the training starts, each trainee approaches the beacon terminal installed in the training environment, so that the victim information corresponding to the beacon is displayed on the tablet terminal. The trainees carry out triage while watching the injured person information.

During training, events such as sudden change of injured people and arrival of ambulance are generated. If a sudden change occurs, the trainees should move to the beacon terminal of the victim who has suddenly changed and triage again. Also, if an ambulance arrives, the trainees need to decide the victim who should be carried. They decide the victim with the highest priority while looking at the information on the injured person list on the tablet. After responding to each event like these, the trainees report a message to the Disaster Countermeasure Headquarter, that is, the trainer. All the records related to the training such as the triage results, the transmitted message, and the occurrence and response of the event, are stored in a database through the network. Message exchange between the disaster site and Disaster Countermeasure Headquarter is also executed via the database. Sharing information is extremely important in coordinating activities. Not only the information about which you are involved but also how you can check all the information, such as what other activities are doing, what messages are exchanged, and what kind of injured people you have found, is necessary. For this reason, we constructed a structure to exchange information via the database.

4.2   Changes in Information Presentation According to Distance

Figure 4 is a search screen of virtual injured people. The trainees search for victims while watching this display.

Fig. 4. Information of virtual victims

When searching for the victims and getting close to them, the amount of information changes. In this system, the information displayed according to the distance to the beacon terminal roughly changes in three steps. When the distance between the beacon terminal and the trainee is 3 m or more, the figure of the victim is not displayed on the tablet. When the distance is less than 3 m from 20 cm, an image showing the appearance of the victims is displayed. In order to reproduce the state where it is impossible to palpate such as acquiring biological information, the image of the injured person was designed so that the size of one step increases as approaching 100 cm although it can look over the injured person from a distance. When the distance to the beacon terminal becomes 20 cm or less, "triage possible" is displayed on the image of the virtual injured people corresponding to the beacon terminal. By touching the image of the victim who is displayed as "triage possible", the screen changes to the screen of vital information of the injured person. The trainee carries out triage based on the information and inputs the result using monocular HMD. In order to reproduce a situation where it is possible to acquire biological information only when it is in close contact with the victims, we designed so that we can not display biological information and enter triage results unless the distance to the beacon terminal is within 20 cm. Therefore, the trainee must triage after approaching the victim in the same way as the actual activity.

Also, during training, an event of sudden change occurs. At this time, "sudden change" is displayed on the image of the virtual injured. When an event of a sudden change in condition occurs, it is necessary to find suddenly changed injured people based on this indication and triage again.

4.3   Changes in Information Presentation According to Proficiency Level for Each Trainee

In this training, the trainees learn how to triage, respond to sudden change, decide the victim to be carried, and share information with each other. In this system, we propose three levels for three factors, including triage, response to sudden change, and decision the victim to be carried, and implement to change levels in each event under training. If the trainees use the system for the first time, all levels are automatically set to 1. The level information of the trainees is kept in the database even after the training is over. The trainees can start next training based on the level information in the database. The level change of the trainees is judged within the server every time they conduct the event. The level is raised by 1 if the trainees process the event correctly, and the level is dropped by 1 if they do incorrectly. However, with regard to triage, the level is raised by 1 if the trainees have correct answer in 2 consecutive times, and the level is dropped by 1 if they have incorrect answer in 2 consecutive times.

Changes in Biometric Information Presentation. When doing triage, you judge the seriousness based on biological information of the injured person. Triage is performed mainly in accordance with the flow chart of the START method, but this method is not familiar for beginners of triage. So, to get used to the triage and the START method, we implement information presentation that let the trainees check hints in the lower level and make them think by themselves as the level gets higher.

Determination of level change is made based on whether correct triage judgment can be made or not.

When the triage level is 1, all biological information expressed by letters and hints of START method are displayed like Fig. 5. The hint of the START method displayed beside the biometric information is a mechanism in which the triage category is displayed when answering "Yes" or "No" to the question. When the triage level is 2, all the biological information expressed by characters is displayed. Unlike level 1, triage must be done without hint of START method. When the triage level is 3, only the image of the injured person is displayed first like Fig. 6.

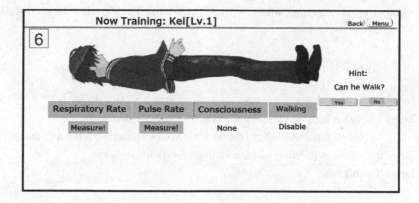

Fig. 5. Triage mode:lv1

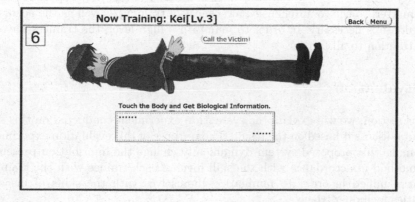

Fig. 6. Triage mode:lv3

In this case, by touching the part of ⊚ displayed on the image of the victims, the trainees can acquire biological information such as respiration rate and pulse rate. Unlike levels 1 and 2, where all the biological information was displayed, it is necessary for the trainees to gather the information while thinking by themselves. Since it takes extra time to gather information, triage must be done accurately and quickly at level 3.

Notification After Event Response. For events such as occurrence of a sudden change and a decision of carried victim, quick response and accurate judgment are required. After responding to events, the trainees should report to the headquarter in order to share on-site information. In this system, support is given to the trainees by displaying hints at the time of happening event. We give hints for beginners to encourage actions and change the expression of information for the experienced to think and act by themselves. Table 1 shows the detail of hints we give to the trainees.

Table 1. Hints given by system according to level of trainee

Level	Sudden change response	Carried victim decision
Level 1	Notice happening sudden change	Hints for decision
	Notice reporting after response	Notice reporting after response
Level 2	Notice happening sudden change	hints for decision
Level 3	No hints	No hints

A notice prompting the trainees to report a message to the headquarter is displayed on the tablet when they update information of the injured by the system. This notice is displayed in case of Level 1 or 2. Even if the trainees properly respond to the event, the level is lowered unless they report it to the headquarter, so the comprehensive awareness of training as well as the accuracy of response is necessary. In order to maintain a high level, the trainees have to pay attention to all factors.

5 Evaluation

In this section, we will explain the evaluation experiment conducted on this system and discuss it based on the result. The purpose of this evaluation experiment is to make this proposed system dynamically change the information presentation method in accordance with the skill level of each trainee with the training scenario unified in order to familiarize themselves with the skills of disaster activities including triage.

5.1 Experiment Description

The feature of this system is to increase the effectiveness of training by providing a training environment of difficulty according to the master level of each trainee. Therefore, we asked the examinees to practice using the proposed system and compare the results with the system that does not change the difficulty level.

Subjects. 12 university students and graduated school students without knowledge about triage were taken as subjects. Experiments were conducted in pairs of two, divided into two groups, three groups using the proposed method and the other three groups using the comparative method. In the proposed method group, experiments were conducted using the prototype system implemented in this research, and in the comparative method group, using a training system in which difficulty does not change dynamically during one training. The practical training was executed four times in total, and the fourth experimental result was evaluated.

Evaluation Criteria. Evaluation criteria focus on the final result of training for one pair of people, not the result of each subject individually. We think of four points as evaluation criteria. Four points are the following: quality of triage training (required time and correct answer rate), response for sudden change, times of sharing information, and questionnaire.

5.2 Procedures

Prior to training, the trainees read materials on triage, response to sudden change, and decision of victim to be carried. Then, using the START method to carry out triage when discovering a victim, if you have a sudden change, immediately rush to triage again and update the information, when an ambulance arrives urgent person. After that, a desk training was carried out based on that knowledge. The desk training uses monocular HMD and tablet, sitting in front of PC. The biological information of the virtual victims is displayed on the screen of PC, so the trainees carried out triage for seven people in total.

After the desk training was completed, a practical training was carried out. In the comparative method, all levels were unified so that they did not change during training. For example, the level varies depending on the response of each event in the proposed method. However, in the comparison method, all of the triage level, sudden change response level, and carrier determination level are fixed at 1. The trainees became one pair of two people, possessing a monocular HMD and a tablet, so that it searched for the beacon which the virtual injured person.

Training is started with the assumption that there are five injured people from the beginning, new discoveries of victims and various events occur with the passage of time. Distribution of the color of triage of each injured person existing from the beginning is 2 red in red, 1 in yellow, 1 green and 1 black, and the distribution of new injured people occurring during training is red 2 people, 2 yellow people, 1 green and 0 black.

In order to prevent the difference in the required time and the correct answer rate due to the difference in biometric information, in the experiment, the biological information of the virtual injured person was input fixed value beforehand so as not to fluctuate during the training. One who changed rapidly was 1 person from red, 1 person from yellow and 2 persons in green, totaling 4 people. Therefore, the number of victims and injured persons is ten in total, and subjects including trials of sudden change will carry out triage a total of 14 times. The event of carrying the injured happens 5 times and the event was generated in the same order by all subjects. Even during this experiment, we allowed both sending and receiving of messages using the system and conversation, and people who worked at the site freely shared information and carried out training.

5.3   Results

Required Time and Correct Answer Rate for Triage. Table 2 shows the time required for subjects to complete triage of all the victims and their correct answers. The required time refers to the time until the completion of the triage input result of all 10 virtual injured people from the start of training. The correct answer rate was calculated by measuring whether the triage category entered by the trainees were correct or not. Regarding the required time, the result was 791 s on the proposal side and 1027 s on the comparison side. From this result, it is understood that the group who trained in the proposed system was able to quickly triage to all the injured. The trainees were able to act while thinking about what kind of activities should be done as individuals in addition to sharing tasks between each trainee for the events. Next, the correct answer rate was 96.7% on the proposal side and 76.7% on the comparison side. Both of them have a high correct answer rate, but it turns out that the proposing side was able to carry out triage more accurately. A t test on the required time and correct answer rate showed no significant difference. One factor is that desktop training with the same content was done. The triage categories are classified into four categories, and the START method is not complicated, so it seems that they were able to master familiarity by repeating the number regardless of the difficulty change. As for the required time, it is expected that a more clear difference will appear by increasing the number of injured people.

Table 2. Required time and correct answer rate result

	Proposal method	Comparison method
Required time (sec.)	791.0	1027
Correct answer rate (%)	96.7	76.7

Table 3. Sudden change response result

	Proposal method	Comparison method
Sudden change response time (sec.)	70.5	124

Sudden Change Response. Table 3 shows the average required time it took for the subjects to complete sudden change response of the injured. The time from the sudden change of the condition of one injured person to the completion of the re-triage was regarded as the sudden change response time, and the average of the time taken for all the sudden change was compared. The result was 70.5 s for the proposed method and 124.1 s for the comparison method. Although the proposed method was able to cope in a shorter time, there was no significant difference in t test. In the proposed method, the required time is short and the variance is small regardless of the corresponding trainees or activity place, but on the comparative method side, the time taken to deal with the response was greatly dispersed depending on the corresponding trainer and place. Unless we know the state and location of the victim who completed the triage, we can not respond promptly when sudden change occurs. Looking at the results of the proposed method with a short average time and small variance, all of the subjects consciously wonder how they can quickly respond to the suddenly changing persons, learn the symptoms and places of each victim and injury unconsciously.

Sharing Information. Table 4 shows the number of site status reports to the disaster countermeasures headquarters conducted by the subjects. In the training conducted this time, there were nine reporting opportunities including response to sudden change and decision of carrier. The result was that the proposed method was 8 times and the comparison method was 4 times. The percentage of correct answers was higher in the proposed method, and when the t test was conducted, a significant difference was observed at the significance level 5 % ($p = 0.036278$, degrees of freedom: 4). From this result, it can be said that the proposal method side became able to act while conscious of information sharing. When events frequently occur during training, they tend to desperately respond to each event and tend to forget information sharing. In the proposal method, the degree of difficulty changes dynamically during training and behavior promotion message is notified or not, so that the subjects are always conscious of what to do when the response of the event ends. It seems that it became possible to report on the activity situation of the work place frequently.

Table 4. Sharing information result

	Proposal method	Comparison method
Reports (times)	8.0	4.0

Table 5. Questionnaire result: was the difficulty of training suitable for you?

Method	5pt	4pt	3pt	2pt	1pt
Proposal method (num. of subjects)	5	1	0	0	0
Comparison method (num. of subjects)	1	0	4	1	0

Table 6. Questionnaire result: do you feel that you are learning by using the system?

Method	5pt	4pt	3pt	2pt	1pt
Proposal method (num. of subjects)	4	2	0	0	0
Comparison method (num. of subjects)	2	4	0	0	0

Questionnaire. Finally, the questionnaire result is shown in Tables 5 and 6. Questionnaires were asked to answer in 5 grades from 1 to 5. 1 is bad, 5 indicates good results. Table 5 shows opinions that the degree of difficulty changes dynamically according to the proficiency level of the trainees, but it was highly appreciated for the proposal method, but from subjects who used the comparison method. The system of the comparison side remains fixed without changing the difficulty level during training, so even though the trainee is not familiar with training at a high level or despite being proficient at a low level. Table 6 shows even if you substitute a beacon terminal without actually using human beings as a victim of actual injury, it can be said that it was established as training.

Based on the above, by using this system to provide subjects with training to dynamically change the difficulty of presenting information according to the level of proficiency of each trainee through evaluation experiments, it was shown to be useful for learning the skill of activities including triage.

6   Conclusion

In order to act quickly and accurately in event of disasters it is necessary to train on a daily basis and acquire knowledge and skills. However, in the current training, since more than one person is trained in the same environment at the same time, training can be conducted only by those with knowledge amount and technical ability. Based on such a background, we proposed a triage training system in which the presentation content of information varies depending on the proficiency level of each trainee. First, victim information shown according to the distance between the injured and the trainees was changed, and the situation of the actual disaster site was reproduced. Actually moving around and searching for injured people, practicing triage approaching the injured and advancing training while responding to each event, so that you can find out the points of action that you can understand only by grasping the action. Experiments were conducted using this system to examine whether it is useful for learning skills of disaster activities including triage by changing the difficulty level of information presentation according to the skill level of each trainer. There was a tendency to be effective for decision of carrier and awareness of information sharing. Not only was the time required to respond to each event shortened, but also it gained a high correct answer rate. Based on these results, it was demonstrated that by implementing training using the proposed system, it is possible to carry out triage quickly and accurately in response to sudden change of persons etc. In addition, we found that it is effective for awareness of important information sharing in collaborative activities. From the above, it is possible to conduct more effective triage disaster drills by providing training in which information presentation difficulty is dynamically changed according to the level of proficiency of each trainer using this system. It is expected that this will lead to more efficient life-saving activities in disasters.

References

1. Takahashi, S.: Triage for Emergency Nurse, Emergency Life - Saving Person - From Preposition to ER and Disaster. Medica Publishment (2008)
2. Team DMAT Japan: Japan DMAT Activity Procedure. http://www.dmat.jp/
3. Miyano, M.: Human damage caused by the 1995 Hyogo ken Nanbu Earthquake (part 5) Interview survey on life-saving activities in Higashi Nada Ward, Kobe City. In: Japan Architecture Conference (1996)
4. NPO corporation disaster, medical care, town planning. http://triage.web.fc2.com/
5. NHK, Hanshin-Awaji Great Earthquake 19 years Great earthquake where rescue does not come. http://www6.nhk.or.jp/special/detail/index.html?aid=20140117
6. Ferrer, M., Hodges, J., Bonnardel, N.: The MoLE project: an international experiment about mobile learning environment. In: Proceedings of the 31st European Conference on Cognitive Ergonomics (ECCE 2013). Article 32, p. 5. ACM, New York (2013)
7. Otim, S.: A case-based knowledge management system for disaster management: fundamental concepts. In: Van de Walle, B., Turoff, M. (eds.) Proceedings of the 3rd International ISCRAM Conference, Newark, NJ, USA, pp. 598–604 (2006)
8. Sherstyuk, A., Vincent, D., Jin Hwa Lui, J., Connolly, K.K., Wang, K.L., Saiki, S.M., Caudell, T.P.: Design and development of a pose-based command language for triage training in virtual reality. In: IEEE Symposium on 3D User Interfaces (3DUI 2007), pp. 40–44, March 2007
9. Vincent, D.S., Sherstyuk, A., Burgess, L., Connolly, K.K.: Teaching mass casualty triage skills using immersive three-dimensional virtual reality. Acad. Emerg. Med. **15**(11), 1160–1165 (2008)
10. van der Spek, E.D., Wouters, P., van Oostendorp, H.: Code red: triage or cognition-based design rules enhancing decisionmaking taining in a game environment. Br. J. Educ. Technol. **42**(3), 441–455 (2011)
11. Tayama, Y., Kato, R., Okada, K.: Triage training system: adjusting the difficulty level according to user proficiency. In: 14th International Conference on Mobile and Ubiquitous Multimedia (MUM 2015), pp. 139–147, December 2015

A Scratch-Based Collaborative Learning System with a Shared Stage Screen

Yusuke Fukuma, Kumpei Tsutsui, Hideyuki Takada$^{(\boxtimes)}$, and Ian Piumarta

Faculty of Information Science and Engineering, Ritsumeikan University,
1-1-1 Noji-Higashi, Kusatsu, Shiga 525-8577, Japan
htakada@cs.ritsumei.ac.jp
http://www.cm.is.ritsumei.ac.jp/~htakada/index_e.html

Abstract. Opportunities for elementary and junior high school students to learn programming have been increasing over the last few years, and programming education in elementary schools will become compulsory in 2020. Applying 'collaborative learning' to programming education can be considered an effective method, but the current environment for collaborative learning in programming education needs to be improved because in many cases the creation and execution of programs are completed on isolated personal computers. To improve this situation we have developed a collaborative learning support system featuring a shared 'stage' screen based on the visual programming environment Scratch. Our system keeps each individual's Scratch programming environment separate from the shared stage screen, but allows each of the individual stages to be displayed together on the shared screen at the same time. The system was used during collaborative learning workshops at a local community center. Evaluations were made with post-workshop survey questionnaires and analysis of the learners' behavior. We confirmed that co-teaching and communication among learners occurred because the programs developed by others were visible on the shared stage screen.

Keywords: Collaborative learning · Programming education · Shared screen

1 Introduction

With the introduction of compulsory programming education in the Japanese standard curriculum for elementary schools in 2020 [3], increasing interest in programming education is gaining the attention of workshop organizers. Programming workshops for elementary and secondary school students are being held by various organizations, including non-profit organizations and companies.

At the same time, the Japanese Ministry of Education, Culture, Sports, Science and Technology (MEXT) is emphasizing collaborative learning as one of the key methods of education for the 21st century [2]. In collaborative learning, a teacher facilitates communication and mutual teaching between children during classes. Collaborative learning can deepen the students' understanding by

© Springer International Publishing AG 2017
T. Yoshino et al. (Eds.): CollabTech 2017, LNCS 10397, pp. 84–98, 2017.
DOI: 10.1007/978-3-319-63088-5_8

encouraging them to exchange ideas, thoughts, and opinions with their peers. Through the advocacy of MEXT, various new methods of classroom teaching (such as collaborative learning) are being introduced to schools, in contrast to the 'one-way guidance' from teacher to students that was normal in the past.

Collaborative learning, involving teaching and learning within a group instead of traditional one-way guidance or individual learning, could also be an effective method for programming education. In most practical situations, however, students are isolated with their own computer on which they create and execute their programs. This is far from an effective environment for collaborative learning. Communication among students must also be promoted for effective collaborative learning, which is outside the scope of conventional methods.

To improve this situation we developed a collaborative learning system based on Scratch [5]. Scratch is a visual programming environment in which users create projects using multimedia and scripts. A typical Scratch user creates programs to control object movement on a 'stage' displayed on their personal computer, leading to isolated project work. We extended Scratch to be suitable for collaborative learning, by allowing multiple users' individually-created moving objects to be displayed on a single, shared stage. It is expected that seeing the movement of objects created by others on the shared stage will promote communication and co-learning between users. We evaluated the effectiveness of our system by using it during programming workshops with young students.

2   Collaborative Learning with Programming

In this section we describe some of the problems faced when introducing collaborative learning into programming education at elementary schools, in order to formulate the requirements for an effective system.

2.1   Programming Education in Elementary School

The MEXT suggests that programming education at elementary schools should address the following four points:

- Children notice that computers are being used in their daily lives.
- Children notice the necessity of solving problems by taking a series of steps.
- Children acquire *programming thinking*.
- Children try to make use of computers in their own lives.

To achieve these learning goals, the MEXT also suggests that it is important to create a method of programming education that encourages "subjective, interactive and deep learning", and that classes should never become silent with students just facing their own computers.

When considering a form of programming education based on the points above, we note that conventional one-way teaching cannot be subjective because in most cases it forces children to learn passively. Similarly, private one-on-one lessons cannot promote interaction among learners. The conventional method is therefore considered inappropriate.

In elementary school programming education, conventional classroom lessons or personal lessons should therefore be replaced by learning methods that promote inter-student interactions in addition to self-directed learning.

2.2   Problems in Collaborative Learning of Programming

To engage in collaborative learning, the following two conditions should be satisfied:

- Learners can share their thoughts through communication with others.
- Learners can incorporate the opinions of others and improve their own performance based on them.

In programming education, however, learners have little chance to be involved with others as they focus on using just the computer in front of them. Communication is subsequently less motivated, and opportunities to incorporate others' opinions are reduced.

To solve this problem it is necessary for learners to be exposed not only to their own project but also to the projects developed by others. By learning in an environment where they can take an interest in other projects, they are naturally encouraged to talk about their projects, ask questions, make suggestions, and teach each other new skills.

2.3   Related Work

The system described in this paper is an extension of Single Display Groupware (SDG) [6]. SDG enables co-located users to collaborate using a single, shared display while simultaneously using multiple input devices. In order to adapt SDG to a visual programming environment such as Scratch, we placed a single stage on a shared display screen while keeping the programming pane on the individual users' personal computers.

Some research work emphasizes collaborative scripting by multiple users for visual programming environments [4,7,8], but they are based on a 'multiple computers, multiple displays' paradigm.

3   Development of the System

In this section we first describe the requirements, functions and implementation of a collaborative learning system based on Scratch. We then describe a scenario for its use in a practical situation.

3.1   Requirements

As mentioned above, Scratch is essentially a single-user application. A single window displays three panes containing command blocks, scripts, and the stage. To make collaborative learning possible, the system should be modified to satisfy the following requirements:

- The stage pane, showing the results of executing scripts, can be shared.
- Both individual development and group development can be performed.

Based on these requirements, the stage pane (where scripted actions are displayed) is separated from the other panes and displayed on a different screen shared among the co-located users. As shown in Fig. 1, in addition to the individual development terminals used by the learners, a 'shared stage screen' displays all the stage panes belonging to the users within the collaborating group. Furthermore, as shown in Fig. 2, the shared stage can be unified into a single project by removing the frames separating one individual stage from the others, allowing objects from different stages to interact with each other on a single, shared stage.

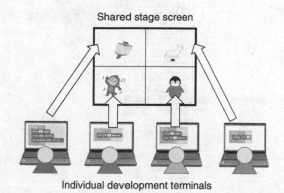

Fig. 1. Sharing the stages on the shared stage screen

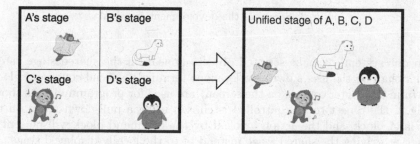

Fig. 2. Removing the frame on the shared stage screen

3.2   Functions

The system has four major functions: a 'programming' function allowing the user to create and execute programs, a 'stage sharing' function for displaying the multiple stages of projects developed on the users' computers, a 'group management' function for choosing which individual computers belong to the shared stage group, and a 'frame removal' function to switch between multiple individual stages and a single, shared stage.

Programming. In Scratch, users can easily develop a program by combining prepared command blocks using drag-and-drop, and then see the resulting motion of their objects on the stage. Figure 3 shows the screen used for program development. It is an extended version of Scratch, displayed on the personal computer of an individual user.

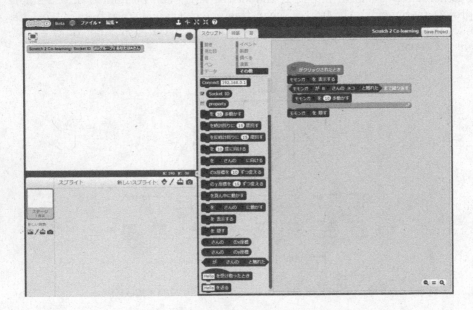

Fig. 3. Screen of the development terminal

In our system, to make scripted objects appear on the shared stage screen (rather than on the user's own development terminal), special command blocks (shown in the center column on the screen) are used for programming. As shown in Fig. 4, the object to be controlled is chosen using a pull-down menu on the command block, and the action invoked by the command block will be sent to the server driving the shared stage instead of to the locally-displayed stage.

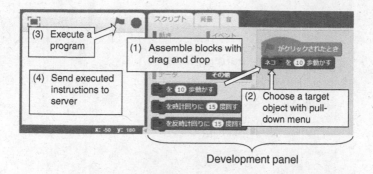

Development panel

Fig. 4. Programming on our Scratch-based system

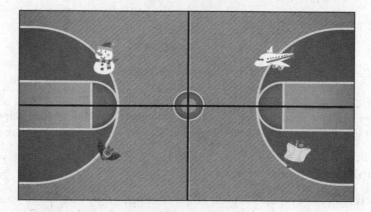

Fig. 5. Shared stage screen

Stage Sharing. Figure 5 shows the shared stage screen. A single display shows the stages from every user in the group. Frames divide the screen into four areas, each of which is assigned to display one of the user stages. In the example shown, each stage contains a single object which will move according to the actions generated from the script running on the user's personal computer.

Group Management. Figure 6 shows the group management Web interface, running on the server, allowing the system operator to manage group membership. The stages for individual development computers can be assigned to a specific quadrant of the group's shared stage screen.

Frame Removal. This server function is also provided by the Web interface, accessed with a Web browser. Pressing the 'toggle frame' button removes the frame separating the stages on the shared display. Removing the frame switches the system from individual development mode to group development mode. In

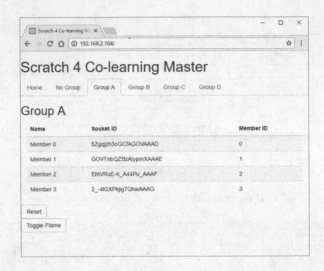

Fig. 6. Management console

group development mode, objects can move beyond the bounds of their 'home' stage and can be programmed to interact with objects created by other users.

3.3   Implementation

The structure of our system is shown in Fig. 7. Each group consists of four development terminals, one shared stage screen terminal, and a server. The development terminals and the shared stage screen terminal communicate with the server using the WebSocket API. Commands executed on the development terminals are transmitted to the shared stage screen terminal via the server. Object coordinates, and collisions between objects, are monitored on the shared stage screen terminal and transmitted back to the server. The server then forwards this information to the individual development terminals.

The individual development environments run in the users' Web browsers. The functionalities of the shared stage screen terminal and the server are provided by Windows applications. The server and the shared stage screen application can be operated on the same computer. Figure 8 shows a picture of the entire system in use.

Development Terminal. Special command blocks for interacting with objects on the shared stage screen were added using ScratchX [1], an extension of Scratch that facilitates the addition of new command blocks written in JavaScript. Our additional command blocks are shown in Table 1.

When a command block in the 'operation' category is executed, the development terminal does not perform the block's operation locally. Instead it transmits the attributes of the executed operation to the server, along with the ID

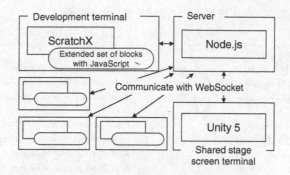

Fig. 7. System structure

Fig. 8. Actual application environment

assigned to the development terminal. Command blocks in the 'monitoring' category are triggered in response to information received from the server about object coordinates and collisions.

Server. The server mediates communication between the development terminals and the shared stage screen terminal. It transmits executed commands from the development terminal to the shared stage screen terminal, and sends information about the monitored status of object coordinates and collisions received from the shared stage back to individual development terminals. The server is implemented using JavaScript, Node.js, and the Apache HTTP daemon.

Group membership is managed by the system operator using the group management interface. When a development terminal is added to a group, the server allocates a unique ID that will be associated with the terminal. Terminal IDs are stored on the server to allow group membership to be determined. When the server receives information from a development terminal, it uses the terminal's ID to identify its group. The information is then propagated to the other terminals belonging to the group.

Table 1. Extended set of blocks

Category	Block	Function
Connection	Connect [A]	Connect to server A
Operation	Move [A] [B] steps	Move object A in B steps
	Turn [A] clockwise [B] degrees	Turn object A clockwise in B degrees
	Turn [A] counter-clockwise [B] degrees	Turn object A counter-clockwise in B degrees
	Point [A] in direction [B]	Point object A in direction B degrees
	Point [A] towards [B]'s [C]	Point object A towards object C of user B
	Change [A]'s x by [B]	Add B to x-axis of object A
	Change [A]'s y by [B]	Add B to y-axis of object A
	Move [A] to center	Move object A to the center of the coordinate
	Move [A] to [B]'s [C]	Move object A to the coordinate of object C of user B
	Show [A]	Show object A in the stage
	Hide [A]	Hide object A in the state
	Send [A]	Send message A to all objects in the group
Monitoring	[A] touches [B]'s [C]	Check if object A touches object C of user B
	x position of [A]'s [B]	X-axis of object B of user A
	y position of [A]'s [B]	Y-axis of object B of user A
	When I receive [A]	An event receiving message A

Shared Stage Screen Terminal. The shared stage screen terminal is implemented using C# and the Unity engine. It renders users' objects according the information received from the server about 'operation' commands executed on the development terminals. It also monitors its own objects' coordinates and collisions, transmitting this information back to the server. Transmissions to the server are made every few tens of milliseconds. From the server, relevant parts of this information are forwarded back to the development terminals where it is used to control 'monitor' command execution.

3.4   Use Case

A typical scenario of multiple users using our system for collaborative programming is described below.

Every user executes the command 'Connect A' at their development terminal, causing the terminal to be connected to server A. After all terminals are connected, the operator forms a group by choosing four development terminals from the list of connected terminals. Each development terminal is assigned to a quadrant of the shared stage.

Figure 9 shows an example of individual development with our system. Users create and then execute a program. Their scripted objects are displayed on the shared stage screen, within the area assigned to their development terminal. Their objects cannot move beyond the frame separating their area from the three other areas.

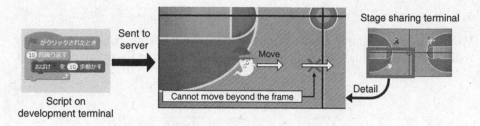

Fig. 9. Example of use for personal development

When the operator presses the 'toggle frame' button on the group management console, the frame separating the four user areas is removed and users can perform group development. In group development, objects are free to move over the entire shared stage as shown in Fig. 10. In addition, objects can be programmed to interact with other objects; for example, one user turns their 'ghost' object towards the 'cat' object created by another user, as shown in Fig. 11.

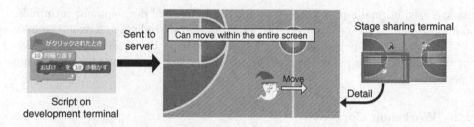

Fig. 10. Use case in group development

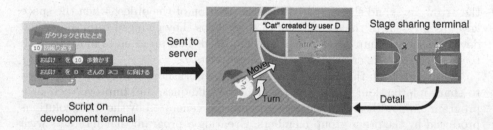

Fig. 11. Interaction between objects in group development

4 Application of the System

In this section we describe our experiences using the system for collaborative learning in practical programming workshops.

4.1 Overview

We held two programming workshops to evaluate our system, which we will refer to as 'Workshop 1' and 'Workshop 2'. Table 2 shows the details of each workshop.

Table 2. Workshops

	Workshop 1	Workshop 2
Place:	Kodomo Mirai-kan (Kyoto City)	
Date:	November 27th, 2016	December 4th, 2016
Duration:	50 min	90 min
Participants:	4 (2 × 3rd + 2 × 4th grade)	7 (4 × 3rd, 1 × 4th, 1 × 6th grade, 1 × 1st grade junior high school)
Groups:	1	2 (3rd grade students, others)

We used normal laptop computers for the individual development terminals, and all-in-one desktop computers for the server and shared stage screen terminal.

Evaluation was performed during the workshops by observing the behavior of children while using the system, and after the workshops by conducting questionnaires.

4.2 Workshop Content

For these workshops we challenged the children to "make a dodgeball game".

Participants created a game in which players throw a ball at each other on a dodgeball court displayed on the shared stage screen. In the first half of the workshops they worked individually to create a script moving an object with the arrow keys, and showing a ball at the position of the object when the space key was pressed. In the second half of workshops they changed from individual development to group development and modified their program to move the ball towards the objects created by other participants.

As they develop this kind of program in the workshop, children are expected to share information, teach each other new techniques, and improve their own programming by observing the different motions generated by the three solutions produced by the other group members. Creating a program that interacts with objects developed by the other participants promotes communication with them.

4.3 Results and Discussion

Tables 3, 4, 5 and 6 show the results of the questionnaires conducted after the workshops. Note that Q1 and Q2 in Workshop 2 (Table 4) are slightly modified from those in Workshop 1 (Table 3), reflecting the experience we gained during the first workshop. Q3 through Q6 were the same in both workshops.

Table 3. Questionnaire results for Q1 and Q2 in workshop 1

	Question	Votes
Q1	When did you look at projects of others? (single choice)	
	1. When I wanted to compare the movement of my project	1
	2. When I wanted to see the movement of others' project	3
	3. When I wanted to know the progress of my project	0
Q2	What did you teach or learn from others? (multiple choice)	
	1. I taught others how to use blocks and choose sketches	2
	2. I taught others how to move objects in a peculiar way	0
	3. I learned how to use blocks and choose sketches	3
	4. I learned how to move objects in a peculiar way	0
	5. Other (free description)	0

Table 4. Questionnaire results for Q1 and Q2 in workshop 2

	Question	Votes
Q1	When did you look at projects of others? (multiple choice)	
	1. When I wanted to compare the movement of my project	2
	2. When I wanted to see the movement of others' project	4
	3. When I wanted to know the progress of my project	2
Q2-1	What did you teach others? (multiple choice)	
	1. I taught others how to use blocks and choose sketches	1
	2. I taught others how to move objects in a peculiar way	2
	3. I didn't teach anything	3
	4. Other (free description)	
	• How to use the sound blocks	1
Q2-2	(If you chose 1, 2 or 4 in Q2-1) Why did you teach? (single choice)	
	1. I was asked a question	1
	2. Others looked troubled when I saw the movement of their project	1
	3. Others looked troubled when I saw the screen of their PC	0
	4. Other (free description)	
	• I wanted to teach	1
	• Others looked misunderstood	1
Q2-3	What did you learn from others? (multiple choice)	
	1. I learned how to use blocks and choose sketches	3
	2. I learned how to move objects in a peculiar way	3
	3. I didn't learn anything from others	3
	4. Other (free description)	0

Table 5. Questionnaire results for Q3 and Q4 in workshop 1 and 2

	Question	Votes
Q3	What was helpful to see the project of others? (multiple choice)	
	1. I used the same sketch because I liked it	2
	2. I liked the movement I didn't imagine	2
	3. I liked the movement with different ways of using blocks	4
	4. I didn't have anything helpful	4
Q4	Do you find anything that you wanted to imitate by seeing the project of others? (single choice)	
	1. I found something to imitate, so I created it by myself	3
	2. I found something to imitate, so I created it by learning from others	4
	3. I found something to imitate, but I couldn't create it	1
	4. I didn't find anything to imitate	3

Table 6. Questionnaire results for Q5 and Q6 in workshop 1 and 2

Q5	What did you think in creating a project with your team mates?
	I tried to make my project less overlapped with others
Q6	Write your impressions of this workshop
	• It was fun because I saw the way of programming of others.
	• It was fun!
	• I learned that I could create a game by programming with others
	• I was happy because I enjoyed Scratch very much and the workshop went well
	• Making a dodgeball game was great
	• I thought it difficult because this is my first experience, but it was good to go well

We will discuss the effectiveness of the system in two major areas, according to the results of the questionnaires and the behavior of the participants observed in the recorded video.

Communication and Co-teaching. As shown in the results of Q2 (Table 3) and with Q2-1 and Q2-3 (Table 4), most of the participants answered that they taught or learned from others during the workshop. We can conclude that active co-teaching occurred during the workshop. We can further conclude that the use of a shared stage triggered co-teaching because of answers similar to, "others looked troubled when I saw the motion of their project" given as reasons why participants felt motivated to teach. Sharing of the stage also generated opportunities to learn from others, as indicated by eight out of eleven participants who answered that, "I found something to imitate"; furthermore, four of these eight participants indicated that they created their programs by learning from others (Table 5).

The recorded video showed that communication among participants increased after the transition from individual development to group development. By collaborating in groups to create a single project, communication within the group increased. In the questionnaires, one participant answered Q5 by saying, "I tried to make my project less overlapped with others" (Table 6). The recorded video also showed that they tried to choose a different dodgeball target object from the other participants, by communicating among themselves.

Improvement of Programs. In response to Q1 ("When did you look at projects of others?"), there is a relatively large number of participants who answered, "When I wanted to compare the movement of my project" or, "When I wanted to see the movement of others' projects". From this we conclude that the shared stage increases the probability of participants referring to the projects and programs developed by others. From Q3 we also see that modification and improvement of programs was actually undertaken. Answers to Q6 similar to, "It was fun because I saw the way of programming of others" support the conclusion that participants were aware of what others were developing during the workshop.

From the discussion above, we conclude that the system is effective for promoting communication and co-teaching, as well as motivating participants to improve their own programs.

5   Conclusion

We described a collaborative learning support system based on Scratch that enables four users to share their stages on a single, shared screen. When the system was used during workshops we observed an awareness of others' projects during development, and communication and co-teaching being triggered by viewing the shared stage screen. It was also observed that sharing the stage and communicating with others led participants to make improvements to their own programs.

The current system limits the number of grouped terminals to four, because the shared stage screen is divided into four areas by the frame. In future we would like to make the system more flexible, for example by making it possible to divide the shared stage screen into six areas allowing six users to engage in group project work.

Acknowledgements. This work was supported by JSPS KAKENHI Grant Number 16H02925.

References

1. ScratchX. http://scratchx.org/. Accessed 21 Mar 2017
2. The Vision for ICT in Education, Ministry of Education, Culture, Sports, Science and Technology (2011). http://www.mext.go.jp/b_menu/houdou/23/04/_icsFiles/afieldfile/2012/08/03/1305484_14_1.pdf. Accessed 21 Mar 2017
3. Japan Revitalization Strategy 2016, Ministry of Education Culture Sports Science and Technology (2016). http://www.kantei.go.jp/jp/singi/keizaisaisei/pdf/2016_zentaihombun_en.pdf. Accessed 21 Mar 2017

4. Engelhard, P., Hirschfeld, R., Lincke, J.: Pitsupai collaborative scripting in a distributed, persistent 3D world. In: Proceedings of the Seventh International Conference on Creating, Connecting and Collaborating through Computing, pp. 87–94. IEEE (2009)
5. Maloney, J., Resnick, M., Rusk, N., Silverman, B., Eastmond, E.: The scratch programming language and environment. ACM Trans. Comput. Educ. (TOCE) **10**(4), 16 (2010)
6. Stewart, J., Bederson, B.B., Druin, A.: Single display groupware: a model for co-present collaboration. In: Proceedings of the SIGCHI conference on Human Factors in Computing Systems, pp. 286–293. ACM (1999)
7. Takada, H.: A 3D collaborative creation environment with tile programming on croquet. In: Proceedings of the Fifth International Conference on Creating, Connecting and Collaborating through Computing, pp. 125–130. IEEE (2007)
8. Umezawa, M., Abe, K., Nishihara, S., Kurihara, T.: NetMorph-an intuitive mobile object system. In: Proceedings of the First International Conference on Creating, Connecting and Collaborating Through Computing, pp. 32–39. IEEE (2003)

AccelChalk: Detecting Writing Actions with Chalk Acceleration for Collaboration Between Teachers and Students

Taishi Okazawa$^{(\boxtimes)}$ and Hironori Egi

Graduate School of Informatics and Engineering,
The University of Electro-Communications, 1-5-1 Chofugaoka,
Tokyo 182-8585, Chofu, Japan
{okazawa,hiro.egi}@uec.ac.jp

Abstract. In this research, we design a system to detect the writing behavior of teachers on a chalkboard. The developed system uses a smart chalk holder with a three-axis accelerometer (AccelChalk) and is used in actual lectures for evaluation. A technique for determining the physical state of learners by using behavior identification has been developed earlier. It has been suggested that this technology could be used to estimate the state of learners in a classroom. We believe that it can also be applied to detect writing behavior on a chalkboard. From an experiment with teachers, the overall recognition rate exceeded 80% in the detection of writing behavior on chalkboard in actual lectures. The teachers suggested that the proposed system was useful for reviewing their lectures. In future work, it will be necessary to make the shape of the AccelChalk more sophisticated.

Keywords: Teacher sensing · Chalk and talk · Smart chalk holder · Classroom collaboration

1 Introduction

In this research, we have designed a system that detects the writing behavior of teachers on a chalkboard. The developed system uses a smart chalk holder with a three-axis accelerometer. The system aims to encourage teachers to self-reflect on their lectures by showing them their of writing action rates. We validated the accuracy of the rates calculated by the implemented system and also evaluated its effectiveness from the results of interviews with teachers after experiments in actual lectures.

Previous research has developed a method of detecting the writing behavior of students [1]. We aim to combine the results of detecting the writing behaviors of both teachers and their students. This is intended to assist teachers in adjusting their writing approaches to the writing abilities of their students.

Teachers often choose different approaches to teaching depending on the characteristics of particular lectures, enabling them to more efficiently convey

© Springer International Publishing AG 2017
T. Yoshino et al. (Eds.): CollabTech 2017, LNCS 10397, pp. 99–106, 2017.
DOI: 10.1007/978-3-319-63088-5_9

the contents of the lecture to students. The patterns of writing behavior on a chalkboard have been classified [2]. Such patterns are considered to be the fundamental elements of any teaching method.

There are several ways for teachers to reflect on their own writing behavior on a chalkboard [3], including memory, peer review, video recordings of their lectures, and student evaluation. However, there are difficulties to carry out in point of costs and to find specific elements to be improved. The advantage of the system proposed in this research is that it presents teachers with their own writing behavior. It is essential that teachers are not burdened by the system or required to change their teaching methods.

The goal of this research is to make a collaborative system that detects the writing behavior of teachers on chalkboards and of students on notebooks.

2   Related Work

2.1   The Significance of Chalkboards

In the recent years, lectures have often been given to students using presentation software such as Microsoft PowerPoint to display pre-prepared lecture materials on a screen in the classroom. Some of the lectures do not need chalkboards at all and only use pre-prepared materials. There is no necessity of a chalkboard in terms of writing phrases to highlight for students. However, even now some lectures are still given by writing on chalkboards. One of the differences between a presentation style lecture and "chalk and talk" style lecture is the presence of writing behavior. This is expected to gain the visual attention of the students by emphasizing not only on the teacher's body movements but also on the process of organizing knowledge in a "chalk and talk" style lecture.

Studies have surveyed the kinds of lectures students prefer [4]. The researchers asked medical and dental school students about three lecture styles, namely PowerPoint presentations, "chalk and talk" and using OHP(overhead projector). The result was that the majority of medical students (65.33%) preferred PowerPoint presentations: whereas, dental students preferred "chalk and talk" (41.84%), OHP (31.21%), and PowerPoint presentations (25.85%) for their lectures.

Therefore, the suitability of a particular lecture style was found to be different depending on the area of study. Also, previous research has confirmed that there is a strong correlation between the amount of note-taking and the score on the post-test [5]. "Chalk and talk" is defined as an important teaching method by the Ministry of Education, Culture, Sports, Science and Technology of Japan [6]. Presentation of information using computers is not regarded as a substitute for "chalk and talk". Moreover, it is important to instruct students to take notes because important information is written on a chalkboard.

As a result, we feel that the presence of writing behavior is a strong advantage of lectures using a chalkboard over lectures using presentation software.

2.2   Pen Motion Sensing

Some researchers have focused on pen sensing for collaborative systems. There has been a study that developed a technique for hand based motion analysis using a radio-frequency inertial measurement unit [7]. That system automatically analyzed characters handwritten in the air in real time using the hand motion analysis technique. It is argued that this method would be useful for designing real-time hand gesture recognition in applications such as computer games. The purpose of the study was to detect written letters and not to detect the subjects' writing behavior.

Research has also been conducted to identify the writing behavior of students by using a ballpoint pen with an acceleration sensor [1]. Four pen movement patterns could be detected using the acceleration sensor. We apply this method to detecting the writing behavior of teachers on a chalkboard.

3   Integrated Classroom Sensing for Collaboration

Previous work recorded the state of the teacher and supported the review of teaching behavior [8]. In that study, the teacher used a pen-sensitive display instead of a chalkboard. The goal of the research was to broaden the reach of distance learning while maintaining the merits of chalkboards. In a similar manner, research has been conducted to develop an interactive system that records "chalk and talk" style lectures of a teacher and shares the recorded lectures with students in remote places. Using such a system, physical aspects of teachers' presentations, like their nonverbal behavior, can be delivered to students.

We consider a method for detecting writing behavior on a chalkboard in this research. In addition, we introduce a method that uses this analyzed data to support teachers in reflecting on their lectures. The writing behavior of students in their notebooks is also detected by ballpoint pens with acceleration sensors and will be combined with the teacher data to form an integrated classroom sensing system for collaboration. Figure 1 shows an overview of the integrated classroom sensing system in the classroom.

The architecture of the proposed system is designed as follows. The values measured by the three-axes accelerometers are sent to the Collecting Servers via Bluetooth. The Collecting Servers are placed in the classroom, and we propose to use handheld devices that have both Bluetooth and Wi-Fi modules. The Collecting Servers process these values, detect the current state of each student (selected from a set of pre-defined state types) and relay those states to the Context Server at the front of the classroom via Wi-Fi. The Context Server estimates the overall classroom situation and sends feedback to the teacher. The teacher is notified about the number of writing students during the lecture.

The teacher can then review their teaching methods by comparing the number of students writing with their own writing behavior. Integrating the teacher's behavior with that of the students is much more effective than considering them separately.

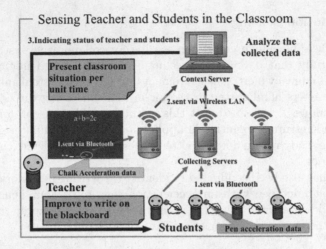

Fig. 1. Overview of the proposed system for sensing the teacher and their students in the classroom

4 Teacher Sensing with Chalk Acceleration

It is necessary to confirm that the movement of a piece of chalk can be measured and used to estimate a teacher's writing behavior. Figure 2 shows an acceleration sensor attached to a chalk holder. A preliminary experiment was conducted to clarify the effectiveness of the movement estimation for the chalk holder. A teacher using the chalk holder is shown in Fig. 3.

Fig. 2. A chalk holder with an acceleration sensor (AccelChalk)

Various kinds of states can be assumed in an actual classroom. From observation of the regularity of chalk movement and the actual behavior of teachers, the following three kinds of states were identified. These three kinds of states and the transitions between them are shown in Fig. 4. "State a," "State b," and "State c" in the figure can be described as follows.

a. The chalk is regularly moved for writing (Write Action)
   When the chalk is continuously and regularly moved in a certain pattern, it is being used by the teacher to write on a chalkboard. In this state, the teacher is estimated to be writing during a lecture.

Fig. 3. A teacher using the chalk holder in the classroom

b. Chalk is moved irregularly (Move Action)
   When the chalk is moved continuously but irregularly, it is being held by the teacher but not used for writing on a chalkboard. In this state, the teacher is estimated to be explaining content already written on a chalkboard.
c. Chalk is stopped (Stop Action)
   When a piece of chalk is fixed in a tilted or horizontal direction, it is stopped. In this state, the teacher is estimated to be thinking about how to best explain the content to the students.

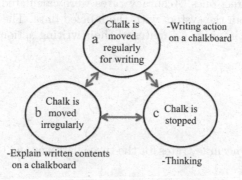

Fig. 4. The three kinds of states and their transitions

The benefit of this method is that it is applicable to the unwritten and unexpressed states of teachers. The ordinary chalks used in classrooms are adopted to encourage a natural "chalk and talk" lecture style. The designed system introduces an acceleration sensor with a battery (WAA-010 by Wireless Technologies, Inc.). The three-axis accelerometer data from the sensor is sent to the Collecting Servers via wireless transmission (Bluetooth).

5   Experiment

5.1   Preparation for the Experiment

Two teachers who give mathematics lectures at a university were chosen to help evaluate the state recognition rates of our system. The position of the acceleration sensor was adjusted so as not to interfere with holding the chalk holder. Attaching the acceleration sensor to the chalk holder had no significant influence on their teaching. The average recognition rates for the demonstration lectures performed by the two teachers exceeded 80% for all patterns. We consider that these rates are sufficient for discriminating the three patterns of writing behavior under controlled conditions.

5.2   Evaluation Experiment

An experiment was conducted with the developed system to evaluate its recognition rates in actual lectures. The topic of the lectures was mathematics for first grade students at a science and engineering university. The writing behavior patterns of the two teachers were detected in a classroom with a chalkboard. The lectures were considered to be typical "chalk and talk" style lectures.

The movements of the chalk holder were collected for the two teachers in the course of their lessons. The lectures were also recorded using a video camera. The detection rates for the three kinds of states recognized by the system were shown to the teachers after the experiment. A set of labeled data was manually prepared by checking the lecture videos. The detection rates using the labeled data were regarded as the correct ones. Accuracy rates were calculated by comparing the recognition data from the system with the labeled data. The teachers were also asked for their own intuitive estimates of their writing action rates during their lectures.

6   Results

6.1   Accuracy

Figure 5 depicts the accuracy rates for the three patterns and the overall accuracy of the system.

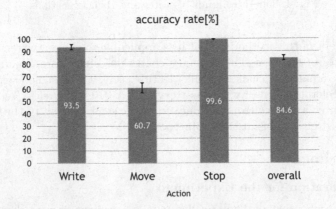

Fig. 5. Accuracy rates for the three individual patterns and the overall accuracy

The overall accuracy rate across all the data sets was 84.6% and the accuracy rate for writing was 93.5%. However, the accuracy rate for moving was only 60.7%, which is lower than that for the other patterns. Many factors differed between the actual lectures and the demonstration lectures, such as the presence of students and the limited lecture time. We consider that the teachers performed differently in the actual lectures than in the demonstration lectures. Subsequently, the data of Move Action in the demonstration lectures were replaced with the data picked up from the actual lectures, which resulted in a higher coincident ratio of the Move Action. Figure 6 depicts the recalculated accuracy rates after the replacement.

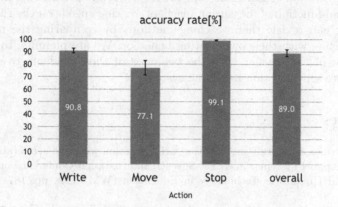

Fig. 6. Accuracy rates after replacement of the Move Action data

6.2   Comparison of Write Action Rates

The teachers were asked to reflect on their lectures and intuitively estimate their writing action rates. Table 1 shows their answers and the actual rates for each teacher.

Table 1. The intuitive estimates given by the teachers and the measured Write Action rates

	Self-reflection	Label	System[a]
Teacher A	45–50%	22.0%	29.7%
Teacher B	25–33%	30.3%	38.7%

[a] After replacement of Move Action.

Both of the teachers had university teaching experience of more than 10 years. Teacher A answered that he had intuitively thought his Write Action rate equaled half of the lecture. It seems to be difficult even for expert teachers to determine their Write Action rates accurately. We anticipate that indicating their writing behavior rates to them will induce self-reflection in teachers.

7   Conclusion and Future Work

In this research, we have developed a system that detects the writing behavior of teachers on a chalkboard. The system uses a smart chalk holder with a three-axis accelerometer. Three kinds of states were recognized, both by the regularity of chalk movement and actual teacher behavior. From an experiment with real teachers, the overall recognition rate exceeded 80% in detecting writing behavior on the chalkboard in actual lectures. The teachers suggested that the proposed system was useful for reviewing their lectures.

In future work, it will be necessary to make the shape of the chalk holder with the acceleration sensor more sophisticated. We are considering introducing the additional function of measuring teachers' writing speeds on the chalkboard. The teacher can review their teaching methods by comparing the number of students writing with their own writing behavior. We are planning to integrate the behavior of the teacher with the behavior of their students to encourage more effective self-reflection using the system.

References

1. Egi, H., Ozawa, S.: AccelPen: detecting writing action with pen acceleration toward learning support systems. In: IEEE Seventh International Conference on Wireless, Mobile and Ubiquitous Technology in Education (WMUTE), pp. 187–189. IEEE (2012)
2. Bonesrønning, H.: Can effective teacher behavior be identified? Econ. Educ. Rev. **23**(3), 237–247 (2004)
3. Kometani, Y., Tomoto, T., Tonomura, T., Furuta, T., Akakura, T.: Video feedback system for teaching improvement using student sequential and overall teaching evaluations. Educ. Technol. Res. **37**(1), 73–85 (2014)
4. Seth, V., Upadhyaya, P., Ahmad, M., Moghe, V.: Powerpoint or chalk and talk: perceptions of medical students versus dental students in a medical college in india. Adv. Med. Educ. Pract. **1**, 11–16 (2010)
5. Nye, P.A., Crooks, T.J., Powley, M., Tripp, G.: Student note-taking related to university examination performance. Int. J. High. Educ. Res. **13**(1), 85–97 (1984)
6. Ministry of Education, Culture, Sports, Science and Technology. http://www.mext.go.jp/en/. Accessed 26 March 2017
7. Patil, S., Kim, D., Park, S., Chai, Y.: Handwriting recognition in free space using wimu-based hand motion analysis. J. Sens. **2016**, 3692876:1–3692876:10 (2016)
8. Friedland, G., Knipping, L., Schulte, J., Tapia, E.: E-Chalk: a lecture recording system using the chalkboard metaphor. Interact. Technol. Smart Educ. **1**(1), 9–20 (2004)

Tourist Information Extraction Method from Tweets Without Tourist Spot Names for Tourist Information Visualization System

Sayuri Watanabe^(✉) and Takashi Yoshino

Graduate School of System Engineering, Wakayama University,
Sakaedani 930, Wakayama, Japan
watanabe.sayuri@g.wakayama-u.jp, yoshino@sys.wakayama-u.ac.jp
http://www.wakayama-u.ac.jp/en/

Abstract. We developed a system to extract tourist information from the web. However, insufficient tourist information is often provided from Twitter. We believe that previous methods could not consider tweets about tourist spots that did not contain the tourist spot name. In this study, we propose a tourist information extraction method from tweets without tourist spot names. In our experiment, we evaluated whether tourist information was contained in tweets before and after tweets containing the tourist spot names, tweets of followers of the user who tweeted tourist spot names, and tweets with images that do not contain tourist spot names. The experiments provided the following three results: (1) Tweets without tourist spot names tweeted before and after tweets containing tourist spot names contain tourist information. (2) Replies to tweets containing tourist spot names contain tourist information. (3) Tweets with images that do not contain tourist spot names contain information regarding the food and entertainment available at tourist spots.

Keywords: Tourist information · Information extraction · Information analysis · Twitter

1 Introduction

The average number of trips taken by Japanese travelers decreased after 2006; this decrease stopped after 2010, based on a national tourism survey by the Japan Tourism Agency [1]. The appearance of new forms of travel in Japan, in which fans visit the locations of dramas and animated programs, is considered to be a factor [2]. In addition, the number of foreign travelers to Japan has increased year-by-year since 2012 including visitor arrivals and overseas Japanese travelers, as determined by the Japan Tourism Agency [3]. Therefore, tourist spot operators want to know the needs of tourists and any problems with the tourist spot so that they can be solved because the tourism behaviors of tourists have changed. In our previous study, we developed a system both to extract tourist information

© Springer International Publishing AG 2017
T. Yoshino et al. (Eds.): CollabTech 2017, LNCS 10397, pp. 107–115, 2017.
DOI: 10.1007/978-3-319-63088-5_10

from the web and to visualize similarities. However, insufficient tourist information was provided by Twitter [4]. We believe that we did not consider tweets about tourist spots that do not containing tourist spot names. In this study, we propose a tourist information extraction method to apply to tweets that do not contain tourist spot names. We evaluated whether we can extract tourist information from tweets that do not contain tourist spot names using tweets with position information regarding the surrounding tourist spot, tweets with images of the tourist spot, tweets before and after tweets containing the tourist spot name, and followers of the user who tweeted the tourist spot name. In the remainder of this paper, TNCT refers to Tweets that do Not Contain Tourist spot names.

2 Related Work

Shimada et al. proposed a tourist information analysis system using tweets containing tourist spot names and words related to the tourist spots [5]. They extracted these tweets and analyzed the polarity of the tweets. Alan et al. proposed a method to extract events using unique representations of tweets and dates [6]. They extracted these tweets containing unique representations that are strongly related to specific times as tweets related to the event. They were using tweets containing tourist spot names and words related to the tourist spots; however, we extracted information about tourist spots from not only tweets containing tourist spot names but also tweets that do not contain tourist spot names.

Oku et al. developed a tourist spot recommendation system using tweets that included position information and images that included position information [7]. They combined the active region of the tourist spot in tweets with both position information and the tourist spot name of the target, in addition to images that include position information. The active region is an area where users often tweet about the target tourist spot. They estimated the active region of the tourist spot, and recommended tourist spots based on the features of the tweets from within the region. Ryong et al. proposed a measurement method for geographical regularity using time and position information from tweets to detect social events [8]. They estimated the normal geographical regularity from the times of tweets based on position information, pose, and the action of the user, and detected irregular events in the region of the target. They extracted tourist information using position information contained in tweets, images, and tweet times. However, the extraction by the position information has a limit, because the number of tweets containing position information is very small. We extracted information about tourist spots from not only tweets containing tourist spot names but also TNCTs.

3 Tourist Information Extraction Method

In this study, we evaluated whether we could extract tourist information from TNCTs. Figure 1 shows the tourist information extraction method.

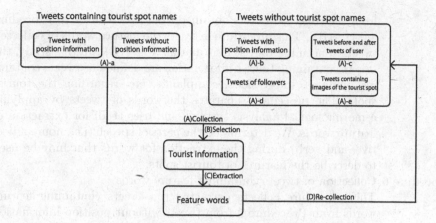

Fig. 1. Tourist information extraction procedure.

Procedure 1 Collection of tweets containing tourist spot names

This procedure collects tweets containing tourist spot names from tweets that include position information and tweets that do not include position information [Fig. 1(A)-a]. This procedure estimates the user location at the time of the tweet about the tourist spot using the active region estimation method suggested by Oku et al. [7]. The procedure also collects tweets within the defined region [Fig. 1(A)-b].

Procedure 2 Collection of tweets before and after tweets containing tourist spot names

This procedure collects tweets within 3 h before and after tweets containing tourist spot names [Fig. 1(A)-c]. In this study, we set the target of collecting within 3 h because we think that you can see the sights within 3 h when you visit the tourist spots. People tend to tweet multiple times in succession within a few hours, rather than tweeting with a long gap between each tweet.

Procedure 3 Collection of tweets of followers

This procedure collects the tweets of the followers of a user whose tweets contained tourist spot names [Fig. 1(A)-d]. This procedure collects neighboring tweets of tweets containing tourist spot names from the tweets of followers because these people might travel together with their followers.

Procedure 4 Collection of tweets with images of tourist spots

This procedure collects tweets with images of the tourist spot [Fig. 1(A)-e]. We use Google Cloud Vision API[1] to detect landmarks for identification of tourist spots.

Procedure 5 Extraction of feature words

This procedure selects tweets that may include tourist information

---

[1] https://cloud.google.com/vision/.

from the collected tweets obtained from Procedure 1 to Procedure 4 [Fig. 1(B)]. This procedure extracts the feature words of collected tweets containing tourist information [Fig. 1(C)]. In this study, the tweets containing tourist information are defined as tweets containing opinions, impressions, complaints, etc. regarding the tourist spots. The procedure separates the words of tweets by applying a morphological analysis system[2] and uses tf-idf for extraction of feature words. We determined the parts of speech (i.e., noun, adjective, and verb) during the extraction for words that may be used to describe the features of tourist spots.

Procedure 6 Collection of tweets containing feature words

This procedure collects extracted the tweets containing feature words from Procedure 5 from tweets without position information [Fig. 1(D)]. We target TNCTs containing feature words in this collection.

Procedure 7 Re-collection of tourist information

This procedure re-collects tourist information from TNCTs by repeating Procedure 5 and Procedure 6.

4   Experiment

In this experiment, we evaluated whether tourist information was contained in tweets before and after tweets containing tourist spot names, tweets of followers of the user containing tourist spot names, and tweets with images that do not contain tourist spot names. In the previous study, we found tweets with position information and feature words to be effective [9]. We extracted the tourist information regarding the tourist spots for a total of 10 points at tourist spots for the first location in nine areas (each in TripAdvisor[3]) and the first location in the Japan tourism ranking (using TripAdvisor[4]). Table 1 shows the tourist spots of the target to be collected in this experiment. We searched for tweets containing tourist spot names using the official keyword search on Twitter, and examined tweets before and after the tweets and the tweets of followers between 0:00 and 23:59 on November 23, 2016, which is a national holiday in Japan. This date was chosen because we think many people used this day to visit family and friends at tourist spots. In this experiment, we evaluated whether there was tourist information contained in tweets containing images but not containing tourist spot names among tweets before and after tweets containing tourist spot names. We made this selection because the number of tweets containing images but not tourist spot names was too large to parse.

---

[2] http://nlp.ist.i.kyoto-u.ac.jp/index.php?cmd=read&page=JUMAN.

[3] https://www.tripadvisor.jp/.

[4] https://www.tripadvisor.jp/Attractions-g294232-Activities-Japan.html.

Table 1. Collection of target tourist spots.

Region	Tourist spot name
Hokkaido	JR Tower (Sapporo, Hokkaido)
Tohoku	Zuihoden (Sendai, Miyagi)
Kanto	Yokohama Minatomirai21 (Yokohama, kanagawa)
Chubu	Atsuta Jingu (Nagoya, Aichi)
Kinki	Dotonbori (Osaka, Osaka)
Chugoku	Atomic Bomb Dome (Hiroshima, Hiroshima)
Shikoku	Matsuyama Castle (Matsuyama, Ehime)
Kyushu	Ohori Park (Fukuoka, Fukuoka)
Okinawa	Shurijo Castle (Naha, Okinawa)
Japan	Fushimi Inari Taisha (Kyoto, Kyoto)

5 Experimental Results and Discussion

5.1 Tourist Information from Tweets Before and After Tweets Containing Tourist Spot Names

Table 2 shows the number of tweets collected for each tourist spot, the amount of tourist information in tweets containing the tourist spot name, etc. Tourism information was collected from TNCTs in all tourist spots. Table 3 shows several examples. We do not know about impressions, we only have tweet (b); however, we may determine the impressions of Ohori Park based on tweet (a), which occurred before the tweets about Ohori Park. From this result, we know that

Table 2. Number of tweets collected for each tourist spot name, the amount of tourist information, and the amount of increase of tourist information.

Tourist spot name	The amount of all collected tweets	The amount of tourist information in tweets containing tourist spot names	The amount of tourist information in TNCTs[a, b]	The amount of increase
JR Tower	34	3	3(1)	1.0
Zuihoden	99	21	8(2)	0.4
Yokohama Minatomirai21	215	4	2(0)	0.5
Atsuta Jingu	321	30	7(1)	0.2
Dotonbori	1147	31	7(2)	0.2
Atomic Bomb Dome	286	19	3(2)	0.2
Matsuyama Castle	71	7	2(0)	0.3
Ohori Park	75	7	4(1)	0.6
Shurijo Castle	145	13	7(2)	0.5
Fushimi Inari Taisha	788	96	64(19)	0.7
Total	3181	230	134(30)	0.6

[a] We have collected tweets tweeted within 3 h before and after tweets containing tourist spot names.
[b] The numbers in parenthesis are the numbers of replies containing tourist information within TNCTs.

Table 3. Examples of tourism information in tweets before and after tweets containing tourist spot names.

Kind of tweet	Contents of tweet
Tweets containing tourist spot names	I started sauntering around because I arrived in Fukuoka and deposited the luggage at the hotel. I intend to chill in Ohori Park if the weather is good (a)
TNCTs	There were many clouds; however, I went because the soft light shined. Runners were running around the large pond. It is the best to chill; many people are eating lunch on a bench (b)

tourist information may be contained in TNCTs tweeted before and after tweets containing tourist spot names.

5.2   Tourist Information from Tweets of Followers

Table 4 shows the amount of tourist information that was contained in tweets of followers and tweets containing images. There are also duplicate tweets because there may be tweets from followers containing images. Results are tweets containing images that contain tourist information for all tourist spots; however, tweets by followers contained tourist information for seven out of ten tourist spots. In addition, the collected tweets of followers containing tourist information were replies to the tweets describing wanting to go to the tourist spots or having gone to the tourist spots, rather than describing going to the tourist spots together. Table 2 shows the amount of tourist information that is contained in replies for each tourist spot. There were TNCTs containing tourist information

Table 4. Amount of tourist information contained in the tweets of followers and tweets containing images before and after tweets containing tourist spot names.

Tourist spot name	Tweet of followers	Tweet containing images
JR Tower	0	2
Zuihoden	0	4
Yokohama Minatomirai211	1	2
Atsuta Jingu	1	5
Dotonbori	1	3
Atomic Bomb Dome	2	1
Matsuyama Castle	0	1
Ohori Park	1	2
Shurijo Castle	1	4
Fushimi Inari Taisha	6	24

Table 5. Examples of tourism information contained in replies before and after tweets containing tourist spot names.

User	Time	Contents of tweet
A	0:05	I am going Kibune, Tofukuji, and Fushimi Inari today (A-1)
B	0:06	Fushimi is good (B-1)
A	0:22	@B I like Senbontorii very much. I like it (A-2)
B	0:23	@A I understand. This is an unusual space. In fact, I have never been there (B-2)

in replies for 30 of 134 pieces of tourist information collected in this experiment; Table 5 shows several examples. When user B tweets the reaction to the tweet about going to Fushimi Inari Taisha (tweeted by user A), user A replied to the tweet (A-2) regarding their impression of Fushimi Inari Taisha. User B replied to a tweet (B-2) regarding their impression of the tourist spot, in addition to this reply. From this result, we know that tourist information was contained in the replies to tweets containing tourist spot names.

5.3   Tourist Information from Tweets with Images

Tweets containing images also contained tourist information for all tourist spots, as shown in Table 4. The images were often of the tourist spots themselves; however, there were images of the food sold at tourist spots and entertainment at tourist spots. Table 6 shows several examples. Tweets about food and entertainment are common kinds of tweets. We learn that we can order jasmine tea at Shurijo Castle because a user wrote tweet (F-2) showing an image of the tea after writing tweet (F-1), among tweets about food. We learn that celebrations of children of three, five, and seven years of age and shrine visits were held at

Table 6. Examples describing food and entertainment available at tourist spots contained in tweets before and after tweets containing tourist spot names.

Contents	Time	Contents of tweet[a, b]
Food	23:04	I went to Shurijo Castle today to spend some time (F-1)
	23:10	I drank the jasmine tea inside. [image of the jasmine tea] (F-2)[b]
Entertainment	12:44	I wrote a formal letter to God for the hope in a sacred place. When I suddenly looked up, the clouds had strange shapes... —#Atsuta Jingu (E-1)
	13:37	The shrine is bustling for the celebration of children of three, five, and seven years of age and shrine visits. In addition, I met a bride in a pure white dress. Because I felt a happy energy, it is a good day today. It was good that I came here. [image of shrine] (E-2)[b]

[a] All of the contents of tweets are originally translated from Japanese.
[b] The text in square brackets provides an explanation of the image in the tweet.

Atsuta Jingu because a user has written tweet (E-2) showing an image of the shrine after tweeting with the hashtag for Atsuta Jingu, among tweets about entertainment. From these results, we know that not only the impressions of the tourist spots themselves but also information about food and entertainment at tourist spots is contained in TNCTs containing images.

5.4 Summary of Discussion

In this experiment, we determined whether there was tourist information contained in TNCTs. The results of the experiments revealed the following.

(1) TNCTs tweeted before and after tweets containing tourist spot names contain tourist information.
(2) Replies to tweets containing tourist spot names contain tourist information.
(3) TNCTs containing images contain information regarding the food and entertainment available at tourist spots.

These results lead to a solution of problem of insufficient tourist information being provided from Twitter (as seen in the previous study), namely, by finding tourist information contained in TNCTs, such as in (1) and (2). Tourist information can be classified into multiple kinds such as history, food, and entertainment at tourist spots, and they can be the main features of the tourist spots in (3). Based on this information, we can express the features of each tourist spot using multiple indices when we visualize the tourist information. The scope of awareness (including similarities and problems) will spread because we can extract different kinds of information regarding the tourist spots. In addition, the amount of tourist information in TNCTs is about 0.6 times the amount of tourist information in tweets containing tourist spot names. From this result, we could collect approximately 1.6 times the amount of tourist information collected by a normal search. Therefore, we conclude that the proposed method is effective for collecting more tourist information from Twitter.

6 Conclusions

In this study, we proposed a tourist information extraction method based on TNCTs. We evaluated whether tourist information can be extracted from TNCTs. The results of the experiments revealed the following.

(1) TNCTs tweeted before and after tweets containing tourist spot names contain tourist information.
(2) Replies to tweets containing tourist spot names contain tourist information.
(3) TNCTs containing images contain information regarding the food and entertainment available at tourist spots.

In the future, we will examine correspondences, because we can not identify landmarks from food and entertainment images that do not photograph the tourist spots. We will determine whether the method can collect tourist information about minor tourist spots from TNCTs.

References

1. Japan Tourism Agency: Research study on economic impacts of tourism in Japan (2014). http://www.mlit.go.jp/common/001136064.pdf
2. Kazuya, H., Yusuke, K.: Research on the regional promotion through anime-tourism. In: 19th Conference of Japan Association for Evolutionary Economics, pp. 1–56 (2015)
3. Japan Tourism Agency: Change of visitor arrivals and Japanese overseas travelers. http://www.mlit.go.jp/kankocho/siryou/toukei/in_out.html
4. Sayuri, W., Takashi, Y.: Tourist Information Visualization System for Improvement Discovery Based on the Similarity among Tourist Spots, Multimedia, Distributed, Cooperative, and Mobile Symposium, pp. 1357–1362 (2016)
5. Kazutaka, S., Shunsuke, I., Hiroshi, M., Tsutomu, E.: Analyzing tourism information on Twitter for a local city. In: 1st ACIS International Symposium on Software and Network Engineering (SSNE 2011), pp. 61–66 (2011)
6. Ritter, A., Mausam, E.O., Clark, S.: Open domain event extraction from Twitter. In: Proceedings of the 18th ACM SIGKDD International Conference on Knowledge Discovery and Data Mining (KDD 2012), pp. 1104–1112 (2012)
7. Kenta, O., Koki, U., Fumio, H.: Mapping geotagged tweets to tourist spots for recommender systems. In: 2014 IIAI 3rd International Conference on Advanced Applied Informatics (IIAI 2014), pp. 789–794 (2014)
8. Lee, R., Sumiya, K.: Measuring geographical regularities of crowd behaviors for Twitter-based geo-social event detection. In: Proceedings of the 2nd ACM SIGSPATIAL International Workshop on Location Based Social Networks, pp. 1–10 (2010)
9. Sayuri, W., Takashi, Y.: Proposal of tourist information extraction methods from tweets without position information by tweets with position information and tweets containing tourist spots names, IPSJ Kansai-Branch Convention 2016, G-15, pp. 1–3 (2016)

Enhancing Participation Balance in Intercultural Collaboration

Mondheera Pituxcoosuvarn[✉] and Toru Ishida

Graduate School of Informatics, Kyoto University, Kyoto, Japan
mondheera@ai.soc.i.kyoto-u.ac.jp, ishida@i.kyoto-u.ac.jp

Abstract. In multilingual collaboration, a paucity of shared language and gaps in the language backgrounds of group members could bring about imbalanced participation, which is likely to hinder problem solving, idea generation and collaborative learning. This paper proposes a model of best balanced communication based on the Quality of Messages among participants using various languages. We describe a method for selecting the languages to be used with machine translators, and how to create the best balanced communication environment. Currently, many studies on machine translators and balancing conversations have been published, but none have attempted to balance asymmetric participation in multilingual groups. Our vision allows machine translation technologies to enhance the communication between humans with different language backgrounds in terms of balancing their participation. We conduct controlled experiments and find the proposed method successfully enables users to interact and communicate with better equality while minimizing the problems that can arise from machine translation usage.

Keywords: Communication support environment · Intercultural collaboration · Multilingual communication · Usability of machine translation

1 Introduction

The common approach to intercultural collaboration is to learn English [1], since English has become the global language [2]. In international discussions, however, the advantage of native speakers may be counter-productive. In fact, disparity in language skill is likely to suppress opportunities for non-native speakers to make significant contributions to intercultural communication. Using English in a group with language diversity can affect socialization and interpretation as it can act as a hidden barrier. Non-native speakers sometimes receive negative assessments and their intelligence be underestimated because of their lack of fluency [3]. We call this phenomenon language asymmetry; the participants in the communication channel have unequal semantics and language abilities.

Some researchers have attempted to improve communication by improving the quality of machine translation as well as using human intelligence. For example, Morita D. [4] introduced a method to use monolinguals to enhance the fluency and adequacy of both sides of two-language translation-mediated discourse. Taking a direction from the outsourcing of human intelligence, we realized that the ability of the users themselves is

© Springer International Publishing AG 2017
T. Yoshino et al. (Eds.): CollabTech 2017, LNCS 10397, pp. 116–129, 2017.
DOI: 10.1007/978-3-319-63088-5_11

another valuable resource. Many people know more than one language and to communicate in a group, we can combine the full abilities of those users and machine translation services to realize best quality communication.

Several methods have been developed to help non-native speakers to effectively take part in conversations, for example, imposing artificial delays to help the non-native speaker understand the conversation [5], signaling the native speaker about the status of non-native speakers [6], helping non-native writers with vocabulary navigation [7], and providing real-time translation using eye gaze input [8]. Though these methods reduce the burden of non-native speakers, they cannot provide a completely balanced communication environment.

Beyond sharing a language, it is also important to understand different cultures. Because one cannot learn every language, machine translation and other technologies on the internet can be a solution [1]. Machine translation can enhance the efficiency and effectiveness of discussions [9]. However, machine translation can cause many communication problems during collaborative work. Because of uncertainty in machine translation accuracy and the different foreign language proficiency of participants, it is difficult to decide which languages or translation services should be used. If a foreign language is chosen, users with lower skill in that language can be left out of the conversation or have less chance to contribute. If machine translators are set between all users, some of whom might have adequate common language skill, the conversation will not be as fruitful as it should be. Polysemy and synonymy [10], common problems with machine translations, can trigger conversation breakdown, since translation output can be erroneous [11].

Beside language problems, balancing participation is also important for effective discussions and collaboration. In many kinds of collaboration, including collaborative problem solving, idea generation, collaborative leaning, and etc., the variety of backgrounds should yield a variety of opinions and ideas. Thus balancing the participation of the participants with different backgrounds is essential to these kinds of collaboration. Several studies have focused on rectifying unbalanced communication. Most focus on giving the users feedback in real time. A previous study provided a system that computes necessary features of speech and provides the users with some feedback via SMS on smartphones and creating animations that depict the participation of each user [12]. Related works use various types of interfaces to inform users about the activities of all users to increase users' awareness of who is participating [12]. Related works use various types of interfaces to inform users about the activities of all users to increase users' awareness of who is participating. For example, [13, 14] use a shared display to show speaker participation rates. They also suggest that providing a peripheral display helps to improve certain types of interaction. A similar study describes an interactive table that works as mirroring tool for group collaboration [15]. This tool also indicates how much each speaker participates in order to create awareness.

The works mentioned above describe various methods to help non-native speakers and balance the discussion. Our research is novel and orthogonal to existing research. Our model can support speakers of different languages with different proficiencies in a shared language skill by creating the best balance in terms of opportunity to participate in communication.

Our approach to balancing the discussion is also different from existing works, since our concept is to level the language burdens. To obtain the best balanced communication environment, we start with an existing study called user-centered QoS [16]. Normally, services are evaluated by users based on the Quality of Service (QoS). Yet, skill or information of users is important in selecting the best machine translation service. Therefore, a new function was introduced to calculate the Quality of Message (QoM) by incorporating the users' skills in writing and reading messages when machine translators were used. In this paper, we extend QoM to define a model of the best balanced channel given the parameters of user language skills and machine translation accuracies. We then test the model in a real-world experiment to investigate the ability of our approach to create highly-effective multilingual communication environments.

2   Scenario

Figure 1 displays the difficult situation possible with multilingual communication. For a conversation between a Chinese user with fair English skill and a Japanese user with limited English skill, it is not complicated to choose the best communication method. In this case, the participants will be more effective if they use machine translation than using English as a shared common language if the machine translation quality is acceptable. Later, a Korean user with good English skill joins the conversation, it becomes more difficult to choose the best method of communication.

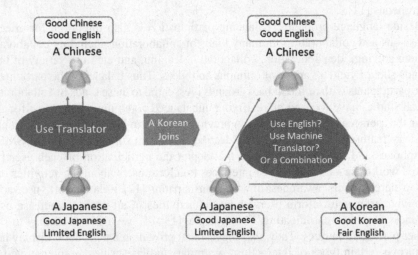

Fig. 1. A multilingual communication problem

It is possible to use the shared foreign language, English, use machine translation, or combine both options. If English is used as the medium for this conversation, it might cause difficulties for the Japanese whose English skill is limited. Machine translation could be a good alternative; however, two participants have good enough English skill to communicate directly, which might be better than using machine translation because of machine translation weaknesses. It is also possible to use both the shared language and machine translation. One might use his native language and the other two might use English. The problem is where machine translation should be used and which languages should be translated.

This situation is an example of asymmetry in collaboration caused by language. In that group, the members have asymmetric opportunity to participate. We believe that the best form of communication is to have mutual understanding and equal chance to participate. As a consequence, we tackle the language asymmetry problem.

3 Modeling Multilingual Communication

3.1 Best Balanced Channel

This paper proposes a model to solve the language asymmetry problem by providing equal opportunity to take part in a conversation even with the asymmetry nature of machine translation as stated above. Our model is called BB, the best balanced machine translation.

Based on existing work [17] on user-centered QoS, we model the Quality of Message (QoM) that user P_i who uses language L_i to send a message to user P_j, who uses language L_j via a machine translation service $MT_{i,j}$. $MT_{i,j}$ translates messages from language L_i into language L_j. We consider the input language writing skill of the message sender, machine translation accuracy of $MT_{i,j}$, and output language reading skill of the message receiver. Then, the quality of message from user P_i to P_j via machine translation service $MT_{i,j}$. QoM $(P_i, MT_{i,j}, P_j)$, or simply $QoM_{i,j}$, can be represented as follows:

$$QoM(P_i, MT_{i,j}, P_j) = writing\_skill(P_i, L_i) \times accuracy(MT_{i,j}) \times reading\_skill(P_j, L_j) \quad (1)$$

This model shows that writing skill of the sender, reading skill of the receiver and accuracy of machine translation impact QoM. As a consequence, selecting the most appropriate language pair is critical.

To increase the overall quality of communication, the quality of message should be maximized, since messages are dominant parts of conversations. BB comes with a method of choosing the language pairs that will maximize the quality of message.

Let $(QoM_{i,j}, QoM_{j,i})$ be a QoM pair between user P_i and user P_j, and $(MT_{i,j}, MT_{j,i})$ be an MT pair between language L_i and language L_j. A QoM pair is called Pareto optimal when it is impossible to make a better QoM, without making another QoM worse off. A QoM pair is called best balanced when it is Pareto optimal and the variance of $QoM_{i,j}$ and $QoM_{j,i}$ is minimum if there is more than one Pareto optimal QoM pair.

If there are more than two users, we need to extend Pareto optimality. Recall that $QoM_{i,j}$ can be maximized by selecting appropriate language pair (L_i, L_j), under the constraint that each user can speak one language. The average QoM of a QoM pair is defined as the average of $QoM_{i,j}$ and $QoM_{j,i}$.

A set of QoM pairs is called Pareto optimal when it is impossible to make a better average QoM, without making any of the other average QoMs worse off. A set of QoM pairs is called best balanced when it is Pareto optimal and the variance of average QoMs is minimum among all Pareto optimal sets of QoM pairs. If there is only one Pareto optima, variance does not need to be calculated.

3.2 Example

Assume there are three users $P1$, $P2$, $P3$, who use languages $L1$, $L2$, $L3$, respectively. From the situation in Fig. 1, let ja, ko, and zh represent Japanese Korean, and Chinese language, respectively. Under the assumption that English can be used by everyone to some degree, possible combinations of languages $Cx = \{L1, L2, L3\}$ for the communication of the three users are as follows:

$$C1 = \{ja, ko, zh\}, C2 = \{ja, ko, en\}, C3 = \{ja, en, zh\}, C4 = \{ja, en, en\},$$
$$C5 = \{en, ko, zh\}, C6 = \{en, ko, en\}, C7 = \{en, en, zh\}, C8 = \{en, en, en\}$$

If there are n users in the group, the language combinations will consist of $n(n-1)/2$ QoM pairs. For example, $C1$ consists of three QoM pairs including $(QoM_{1,2}, QoM_{2,1})$, $(QoM_{2,3}, QoM_{3,2})$, and $(QoM_{3,1}, QoM_{1,3})$. C1 utilizes three pairs or six of machine translation services, including $(MT_{ja,ko}, MT_{ko,ja})$, $(MT_{ko,zh}, MT_{zh,ko})$, and $(MT_{zh,ja}, MT_{ja,zh})$.

With the machine translator qualities and our user profiles in the example situation, the only combination that is Pareto optimal is C4, which means the conversation will be best balanced when the Japanese user uses Japanese while Korean and Chinese user use English, and the machine translation service needed is $(MT_{jp,en}, MT_{en,jp})$; $(MT_{en,en}, MT_{en,en})$ represents no translation.

In many cases, there is more than one Pareto optimal combination. The best balanced combination can be determined by evaluating the differences among the QoMs using variance. Lower differences raise the equality of the conversation.

4   Experiment

We designed and conducted a preliminary experiment to investigate our model. This experiment was designed to compare our best balanced channel with other channels including using English as a common foreign language and using a full translation service among all language pairs. However, in some cases, full machine translation can be the best balanced machine translation channel.

4.1   Task

In this experiment, the participants were instructed to play three games together using a multilingual embedded chat system.

As the games we set three survival problems: desert survival problem (DSP) [18], winter survival problem (WSP) from the project ARISE [19], and lunar survival problem (LSP) from NASA [20]. DSP is a popular collaborative task that asks the participants to arrange items in a list by their importance after a crash landing in a desert, in order to survive and reach the destination safety. WSP is similar to DSP, but the environment is in the woods and the weather is extremely cold. The item list is thus different from that the first game. LSP gives a slightly unique situation, landing on the moon but 80 km from the target place. Yet, LSP task is also the same as the first two but with a different item set.

Whereas, the original problems describe the situation using a number of paragraphs in English, we narrated the situation using short easy sentences in English and figures. Our games were simplified to cover the English proficiencies of the players. Each story explains time, location, and events that happened while the participants acted as survivors in the story. Participants were asked to rank a set of 6 items by their importance for each situation.

First, the participants were asked to rank the items individually, then they were asked to communicate with the other participants and negotiate with each other to make a team answer.

4.2 Experiment Design

At the beginning, we introduced each game and its instructions. Then, we demonstrated how to use Online Multilingual Discussion Tool (OMDT) which is a software created for multilingual symposia that enables multilingual chat, using services from the Language Grid. The Language Grid is a services-oriented collective intelligence that allows users to create language services by combining the existing language services [22].

In the OMDT web application, the user can choose the language to be shown on the right-top of the screen. He or she can type the target language into the message box. When the user clicks send, the message appears below. On the screen of the other users, the same message also appears but in the language selected by that user.

We played an example game, the results of which were ignored, for twenty minutes. During this example game, participants could ask questions and talk. After we made sure the participants understood how to play and how to use OMDT, the participants were asked to move and sit separately so they could not see each other.

The games were played using three strategies. The participants played the first game using English (EN), full machine translator (MT), or best balance (BB). The strategy was chosen randomly. The second game was played using one of the strategies not selected for the first game. The last game was played with the remaining strategy.

In each game, the participants had approximately 35 min in total. First, they had to try to understand the given problem, then write down their personal answers before discussing the selections with the other participants online by chatting or using machine translation. Afterwards, they discussed with the other participants to create the team answer. At the end of the game, the participants could give a new personal answer set if the discussion changed their mind.

After those three games were played with different communication channels, we interviewed the participants as to how they felt when they play the games with different communication modes.

4.3   Participants

Our nine research subjects were divided into three groups. Each group consisted of a Chinese, a Japanese, and a Korean. All were either undergraduate, graduate, or research students from various fields.

English skill profiles of the participants, displayed in Table 1, consisted of (*writing_skill*, *reading_skill*) normalized to the range of 0 to 1. English skills were measured using normalized standard test score from TOEIC, TOEFL, or IELTS. Gender is described as M, for male, and F, for female.

Table 1.   Profile of Participants

Group/ participant	Chinese		Japanese		Korean	
	English skill	Gender	English skill	Gender	English skill	Gender
Group 1	(1, 1)	M	(0.75, 0.5)	F	(1, 0.75)	M
Group 2	(1, 1)	F	(0.75, 0.5)	M	(1, 0.75)	F
Group 3	(1, 1)	M	(0.75, 0.5)	M	(1, 0.75)	F

4.4   Machine Translation

The Language Grid [12] currently offers a number of machine translation services. The services used in this experiment included J-Server and Toshiba English-Chinese Machine Translation. J-Server was used for all translations except between English and Chinese. To evaluate the quality of machine translation services, we randomly chose twenty sentences from a corpus provided by the Japan Electronics and Information Technology Industries Association (JEITA) in English.

We translated the original 20 sentences into three languages, including Chinese, Japanese, and Korean. After that, twenty sentences in each language were translated by machine into the other three languages. For example, Japanese sentences were translated into Chinese, English, and Korean.

Even though quantitative metrics are valuable for evaluation purposes, they cannot completely replace human assessment [20]. The translated sentences were rated by educated native speakers holding at least a bachelor's degree. At this stage, each language had only one evaluator. This methodology of rating fluency and adequacy is widely used to measure machine translation as proposed by LDC [21] Our criteria include fluency of the sentence and its adequacy. Fluency of the translated sentences was rated from 0 to 5. Adequacy was rated as how much meaning of the original sentence was expressed by the translated sentence with score from 0 to 5.

The translation rating for each sentence was averaged to decide the quality of the translation service from one language to another language. Fluency and adequacy scores rated by the judges were added up and normalized to the scale of 0 to 1 as displayed in Table 2.

Table 2. Quality of translation services

From > To	Japanese	Chinese	Korean	English
Japanese	1.000	0.787	0.750	0.881
Chinese	0.756	1.000	0.662	0.662
Korean	0.675 ·	0.419	1.000	0.587
English	0.700	0.587	0.737	1.000

4.5 Communication Channel

Using the participant profile from Table 1, and quality of translation services from Table 2, the value of QoM pairs for each combination, $C1$ to $C8$, can be calculated, as in Table 3. In this case, the only row containing Pareto optimal sets of QoM pairs is $C4$, so variance does not need to be calculated and the best balanced channel is $C4$.

Table 3. QoM values of all possible combinations

Combination / QoM	QoM Pair1	QoM Pair2	QoM Pair3
$C1$	0.771875	0.540625	0.712500
$C2$	0.771875	0.625000	0.790625
$C3$	0.790625	0.570313	0.712500
$C4$	0.790625	0.875000	0.790625
$C5$	0.468750	0.540625	0.404688
$C6$	0.468750	0.625000	0.750000
$C7$	0.500000	0.570313	0.404688
$C8$	0.500000	0.875000	0.750000

From the previous section, $C4$ contains {*ja, en, en*}, which means, using best balanced channel or BB, Japanese participant should use Japanese while Chinese and Korean participants should use English. The only machine translation used is Japanese – English machine translation.

As shown in Fig. 2 below, the strategy used in the experiment includes EN, MT, and BB. We also selected $C1$ and $C8$ combination since they are common methods used in multilingual communication. EN channel represents $C8$ {*en, en, en*}, which indicates that everyone uses English and no machine translation is used. MT represents $C1$ {*ja, ko, zh*}; all the members use their mother language and communicate fully via machine translations.

Messages in MT scenario are translated in to the languages used by the participants, for example, the message from Chinese participant in Chinese is translated into Japanese and Korean. The Japanese and Korean participants can see the message in their language and can reply using their native language. Reply messages from the Japanese or Korean user will also be translated into the other two languages for the other two participants.

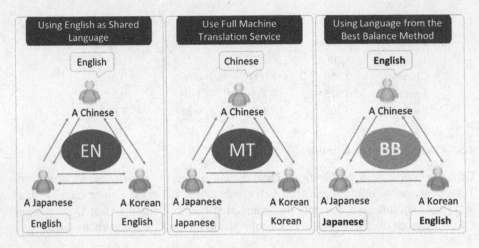

Fig. 2. Strategies of communication in this experiment

5   Behaviors of Participants with Low Shared Language Skill

5.1   Simpler Sentences Used by Japanese When Using English

Using EN channel, sentences typed by Japanese users were simpler and shorter. To illustrate, a participant with limited English skill used only simple words and phrases for most parts of the English conversation, for example, "*mirror* is second", "no need for *aid*", without any further explanation. The longest sentence the participant used in English conversation was "*transmitter* tells us location or way". The same participant expressed his opinion more fully using more complex sentences when he communicated in his own language via translation, for example "*Raincoat*. The reason is to protect ourselves against the direct sun. Not to wear but to use as a shade". Simple sentences are not signs of bad quality of conversation but complex sentences might be more natural and can more easily trigger new assessments or interesting discussions.

5.2   Ignorance of Incomprehensible English Sentence

Incomprehensible sentences can be caused by low language proficiency. The conversation below shows a part of a conversation when all participants used English (EN channel) for the WSP game.

(Using EN Channel)

Ko   We can make fire with *lighter* and tree
Zh   But it is so cold and wet, I wonder if we can make it.
Zh   Do you agree that the *chocolate* is the most useless one?
***Ja*   can we solve *shortening*…?**
Ja   *chocolate* is most useful

Ko Wait a minute we can get fire from crash

They were discussing about which items to be selected based on the idea of how to start fire. *Ko* thought that item *lighter* was useful for making fire by using it with wood, while *Zh* doubted if this were really possible since the given situation was cold and wet, He also expressed his idea that the *chocolate* was the most useless choice and asked if the others agreed or not. Then the Japanese suddenly asked something about *shortening* in English, in which "solve" was not understandable, since her English skill is very limited.

Sentences which are not understandable are normally ignored by other parties [22]. When a low-English skill participant entered an incomprehensible sentence, sometimes the other participants just simply ignored that sentence as happened in this case. Instead, they continued the conversation without referring to what *Ja* said earlier.

This specific situation might not harm the quality of the conversation result. However, understanding all messages might trigger some interesting topic or idea to be discussed further. There might also be something important or useful in non-understandable sentences.

5.3 Less Engagement in Conversation of Japanese Users When Using English

Japanese users tend to engage less in conversations when English is used. The same Japanese participant can be more talkative when he/she uses machine translation. Machine translation makes people with low language skill worry less about what to say. They can easily think in their own language and simply type in that language. Using the mother tongue is more comfortable for the participants who have limited shared language skill and can provide more confidence in joining the conversation.

Table 4 shows the number of utterances in each game by each participant which reflects how talkative each participant was. Before the measurement, sentences not related to the collaborative task were excluded, such as greeting, self-introduction, etc. With machine translation, low language skill participants engaged in the conversation more often, since they took less time to come up with a sentence. We can see the degree of engagement in the conversation by comparing the talkativeness.

Table 4. Number of utterances in each game by each participant

Group	Participant	EN	MT	BB
Group 1	Korean	48 (37%)	35 (38%)	36 (32%)
	Chinese	57 (44%)	29 (31%)	45 (40%)
	Japanese	23 (17%)	27 (29%)	31 (27%)
Group 2	Korean	13 (33%)	14 (35%)	13 (32%)
	Chinese	17 (43%)	12 (30%)	14 (35%)
	Japanese	9 (23%)	13 (33%)	13 (32%)
Group 3	Korean	8 (32%)	12 (32%)	12 (37%)
	Chinese	10 (40%)	15 (40%)	11 (34%)
	Japanese	7 (28%)	10 (27%)	9 (28%)

Figure 3 shows the percentage of utterances made by each participant, and Fig. 4 shows the average percentage of utterances created by each nationality with similar English-skill level. From Figs. 3 and 4, the EN channel yielded unequal participation in the conversation. The Japanese tended to talk much less when using EN, while the balance became better when they used MT and BB.

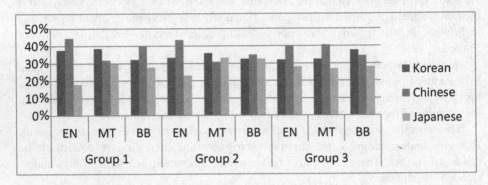

Fig. 3. Talkativeness of each participant in each group as measured by percentage of utterances each participant made

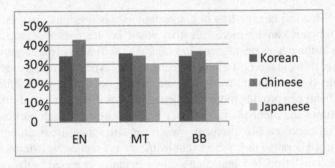

Fig. 4. Average talkativeness grouped by country of origin measured by percentage of utterances

Conversation Encouragement

In games using the English Channel, sometimes one participant become quiet for a long period. For example, the Japanese user was asked for her opinion many times at different parts of a conversation by the other two participants.

(Using EN channel)

15:37:39 *Zh* *Ja*, what do you think?

...

15:48:19 *Ko* How to you think about *Ja*?

...

15:57:42   How about Ja?

The reasons why a participant stopped talking include, not understanding the current conversation, taking time to express her opinion due to the language barrier, having no opinion, or her personality. Using machine translation can help the participant facing a language barrier in terms of expression and understanding and might increase confidence as the mother language is used. Asking for a specific participant's opinion appeared much less when the MT or BB channel was used.

6   Benefit of Best Balance Machine Translation for Conversation Grounding

Machine translation is obviously useful for people who speak different languages to collaborate, however it also creates problems, for instance, translation mistake, conversation breakdowns, etc. One of the difficulties caused by using machine translation is building mutual understanding. In a group conversation, especially in an intercultural group, having a common ground is essential for people to collaborate.

An existing work [23] showed that using machine translation makes it more difficult to ground conversations. The study found that using machine translation violates the requirements for establishing common ground, especially when the number of languages exceeds two. It is difficult for the users to share the same content because of discrepancy between the translations and the users cannot be aware of the content that they share or do not share since they cannot monitor how the messages are translated.

However, both full machine translation and our proposed best balanced machine translation created more distributed talkativeness and more equal participation compared to using English as the mediated language. In many cases, using best balanced machine translation might need a fewer machine translation usages, which can decrease the difficulty of grounding the conversation.

7   Conclusion

The main contribution of this paper is proposing a best balance machine translation model that harmonizes participation rates in multilingual communication via the selective use of machine translation based on users' language skills and quality of available machine translation services.

We conducted an experiment to study how our proposed method works compared to using users' shared second language and simply use mother tongue for all participants by using machine translation. We asked the participants to collaborate on ranking importance of items in three survival games using a machine translation embedded chat system. Observations made during the experiment showed that utterances of participants who had limited skill in a shared foreign language increased when using machine translation services. This indicates that balance of participation among users is enhanced when machine translation is used.

Using our model helps to deal with imbalanced participation in multilingual conversations while raising the probability of successful conversation grounding. It also helped to reduce the chance of machine translation problems that can occur when the quality of machine translation is too low but the language skills of the users are acceptable. Our original model enhances communication quality by selecting the language combination for the best-balanced conversation, allowing people with different backgrounds to participate in conversations equally. Our concept is to harness the intelligence of both machines and people to boost participation balance in multilingual communication and collaboration.

Acknowledgements. This research was partially supported by a Grant-in-Aid for Scientific Research (A) (17H00759, 2017-2020) from Japan Society for the Promotion of Science (JSPS), and the Leading Graduates Schools Program, "Collaborative Graduate Program in Design" by the Ministry of Education, Culture, Sports, Science and Technology, Japan.

References

1. Ishida, T.: Intercultural collaboration and support systems: a brief history. In: Baldoni, M., Chopra, A.K., Son, T.C., Hirayama, K., Torroni, P. (eds.) PRIMA 2016. LNCS, vol. 9862, pp. 3–19. Springer, Cham (2016). doi:10.1007/978-3-319-44832-9_1
2. David, C.: English as a Global Language. Cambridge University Press, Cambridge (1997)
3. Henderson, J.K.: Language diversity in international management teams. Int. Stud. Manag. Organ. **35**, 66–82 (2005)
4. Morita, D., Ishida T.: Collaborative translation by monolinguals with machine translators. In: 14th International Conference on Intelligent User Interfaces (IUI 2009), pp. 361–366. ACM, New York (2009). doi:10.1145/1502650.1502701
5. Yamashita, N., Echenique, A., Ishida, T., Hautasaari, A.: Lost in transmittance: how transmission lag enhances and deteriorates multilingual collaboration. In: 16th ACM Conference on Computer Supported Cooperative Work and Social Computing (CSCW 2013), pp. 923–934. ACM, Texas (2013). doi:10.1145/2441776.2441881
6. Gao, G., Yamashita, N., Hautasaari, A.M., Fussell, S.R.: Improving multilingual collaboration by displaying how non-native speakers use automated transcripts and bilingual dictionaries. In: 33rd Annual ACM Conf. on Human Factors in Computing Systems, pp. 3463–3472. ACM, Seoul (2015). doi:10.1145/2702123.2702498
7. Nikolova, S., Ma, X., Tremaine, M., Cook, P.: Vocabulary navigation made easier. In: 15th International Conference on Intelligent User Interfaces (IUI 2010), pp. 361–364. ACM, Hong Kong (2010). doi:10.1145/1719970.1720031
8. Toyama, T., Sonntag, D., Dengel, A., Matsuda, T., Iwamura, M., Kise, K.: A mixed reality head-mounted text translation system using eye gaze input. In: 15th International Conference on Intelligent User Interfaces (IUI 2010), pp. 329–334. ACM, Haifa (2014). doi: 10.1145/2557500.2557528
9. Aiken, M.: Transterpreting multilingual electronic meetings. Int. J. Manag. Inf. Syst. **13**(1), 35–46 (2009). doi:10.19030/ijmis.v13i1.4940
10. Fellbaum, C.: WordNet. In: Poli, R. (ed.) Theory and applications of ontology: computer applications, pp. 231–234. Springer, Dordrecht (2010). doi:10.1007/978-90-481-8847-5_10
11. Yamashita, N., Ishida, T.: Effects of machine translation on collaborative work. In: Computer Supported Cooperative Work and Social Computing 2006 (CSCW 2006), pp. 515–524. ACM, Alberta (2006). doi:10.1145/1180875.1180955
12. Sarda, S., et al.: Real-Time Feedback System for Monitoring and Facilitating Discussions. In: Mariani, J., Rosset, S., Garnier-Rizet, M., Devillers, L. (eds.) Natural Interaction with Robots, pp. 375–387. Knowbots and Smartphones. Springer, New York (2014). doi: 10.1007/978-1-4614-8280-2_34

13. DiMicco, J.M., Pandolfo, A., Bender, W.: Influencing group participation with a shared display. In: Computer Supported Cooperative Work and Social Computing 2004 (CSCW 2004), pp. 614–623. ACM, Illinois (2004). doi:10.1145/1031607.1031713

14. DiMicco, J.M., Hollenbach, K.J., Pandolfo, A., Bender, W.: The impact of increased awareness while face-to-face. Hum. Comput. Interact. **22**(1), 47–96 (2007)

15. Bachour, K., Kaplan, F., Dillenbourg, P.: An interactive table for supporting participation balance in face-to-face collaborative learning. IEEE Trans. Learn. Technol. **3**, 203–213 (2010). doi:10.1109/tlt.2010.18

16. Bramantoro, A., Ishida, T.: User-centered QoS in combining web services for interactive domain. In: 5th International Conference on Semantics, Knowledge and Grid, pp. 41–48. IEEE Press, Guangdong (2009). doi:10.1109/skg.2009.106

17. Lafferty, J.C., Eady, P.M., Elmers, J.: The desert survival problem. In: Experimental Learning Methods, Michigan (1974)

18. Fermilab Project ARISE. http://ed.fnal.gov/arise/guide.html

19. NASA. http://www.nasa.gov/audience/foreducators/5-8/features/F_Exploration_Then_and_Now.html

20. Callison-Burch, C., Fordyce, C., Koehn, P., Monz, C., Schroeder, J.: (Meta-) evaluation of machine translation. In: 2nd Workshop on Statistical Machine Translation, pp. 136–158. ACM, Prague (2007). doi:10.3115/1626394.1626403

21. Linguistic Data Consortium: Linguistic data annotation specification: assessment of fluency and adequacy in translations. Technical report (2005)

22. Ishida, T. (ed.): The Language Grid: Service-Oriented Collective Intelligence for Language Resource Interoperability. Springer, Heidelberg (2011). doi:10.1007/978-3-642-21178-2_1

23. Yamashita, N., Inaba, R., Kuzuoka, K., Ishida, T.: Difficulties in establishing common ground in multiparty groups using machine translation. In: SIGCHI Conference on Human Factors in Computing Systems, pp. 679–688. ACM, Massachusetts (2009). doi: 10.1145/1518701.1518807

A Culturally-Situated Agent to Support Intercultural Collaboration

Victoria Abou Khalil[1(✉)], Toru Ishida[1], Masayuki Otani[2], and Donghui Lin[1]

[1] Department of Social Informatics, Kyoto University, Kyoto, Japan
v.aboukhalil@gmail.com, ishida@i.kyoto-u.ac.jp
[2] Kinki University, Higashi-osaka, Japan
m-otani@i.kyoto-u.ac.jp

Abstract. While traveling, foreign visitors encounter new products that they need to understand. One solutionis by making Culturally Situated Associations (CSA) i.e. relating the products they encounter to products in their own culture. We propose the design of a system that provides tourists with CSA to help them understand foreign products. In order to provide tourists with CSA that they can understand, we must gather information about their culture, provide them with the CSA, and make sure they understand it. To deliver CSA to foreign visitors, two types of data are needed: data about the products, their associated properties and relationships, and data about the tourist cultural attributes such as country, region, language. The properties and relationships about countries, regions and products, can be extracted from open linked data on the web, and CSA can then be constructed. However, information about the tourist's cultural attributes and the knowledge they can relate to is unavailable. One way to tackle this problem would be to extract the tourist's cultural attributes that are needed in each situation through dialogue systems. In this case, a Culturally Situated Dialogue (CSD) must take place. To implement the dialogue, dialogue systems must follow a machine-learned dialogue strategy as previous work has shown that a machine-learned dialogue strategy outperform the handcrafted dialogue approach. We propose the design of a system that uses a reinforcement learning algorithm to learn CSD strategies that can support individual foreign tourists. Since no previous system providing CSA has been implemented, the system allows the creation of CSD strategies when no initial data or prototype exists. The method is used to generate 3 different agents that learn 3 different dialogue strategies.

Keywords: Automatic dialogue strategies · Reinforcement learning · Culturally situated associations · Wizard of Oz

1 Introduction

Japan, rich in both traditional culture and technical innovation, attracts people from all around the world and is a popular destination for tourists. Every year, tens of millions of visitors are walking in Zen gardens, shopping for strange gadgets, and experimenting with Japanese cuisine. However, the first complaint from foreign tourists is the paucity of foreign language services [1]. Some reported concerns with communication

© Springer International Publishing AG 2017
T. Yoshino et al. (Eds.): CollabTech 2017, LNCS 10397, pp. 130–144, 2017.
DOI: 10.1007/978-3-319-63088-5_12

difficulties while shopping, particularly for food. This highlights a problem in intercultural collaboration. This area of research is becoming essential in a world that is losing its physical borders and in which people and cultures are more and more on the move and in contact [2].

To help tourists understand the food products they are about to buy, one possible solution is to display, in the tourist's language, a complete listing of the ingredients as well as a description of the food product. However, this kind of information might leave them with questions like: What does it taste like? What is the texture? How do we cook it?

In situations where providing a simple description of a product fails to deliver a complete understanding of the product, an efficient alternative is to relate the product to a similar product in the tourist's culture. This would mean offering Culturally Situated Associations (CSA) that allow foreign visitors to understand the usage, and taste of the food product they are inquiring about.

To be able to provide tourists with CSA, two types of data are needed: data about food products, their associated properties and relationships as well as data about the tourist's cultural attributes like country, region, and language. With today's available technologies and the prevalence of data on the web, we are able to offer solutions that use cultural associations to explain concepts and products. With the increased popularity and presence of open data on the web, we are able to query relationships and properties about products. Properties and relationships about countries, regions and food products can be found, and cultural associations can then be extracted. However, information about tourists' cultural attributes and the knowledge they can relate to is unavailable. One way to tackle this problem would be to extract the tourists' cultural attributes that are needed in each situation through dialogue systems.

A dialogue system that supports foreign tourists with CSA must deliver the associations and make sure that those associations were understood. The first requirement can be fulfilled by developing Culturally Situated Dialogue (CSD) strategies that support the realization of those objectives. However, when no initial observations or system exists, learning a dialogue strategy is a challenging task as developers or designers of the system may not be able to predict the most appropriate action to be taken by the system at each moment. Developers and designers would have to undertake the time consuming process of predicting what would be the most appropriate action in each situation. Moreover, a dialogue system is likely to need a considerable number of different utterances and previous work showed that automatic dialogue strategies outperform handcrafted dialogue strategies [3].

In conjunction with the demand for CSA and the challenge of automating CSD strategy generation where no initial system exists, reinforcement learning algorithms are needed to learn CSD strategies to support foreign tourists when no data or working prototype exists. To model the possible state spaces of the reinforcement learning algorithm, we first identified common dialogue patterns that take place between tourists and shop owners in Nishiki Market. Then, we extracted the attributes related to the tourists' culture as well as food properties that interest the tourists. By breaking down the extracted attributes into more fine grained attributes we created three attribute sets with different levels of granularity. Each of these three attribute sets was mapped into a different state space, resulting in the creation of three different agents.

2 Background

2.1 Culturally Situated Associations

A variety of intercultural communication models have been proposed by researchers. However, the most influential model is attributed to Byram because his approach provides holistic intercultural competence and has defined objectives and practical derivations [4].

Byram's model defines the five skills needed in order to accomplish successful intercultural communication: *intercultural attitudes, knowledge, interpreting and relating, discovery and interaction* as well as *critical cultural awareness* [5]. Two of those skills are necessary in the initial stages of becoming familiar with a new culture and are essential to understand foreign concepts or products [5]:

- *Discovery* or *knowledge*: knowledge about a social group and their products and practices in the foreign visitor's own country.
- *Interpreting and relating*: foreign visitors relate the information they get to information from their own culture.

Byram defines the skills of discovery as "the ability to recognize significant phenomena in a foreign environment and to elicit their meanings and connotations, and their relationship to other phenomena [4]". Those skills are of particular importance in contexts where the foreign visitor has very little information about the foreign culture and its related concepts or products, as it is the case of tourists in Japan. The skill of interpreting and relating consists of putting concepts or products from two or more cultures side by side and seeing how each might look from the other perspective [4]. However, in real life situations, interpreting and relating cannot be achieved in real time by tourists or shop clerks as CSA requires deep knowledge about the foreign culture. Automatic dialogue systems might be useful in this situation as they allow the identification of the tourist's culture and the retrieval of the needed association.

2.2 Linked Data

The term Linked Data was created in 2007 to describe a set of best practices for publishing and connecting structured data on the web. The data can be linked to form relationships and becomes more useful with the use of semantic queries. Linked Data allows the connection and query of data from different sources [6].

One of the main projects associated with the use of Linked Data has been the Linking Open Data project; it allows anyone to participate by publishing a dataset following the Linked Data recommendations and linking them with existing datasets. DBpedia is one of the biggest existing datasets. The DBpedia dataset contains data extracted from Wikipedia and consists of 3.4 million concepts described by 11 billion triples. As the information contained in DBpedia results from a crowd sourcing process and is extracted from unstructured and semi-structured information, there are still many problems with the dataset. The error rate in the DBpedia Dataset is 11.93%, which is considered moderate [7]. Previous studies explored the possibility of using Linked Data in combination with dialogue systems [8].

2.3 Automatic Dialogue Strategies

The recent literature shows a growing interest in the implementation and use of automatic dialogue systems. The development of such dialogue systems, and more particularly the development of dialogue strategies is challenging [9]. In order to achieve an application goal in an efficient way through a series of interactions with the user, dialogue strategies are needed. By quantifying the incremental achievements made as well as the efficiency, is it possible to describe the system as a stochastic model that can be used for learning those dialogue strategies. This method has many advantages including the possibility of automating the evaluation of the dialogue strategies as well as an automatic design and adaptation [10]. Moreover, this approach naturally utilizes large amounts of data [11].

Previous works on dialogue systems used reinforcement learning in order to learn Wizard of Oz' (WoZ) dialogue strategies of presenting information and replicating them. WoZ allows the learning of dialogue strategies when no initial system exists. The results showed that reinforcement learning combined with WoZ experiments allows the development of optimal strategies when no working prototype is available [12]. However, unlike standard dialogue systems that take into account user-related properties, the challenge in learning optimal CSD strategies consist of learning which information about the tourist's culture, if any, should be acquired and in which order.

3 Overview of the System

Figure 1 shows the system architecture. The WoZ experiment is used as no working prototype or initial CSD system is available. The tourist and the wizard communicate through Skype to allow the wizard to see the product the tourist is asking about. In order to provide the wizard with the optimal dialogue strategy, an agent is trained based on a reinforcement learning algorithm, and passes the optimal strategy to take at each step to the wizard. The wizard first reports its state of knowledge to the agent through a web interface (e.g.: I don't have any information yet). Once the agent receives the current state of knowledge of the system, it provides the wizard with the appropriate action to take (e.g.: Ask for the tourist's country). If the agent issues a query of the associated concept, the wizard retrieves the CSA from DBpedia. The dialogue, directed by the agent, and executed by the wizard is iterated until the CSA is provided to the tourist and understood. In practice, the dialogue would be translated into the tourist's language using Language Grid, a service-oriented collective intelligence that allows users to create language services from existing language resources [13].

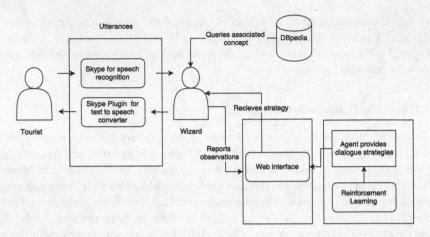

Fig. 1. System architecture

4 Extraction of Dialogue Patterns

In order to extract the necessary components needed to build the feature space of the reinforcement algorithm and create the automatic dialogue strategies, we first identify common natural dialogue patterns that should provide CSA to tourists.

To identify the possible dialogue patterns, we first conducted interviews with tourists in Nishiki Market, a traditional food market in Kyoto. We interviewed 15 tourists coming from western countries, chosen randomly during their visit to the market. The breakdown of genders was balanced and the participants were from Europe, New Zealand and U.S.A. The tourists were asked to list the questions that they would have wanted to ask if it was possible to get an answer. We received 34 questions from the participants. Similar questions were put together and the tourists' questions were categorized by question topic.

The questions of the tourists were classified into three categories shown in Table 1. The first category contains questions about the ingredients of a particular food. The second category covers questions about usage. The last category includes general questions about the composition and usage of the food.

Table 1. Categorization of questions asked by tourists by question topic

Category	Associated tourists' questions
Ingredients	What does it taste like?
	Is it suitable for vegetarians?
	Can I take it through customs?
Usage	How is it used?
	How do we eat it?
Ingredients and usage	What is this?
	What is the difference between X and Y?

Based on the questions provided by the tourists, we developed "typical" dialogues that could happen between the shop owners and the tourists. During those conversations, shop owners follow a CSD strategy to answer the questions of the tourists with CSA. We match each of the previous examples to a particular CSD pattern. To understand CSD, we define several terms as follows:

- *Target concept:* is the concept that needs to be explained.
- *Associated concept:* is used to explain a target concept. It is a concept that belongs to a different culture from the target concept.
- *Common attribute:* is an attribute or a property that belongs to both the target and the associated concepts.

Cultural attribute, such as a *location*, *language*, etc., is a common attribute which contributes to identifying a culture.

Using the previous terms, we classified culturally situated conversations into several CSD patterns, see the examples below.

Example conversation 1:

Tourist: "What is this and what does it taste like?"
Shop Owner: "It is Neri Goma. It is a paste made out of roasted sesame seeds. Where are you from?"
Tourist: "Iraq"
Shop Owner: "It is like Tahine."

Dialogue Pattern 1: Using cultural attribute as a pivot

Tourist: Question about the taste of the *target concept*.
Shop Owner: Question to identify the *cultural attributes* of the tourist.
Tourist: Tourist provides the *cultural attributes*.
Shop Owner: Finds the *associated concept* that possess *cultural attributes* that match the tourist's cultural attributes and *common attributes* related to the taste that are identical to the common attributes of the *target concept*.

Example conversation 2:

Tourist: "What is this? How do we use it?"
Shop Owner: "It is Neri Goma. It is a paste made out of roasted sesame seeds. Where are you from?"
Tourist: "Iraq."
Shop Owner: "It is like Tahine, but in Japan it is mainly used in sweets."

Dialogue Pattern 2: Comparative association

Tourist: Question about a *target concept*.
Shop Owner: Question to identify the *cultural attributes* of the tourist.
Tourist: Tourist provides the *cultural attributes*.
Shop Owner: Finds the *associated concept* that possess *cultural attributes that* match the tourist's cultural attributes and *common attributes* related to the taste that are identical to the common attributes of the *target concept*. If other common attributes differ

from the *target concept*'s *common attributes,* the differences are presented to the tourist.

Example conversation 3:

Tourist: "What is this?"
Shop Owner: "It is Udon, noodles made out of wheat and flour. They are usually served in a broth."
Tourist: "What is the difference from Soba?"
Shop Owner: "Udon is made out of wheat and Soba out of buckwheat Where are you from?"
Tourist: "Italy"
Shop Owner: "Udon is more like Spaghetti and Soba like Pizzoccheri"

Dialogue Pattern 3: Intra-Cultural Comparison

Tourist: Question about the difference between two *target concepts.*
Shop Owner: Question to identify the *cultural attributes* of the tourist.
Tourist: Tourist provides the *cultural attributes.*
Shop Owner: The difference between the two *target concepts* is identified by comparing all their common attributes. Based on the cultural attributes of the tourist, two *associated concepts* with the same difference to the common attributes are found.

Based on the previous dialogue patterns, we extract the components essential to conduct different types of CSD strategies:

- Target Concept
- Associated concept
- Cultural Attributes
- Common Attributes

5 Extraction of Culturally Situated Associations

In order to provide tourists with CSA about food products and answer their questions we need access to an adequate data source. DBpedia contains 3.4 million concepts including concepts about food and dishes, and also provides relationships between foods, countries, and usages.

5.1 Mapping the Common Attributes to DBpedia Properties

Based on the categorization of the questions of the foreign visitors and on the previous dialogue patterns, we map the questions asked by the tourists to the DBpedia properties that we need to answer those questions. Every set of questions could be answered by comparing the common attributes of a particular product from a foreign culture to the common attributes of another product from the tourist's culture. The DBpedia properties shown in Table 2 are the ones used to extract and compare the common attributes.

Table 2. Mapping of tourists questions to DBpedia properties needed to answer them

DBpedia properties	Tourists' questions
dbo:ingredients,	What does it taste like?
dbp:type,	Is it suitable for vegetarians?
dbp:similarDish	Can I take it through customs?
dbo:course, dbp:served,	How is it used?
dbp:similarDish	How do we eat it?
dbo:ingredients, dbp:type, dbp:similarDish,	What is this?
dbo:course, dbp:served, dbp:similarDish	What is the difference between X and Y?

5.2 Mapping the Cultural Attributes to DBpedia Properties

The cultural attributes allow the culture of the tourists to be identified in order to provide them with an associated concept from their own culture. As each country has different food, relating the target concept to an associated concept from the tourist's country is essential in realizing CSA. However, in several cases, particularly in big countries, different regions have different food products. Providing the tourists with an associated concept from their own region will either permit more precise information and/or allow them to understand the food better. We mapped the cultural attributes to existing DBpedia properties below:

> *Dbo:country:* Country to which the associated concept belongs, usually country of the tourist
>
> *Dbp:region:* Region to which the associated concept belongs, usually region of the tourist

5.3 Extraction of Culturally Situated Associations

We draw the knowledge representations to visualize the relationships, based on DBpedia's existing properties and relationships. The example below shows the knowledge representations for dialogue type 1. Figure 2 represents the products' similarity that answers the first type of conversation. In this case, the tourist from Italy asks 'What does Soba taste like?'. To answer this question, Soba is queried, as well as all the products that have the same ingredients and originate from Italy. The query gives us *Pizoccheri*. The red parts show the relationships and concepts that are taken into consideration to find the CSA for this particular question.

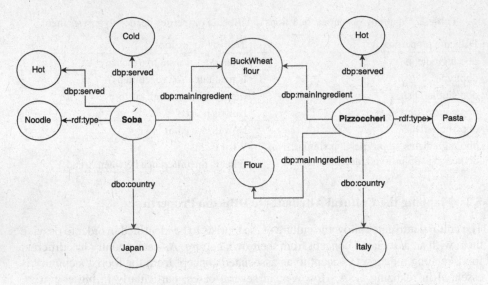

Fig. 2. Knowledge representation for conversation type 1 (Color figure online)

6   Reinforcement Learning Algorithm

6.1   Reinforcement Learning Algorithm

The Markov Decision process is a mathematical formalism that is used to implement the reinforcement learning algorithm. Reinforcement learning is the problem faced by an agent that must learn a behavior through trial-and-error interactions with a dynamic environment [14]. The main components of this formalism and their implementation are explained below. The algorithm was implemented using Python, following Nathan Epstein's implementation[1].

The State Space and Action Space
The state space represents the complete list of states that the system can be in. The action space is the all-inclusive list of actions that can be taken in the environment. The states and actions are usually set a priori.

The Transition Probabilities
The probabilities of transitioning between state s to state s' given action a taken are estimated from observed data. The estimated transition probability is computed as follows:

$$P(s, a, s') = \frac{\text{Number times we transitioned from state } s \text{ to state } s' \text{ given action } a}{\text{Number of times we took action } a \text{ in state } s}$$

---

[1] https://github.com/NathanEpstein/reinforce/tree/
664949173dfaabcc359f46c4f4c640fd577682b4.

In the case that action *a* was never taken in state *s*, we set the value of *P(s, a, s')* to *1/number of states* in order to avoid the ratio of 0/0. In this situation we assume that the probability is equality distributed over all states. With an incremented number of observations, the state transition probability will be updated to become more precise.

The Reward
Our algorithm assumes that the reward is unknown. We can also compute the expected immediate reward in a specific state, as the average reward observed in state *s*. The goal is to find a policy that will produce the biggest possible cumulative reward.

Value Iteration and Policy
A policy is any function that maps states to actions. The value function for policy π is the expected sum of discounted rewards when we start in state s and take actions according to π. The value function of policy π is given by Bellman's equation.

$$V^\pi(s) = R(s) + \gamma \sum_{s' \in S} P_{s\pi(s)}(s') V^\pi(s')$$

Bellman's equation states that the expected sum of discounted rewards $V^\pi(s)$ consists of the sum of the immediate reward as the expected sum of future rewards. We define as well the optimal value function given by:

$$V^* = \max V^\pi(s)$$

$V^\pi(s)$ is the best expected sum of discounted rewards that can be reached using any policy. Based on the equations above, we will describe the algorithm that we use to calculate the value function and to get the best policy.

- For each state s, initialize $V(s) = 0$
- Repeat until convergence:
  - For each state, update:

$$V^\pi(s) = R(s) + \gamma * \max(a \in A) \sum_{s' \in S} P_{s\pi(s)}(s') V(s')$$

  - Policy in state s is the $a \in A$ that maximizes $V(s)$

In this algorithm we update the estimated value function based on Bellman's equation. For every state s, we calculate the new value of $V(s)$. After a certain number of iterations, the value is supposed to converge on $V*(s)$. We then choose the optimal policy that always maximizes $V(s)$.

The State Action Space
The states of the reinforcement learning algorithm amounts to all the states that the system (the wizard in our current system) possesses about internal and external resources that it is interacting with (e.g. input from the tourist, associated concepts). The action set of the dialogue system includes all possible actions it can accomplish. It includes the interactions with the user (e.g. asking the tourist for input, providing the tourist with output) as well as the interactions with other resources (e.g.: searching for the associated

concepts). When the system's current state is *s* and action *a* is taken, the state changes to *s′*. For example, when the system is in an initial state and the wizard doesn't not have any information, the agent will ask the wizard to interact with the tourist and obtain specific information. The next state, *s′*, will depend on whether the wizard obtained the information or not.

We identify the possible state spaces based on the components extracted from the dialogue patterns. The target concept is assumed to be known as the wizard would be interacting with the tourist and would be able to identify it. The cultural attributes are necessary in order to determine the culture of the tourist, and thus, in which culture the associated concepts should be found. Tourists usually have a question that is related to a particular common attribute (e.g.: usage, ingredients). The common attributes are necessary as they will be the basis of the comparison between the target concept and the associated concept. The action space is directly extracted from the state.

Based on the previously defined components, we create three levels of state spaces with different granularity in terms of the minimum number of observations to learn the dialogue strategies. In this work the minimum number of observations was calculated taking into consideration the case where every state is visited by every action. The three different agents are named: Novice agent, Intermediate agent and Advanced agent.

The Novice agent needs few observations to cover all the actions that could be taken from every state, however, it is expected to produce low quality dialogue strategies. The Intermediate agent needs more observations than the Novice agent to cover all the actions that could be taken from every state, but is expected to produce better quality dialogue strategies. The Advanced agent needs the most observations to cover all the actions that could be taken from every state, but is expected to produce the best dialogue strategies. Figure 3 plots the minimum number of observations versus the number of states.

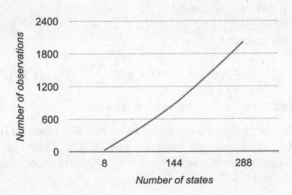

Fig. 3. Minimum number of observations needed versus number of states

6.2   The Novice Feature Space

The first level feature space produces the *Novice agent*. This State space includes only 3 entries that represent the mental state of the system, in other terms, the current state of the wizard.

- Doesn't Know the user's culture/Knows the user's culture
- Doesn't know the associated concept/Knows the associated concept
- Knows that the user doesn't understand the concept/Knows that the user understands the concept.

Every entry can take one of two values, giving us a total number of 8 states(includes 2 final states):

- Knows the user culture
- Knows the associated concept
- Knows that the user understands the concept

and

- Knows the associated concept
- Knows that the user understands the concept

For the first level feature space, the action space includes only three actions:

- Identify the user's culture
- Identify the associated concept
- Confirm that the user understood the concept

6.3   The Intermediate State Action Space

The second level State Action space produces the *Intermediate agent*. The second level state space is the result of breaking down the first level state space into more precise states of knowledge. It includes 6 entries that represent the mental state of the system.

- Doesn't know the user's country/Knows the user's country
- Doesn't know the user's region/Knows the user's region
- Doesn't know the common attributes/Knows the common attributes
- Doesn't know if there is an international associated concept/Knows that there is an international associated concept/Knows that there is not an international associated concept
- Doesn't know the cultural associated concept/Knows the cultural associated concept
- Doesn't know if the tourist understood the associated concept/Knows that the tourist understood the associated concept/Knows that the tourist didn't understand the associated concept

Every entry can take one of two values; with all permutations we get a total of 144 states, including 15 final states. To be in a final state, the agent should know the associated concept and should know that the user understood the associated concept. Moreover, the knowledge of the system should be consistent (E.g.: the system knows the cultural associated concept but doesn't know either of the cultural attributes, is not a final state). For the second state space, the action set includes seven actions:

- Identify the user's country
- Identify the user's region
- Identify the common attributes
- Identify if there is an international associated concept
- Identify if there is a cultural associated concept
- Confirm that the user understood the concept

6.4   The Advanced State Action Space

The third level State Action space produces the *Advanced agent*. The third level state space is the result of breaking down the second level state space in more precise states of knowledge. It includes 7 entries that represent the mental state of the system:

- Doesn't know the user's country/Knows the user's country
- Doesn't know the user's region/Knows the user's region
- Doesn't know the common attributes/Knows the common attributes
- Doesn't know if there is an international associated concept/Knows that there is an international associated concept/Knows that there is not an international associated concept
- Doesn't know the country associated concept/Knows the country associated concept
- Doesn't know the region associated concept/Knows the region associated concept
- Doesn't know if the tourist understood the associated concept/Knows that the tourist understood the associated concept/Knows that the tourist didn't understand the associated concept

Every entry can take one of two values; with all permutations we get a total number of 288 states, including 17 final states. To be in a final state, the agent should know the associated concept and should know that the user understood the associated concept. Moreover, the knowledge of the system should be consistent (e.g.: The system knows the cultural associated concept but doesn't know either of the cultural attributes is not a final state). For the third level state space, the action set include seven actions:

- Identify the user's country
- Identify the user's region
- Identify the common attributes
- Identify if there is an international associated concept
- Identify if there is a country associated concept
- Identify if there is a region associated concept
- Ask if the user understood the concept

7   Conclusion

This paper proposed a system that uses a reinforcement learning algorithm to learn Culturally Situated Dialogue strategies to support foreign tourists. Since no previous system has been implemented, the method allows the creation of dialogue strategies when no initial data or prototype exists.

As a first step, and in order to model the possible state spaces of the reinforcement learning algorithm, we identified common dialogue patterns that take place between tourists and shop owners in a market in Kyoto and extracted the attributes needed to implement Culturally Situated Dialogues. By breaking down the extracted attributes into more finely grained attributes we created three attribute sets with different levels of granularity. Each of these three attribute sets was mapped into a different state space, resulting in the creation of three different agents: The *Novice agent*, the *Intermediate agent* and the *Advanced agent*. Each agent needs a different minimum number observations and produces a different dialogue strategy. In order to provide the system with consistent data, we gathered open linked data concepts from DBpedia, after mapping the attributes with DBpedia properties.

Future work includes exploring the possibilities of automating the process of migrating to more complex agents depending on the available number of observations at each moment. This would allow the application of this technology to a variety of situations where Culturally Situated Associations are needed and no initial system or little observations exist.

Acknowledgments.   This research was partially supported by a Grant-in-Aid for Scientific Research (A) (17H00759, 2017-2020) from Japan Society for the promotion of Science (JSPS), and the Leading Graduates Schools Program, 'Collaborative Graduate Program in Design', by the Ministry of Education, Culture, Sports, Science and Technology, Japan.

References

1. https://www.jnto.go.jp/eng/ttp/sta/PDF/E2016.pdf
2. Ishida, T.: Intercultural collaboration and support systems: a brief history. In: Baldoni, M., Chopra, Amit K., Son, T.C., Hirayama, K., Torroni, P. (eds.) PRIMA 2016. LNCS, vol. 9862, pp. 3–19. Springer, Cham (2016). doi:10.1007/978-3-319-44832-9_1
3. Scheffler, K., Young, S.: Automatic learning of dialogue strategy using dialogue simulation and reinforcement learning. In: Proceedings of the Second International Conference on Human Language Technology Research, pp. 12–19. Morgan Kaufmann Publishers Inc. (2002)
4. Yang, S., Chen, J.: Fostering foreign language learning through technology enhanced intercultural projects. Language Learn. Technol. **18**(1), 57–75 (2014)
5. Byram, M.: Teaching and assessing intercultural communicative competence, p. 34. Multilingual Matters, Clevedon (1997)
6. Berners-Lee, T.: Linked Data - Design Issues (2006). http://www.w3.org/DesignIssues/LinkedData.html. Accessed 23 July
7. Zaveri, A., et al.: User-driven quality evaluation of dbpedia. In: Proceedings of the 9th International Conference on Semantic Systems, pp. 97–104. ACM (2013)

8. Sonntag, D., Kiesel, M.: Linked data integration for semantic dialogue and backend access. In: AAAI Spring Symposium: Linked Data Meets Artificial Intelligence (2010)
9. Eckert, W., Levin, E., Pieraccini, R.: User modeling for spoken dialogue system evaluation. In: Proceedings of the IEEE Workshop on Automatic Speech Recognition and Understanding, pp. 80–87. IEEE (1997)
10. Levin, E., Pieraccini, R., Eckert, W.: Using Markov decision process for learning dialogue strategies. In: Proceedings of the 1998 IEEE International Conference on Acoustics, Speech and Signal Processing, vol. 1, pp. 201–204. IEEE (1998)
11. Levin, E., Pieraccini, R., Eckert, W.: A stochastic model of human-machine interaction for learning dialog strategies. IEEE Trans. Speech Audio Process. 8(1), 11–23 (2000)
12. Rieser, V., Lemon, O.: Learning Effective Multimodal Dialogue Strategies from Wizard-of-Oz Data: Bootstrapping and Evaluation, pp. 638–646. ACL (2008)
13. Ishida, T. (ed.): The Language Grid: Service-Oriented Collective Intelligence for Language Resource Interoperability. Springer, Heidelberg (2011)
14. Schmidhuber, J.: A general method for multi-agent reinforcement learning in unrestricted environments. In: Adaptation, Coevolution and Learning in Multiagent Systems, Papers from the 1996 AAAI Spring Symposium, pp. 84–87 (1996)

Enhancing Learners' Cross-Cultural Understanding in Language and Culture Class Using InCircle

Noriko Uosaki[1(✉)], Takahiro Yonekawa[2], and Chengjiu Yin[3]

[1] Osaka University, Osaka, Japan
n.uosaki@gmail.com
[2] HUB Networks, Inc., Tokyo, Japan
[3] Kobe University, Kobe, Japan

Abstract. This paper describes the development and evaluation of a chat system called InCircle. The importance of cultural understanding in the development of intercultural competence in foreign language learning has been pointed out for a long time. Besides, one of the trends in a pedagogical field is the shift from teacher-centerd to student-centered learning. Recent advancement of IT technology has accelerated its trend. With the spreads of educational application of SNS (social network services), it has enabled us to share information and knowledge in real time. In order to promote student-centered learning, it is necessary to facilitate interaction among students. For these purposes, InCircle was introduced in a language and culture class at university in Japan. The objectives of our research study is to examine whether InCircle contributes to the enhancement of mutual cross-cultural understanding and the facilitation of interaction among students. The number of the students' posting dramatically increased after it was introduced compared with the blog comment function. The result of the questionnaire endorsed its usability and effectiveness as a communication tool.

Keywords: Collaborative learning · Cross-cultural understanding · InCircle · Language and culture class · Student-centered learning

1 Introduction

Language is part of culture. Numerous publications emphasize the importance of cultural understanding in the development of intercultural competence in foreign language learning [1]. In addition, student-centered collaborative learning has been drawing attention. It is reported that student-centred and small-scale course programmes resulted in more academic success than lecture-based course programme [2]. Collaborative learning has a "social constructivist" philosophical base, where learning is regarded as construction of knowledge within a social context [3]. It is also reported that a student-centred collaborative learning is one of the most effective ways of learning in language class [4]. In fact, most studies investigating the link between the extent to which course programmes are student-centred on the one hand and promote academic success on the other hand, find positive relationships between the two [2]. Recent prevalence of high-performance mobile devices has enhanced the potential of students' active interaction via mobile-based communication tools. We have seen a good deal of researches on

© Springer International Publishing AG 2017
T. Yoshino et al. (Eds.): CollabTech 2017, LNCS 10397, pp. 145–152, 2017.
DOI: 10.1007/978-3-319-63088-5_13

communications applications such as educational application of SNS (social network service) [5–8]. Our communications application project, InCircle system, is among them. In this study InCircle was introduced for the purpose of facilitating interaction among students and enhancing learning opportunities.

2   InCircle

InCircle System is a client-server application. The server side runs on Linux OS and Windows Server. The client side is working on iOS, Android, and PC web browser. Chat messages are transmitted and received through the network (Fig. 1).

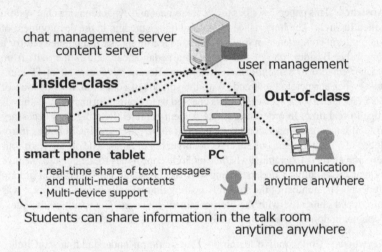

Fig. 1. InCircle system configuration

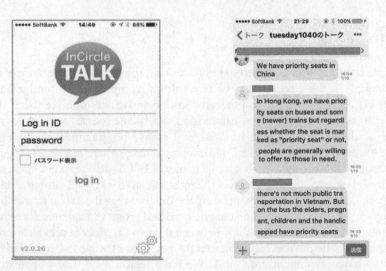

Fig. 2. InCircle log-in interface (left) and chat room interface (right)

The system allows users to create groups. Group members are able to send and receive messages and multimedia files in their chat room with an easy operation. Chat messages are synchronized in real-time to realize smooth communication. Figure 2 shows its log in interface (left) and chat room interface when it was first introduced in class (right).

In our system, we have mainly four major advantages:

(i) Teachers can be administrators of the system.

  Teachers can be administrators of the system so that they can watch the users/their students' behaviors. Therefore they can avoid their students' malicious behaviors via InCircle. Even if some case happens such as a harassment case, teachers can abort the student's accounts.

(ii) User accounts are pre-registered.

  Unlike other SNS or chat tools such as Facebook and LINE, user accounts are pre-registered. Teachers create accounts for their students and make a group for the class in advance. There are always some students who do not want to use the existing SNS systems. In fact in one of the authors' class that some students rejected to create a Facebook account and some students did not want to use LINE. Unless all the students agree to use it, it is next to impossible to use it as a communication tool in class. Besides, the existing SNS users usually post their private information on their profiles. However some students may not wish to share private information with some of their classmates. In our system, on the contrary, there is no page in the first place to fill in their private information such as school career, birth place/date.

(iii) Ensured security

  Every effort was made in order to ensure the security, such as encryption of the cache data in the client terminal, channel coding, encryption of database, the use of different cryptography keys for each company or school in the server side. Therefore it is highly protected against divulging of information or account hacking.

(iv) To be able to delete the sent messages.

  In our system, we can delete messages after it is sent not only on the sender's side but on the recipient's side. It is likely to happen that we send messages by mistake. Out system can handle such human errors.

Our research questions are:

(i) Can InCircle contribute to the enhancement of the students' mutual cross-cultural understanding?

(ii) Can InCircle contribute to the enhancement of interaction among the students?

3 The Target Class

The class was one of "international exchange subjects" which was targeted mainly for international exchange students. Japanese students who are interested in class held in English can also join it. The target class was held 14 times on a once-a-week-basis in a

CALL (computer assisted language learning) room during the fall semester, 2016. The class language was mainly in English. The objectives of the target class were (1) to enhance cross-cultural understanding and (2) to improve the skills of their target languages, which were Japanese or English.

4 Evaluation

4.1 Procedures

An evaluation was conducted in one of the authors' class at university in the western part of Japan. It consisted of 17 students (4 Japanese, 3 Germans, 2 Chinese, 2 Indonesians, 2 Taiwanese, 1 American, 1 Egyptian, 1 Hong Konger, 1 Vietnamese). All the participants were owners of mobile phones.

In order to examine the effectiveness of InCircle system, the comparison was made between InCircle and blogger's comment function. A class blog and a mailing list (ML) were created by the teacher as communication tools because not all the students had facebook accounts, nor LINE accounts, nor Twitter accounts. Google Blogger service was used for creating the class blog. It was used throughout the semester from October 4, 2016 to January 24, 2017. She posted contents which were useful for classroom learning as well as each class schedule. As for the mailing list, even though the teacher instructed the students to use ML as a communication tool among classmates, it turned out that it did not play any role as a communication tool. Therefore the mailing list was used only by the teacher when she needed to share necessary information with the students.

InCircle was introduced in the latter half of the semester and was used from November 29, 2016 to January 24, 2017. Therefore during the period, both Blogger and InCircle were used as communication tools. For the enhancement of the mutual cultural understanding, the teacher posted theme topics on both sites, where interrogative sentences were often posted so that the students felt it easy to post comments and interact each other on the both media (e.g. "Is your language stress-timed or syllable timed?", "Is kindergarten compulsory education in your country?", "Do you have priority seat in your country?"). The students were instructed to post comments on both media. They were informed that their posting would reflect their grades.

4.2 The Resutls

Table 1 shows the comparison of the numbers of posts between the blog comment columns and InCircle talk room. Even though the length of the trial use of InCircle was short (November 29, 2016 – January 24, 2017 for InCircle and October 4, 2016 – January 24, 2017 for Blogger) and the number of the theme topics were small (17 for InCircle and 76 for Blogger), the total number of posts was 146, which overwhelmed the number of blogger comment posts, 16.

Table 1. Comparison between InCircle and Blogger

	InCircle	Blogger
Period of use	11/29/16 – 1/24/17	10/4/16 – 1/24/17
The number of talks (InCircle) The number of blog pages (Blogger)	**17**	**76**
	The number of posts	The number of comments
Teacher	48	4
Students	**86**	**12**
TA(teaching assistant)	12	8
	146	**16**

As the number of the post shows, the students were more active in posting messages in InCircle. As for Blogger comment function, its users cannot post multimedia files. InCircle's easy operation facilitated interaction among classmates. As one example, when the teacher posted a question: Have you ever heard of '*amida kuji*' (a kind of lottery popular in Japan)? in InCircle (Fig. 3 left), 9 students responded and posted their comments such as "I have only seen this as a game in Dr. Kawashimas Brain Training, when I played this on my Nintendo DS:D", "Never played Brain Training like XXX but I also think I've seen this in a game before". One student's post leaded to another student's post. Apparently inCircle facilitated interaction among students. On the contrary, when the teacher posted a question in Blogger site, how they usually made themselves or their rooms warm, 9 students also posted comments in the comment column. This topic was expected to stimulate the students' interactions since for the most students, 2016 winter was their first winter in Japan, it was useful for them to get some tips to keep the room warm. But unlike the teacher's expectation, one student's post did not lead to another students' reaction (Fig. 3 right).

Table 2. The results of the 5-point-scale questionnaire

	Questions	Mean	SD
Q.1	Was it easy for you to use InCircle?	4.8	0.39
Q.2	Was it fun for you to use the system?	4.5	0.66
Q.3	Was it helpful as a means of communication with your classmates and teacher?	4.5	0.78
Q.4	Was it helpful for your class room learning?	4.3	1.21
Q.5	Was it helpful for your target language learning?	3.4	1.30
Q.6	Please rate its interface	4.1	0.51
Q.7	Please rate the whole system.	4.0	0.60

At the end of the phase, they were asked to answer the five-point-scale-questionnaire as shown in Table 2. Q1 and Q3 were created based on the technology acceptance model

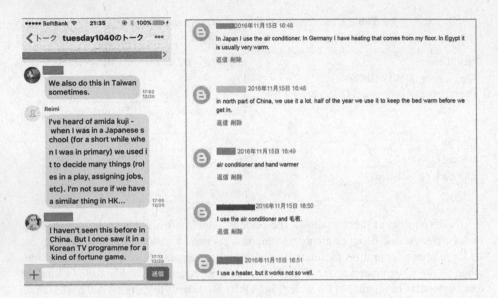

Fig. 3. InCircle posts (left) and Blogger comments (right)

proposed by [9]. Q2 was created to examine the fun factor of our system. Q4 and Q5 were created to examine its usefulness of the class learning. Q6 and Q7 were created for examining the user acceptance of its interface and the whole system.

The highest score, 4.8 was given when they were asked the usability of the system (Q.1). As some students felt it was like other existing apps (Table 2 Comments #1, and 4), most students had already used other similar apps, which lead to the high score of the usability of InCircle. The lowest score, 3.4 was given when they were asked if it was helpful for their target language learning (Q.5). Since the class was held in English, communication language in InCircle was mostly English. Therefore it was helpful for English language learners, but it was not so helpful for Japanese language learners as a language learning tool. In fact, 15 out of 17 students' target language was Japanese. In order to contribute to the improvement of their Japanese language skills, it is necessary to consider how to use this tool more effectively for Japanese language learning, which will be included in one of our future works.

4.3   Discussions

Our research questions were (i) Can InCircle contribute to the enhancement of the students' mutual cross-cultural understanding? (ii) Can InCircle contribute to the enhancement of interaction among the students? As for (i), our system contributed to enhancement of mutual cross-cultural understanding with the following reasons:1) As Figs. 2(right) and 3(left) show, and as the students #5 in Table 3 pointed out, they could gain knowledge and enhance cross-cultural understanding through InCircle communication. Besides, the fact that the average point of Q.4 (Was it helpful for your class room learning?) was as high as 4.3 endorsed it. In traditional teacher-centered lecture style class, the students are not able to gain knowledge from other students. For instance, they could learn job hunting systems in other countries by using InCircle. These are among what the teacher cannot provide. As for (ii), our system contributed to enhancement of interaction among the students with the following reasons: (1) The students' posting via InCircle outnumbered Blogger comments. (2) As the students #2 and #7 in Table 3 pointed out, knowledge can be shared via our system instantly so that they were able to interact each other in a very effective way. In traditional class, most possible way to share knowledge with other classmates was to present them one by one in turns, which takes time, thus ineffective. Besides, in pair work or group work, which are regarded as typical collaborative learning methods, it is difficult to share knowledge with other pairs or groups. Therefore it can be safely be said that InCircle contributed to the enhancement of both students' mutual cross-cultural understanding and interaction among the students. As mentioned earlier, other SNS tools such as facebook, LINE, twitter have a weakness as a communication tool in class. InCircle could be a powerful communication tool to run effective student-centered collaborative learning class.

Table 3. The students' impression of InCircle

#1	It is just a messenger and i do not feel the difference between incircle and other messenger apps such as google hangouts, or line.
#2	It was an interesting way of communication with teachers and peers
#3	Fun way to communicate
#4	its like whatsapp
#5	use it in class to share with others
#6	Feel interested in chatting with friends
#7	It was easy to use and good for classroom discussion use.

As for the last question in the questionnaire: "Is there any functions that you feel great if InCircle could provide?", Student #1 suggested "easier login access". In our system, we can maintain the login state for 30 days. Therefore frequent users like users who use every week in class can keep the login state so that they do not need to text their ID and password when they log in. The login state for 30 days was set for the security reason. To enhance both security and convenience is a trade-off situation. In order to enhance convenience without losing high security, a new function, passcode input at regular intervals, has been under development. This function is expected to facilitate its users' login procedure.

5   Conclusion and Future Works

In this study, we describe enhancing communication among students using InCircle. When InCircle was introduced in the mid-semester, the number of the students' posting dramatically increased. The high points of the questionnaire results showed that the participants were satisfied with its usability, its fun factor, its interface and the whole system. Our hypotheses (research questions (i), (ii), and (iii)) were proved to be correct. However it was found out that our system was not supportive for their target language learning. Since it is one of the two objectives of the target class, it is needed to consider how to introduce InCircle from the pedagogical viewpoint in order to support their language learning. It is among our future works to find out some solutions to improve the skills of their target languages via InCircle.

Acknowledgements. Part of this research work was supported by the Grant-in-Aid for Scientific Research No. 26350319 and No. 16H03078 from the Ministry of Education, Culture, Sports, Science and Technology (MEXT) in Japan.

References

1. Schulz, R.A.: The challenge of assessing cultural understanding in the context of foreign language instruction. Foreign Lang. Ann. **40**(1), 9–26 (2007). doi:10.1111/j. 1944-9720.2007.tb02851.x
2. Severiens, S., Meeuwisse, M., Born, M.: Student experience and academic success: comparing a student-centred and a lecture-based course programme. High. Educ. Int. J. High. Educ. Educ. plann. **70**(1) (2015). doi:10.1007/s10734-014-9820-3
3. Oxford, R.L.: Cooperative learning, collaborative learning, and interaction: three communicative strands in the language classroom. Modern Lang. J. **81**(1), 443–456 (1997). doi:10.1111/j.1540-4781.1997.tb05510.x
4. Chen, T.X.: Interactive learning of a foreign language. J. Acoust. Soc. Am. **114**(1), 30 (2003). doi:10.1121/1.1601085
5. Munoz, C., Towner, T.: Opening facebook: how to use facebook in the college classroom. In: Gibson, I., Weber, R., McFerrin, K., Carlsen, R., Willis, D. (eds.) Proceedings of Society for Information Technology & Teacher Education International Conference 2009, pp. 2623–2627 (2009)
6. Hung, T.-H., Yuen, S.C.-Y.: Educational use of social networking technology in higher education. Teach. High. Educ. **15**(6), 703–714 (2010)
7. Kim, S.-Y., Kim, M.-R.: educational implication of reflection activities using SNS in cooperative learning. In: Proceedings of the 13th International Educational Technology Conference, pp. 340–347 (2013)
8. Kwak, K.T., Choi, S.K., Lee, B.G.: SNS flow, SNS self-disclosure and post hoc interpersonal relations change: focused on Korean Facebook user. Comput. Hum. Behav. **31**, 294–304 (2014)
9. Davis, F.D.: Perceived usefulness, perceived ease of use, and user acceptance of information technology. MIS Q. **13**(3), 319–339 (1989)

Children's Social Behavior Analysis System Using BLE and Accelerometer

Shuta Nakamae(✉), Shumpei Kataoka, Can Tang, Simona Vasilache,
Satoshi Saga, Buntarou Shizuki, and Shin Takahashi

University of Tsukuba, Tsukuba, Japan
{nakamae,shizuki}@iplab.cs.tsukuba.ac.jp, kataoka@adapt.cs.tsukuba.ac.jp,
tangcan@padc.cs.tsukuba.ac.jp, {simona,saga,shin}@cs.tsukuba.ac.jp

Abstract. We present an IoT-based children's social behavior analysis system aimed at young children and elementary school students. Our system uses BLE-based ID logs to analyze daily social behaviors, such as how a child spent the day with his/her friends. Furthermore, we also use accelerometer logs to detect the period when the user (i.e., a child) was with friends or not, and what kind of activity (e.g., walking or staying in one place) the user was involved in. We conducted a five-day experiment with four families using our system. We also interviewed the families' parents and compared their responses with the analyzed results to investigate the accuracy of the above detection and usability of our system. The result shows that our system can detect the period when the child was with other friends or alone, as well as the activity (s)he was involved in.

Keywords: Bluetooth low energy · Activity log · Activity recognition · Crime prevention · Wireless communication · Wearable device · Data visualization

1 Introduction

In Japan, most kidnappings of young children and elementary school students occur when the children are alone [14]. To address this issue, numerous tools and systems have been developed by companies for crime prevention. A crime preventing tool "Amber Alert GPS Locator" developed by "Amber Alert" [1] can track a child and can send emergency alerts to his/her parents by using GPS. These systems can detect the location of the child and they are effective when such incidents occur. However, to prevent such incidents the parents need to know what their child is doing in his/her daily life.

In this paper, we show a system that enables parents to guide the child by knowing what the child is doing when they are apart from each other. The system records children's behavior with accelerometers and Bluetooth low energy (BLE). The use of accelerometer logs allows the user (for example, parents) to analyze the child's behavior in a single device scenario. Furthermore, it allows the user to analyze children's social behavior, such as, whether the child's friends are nearby

© Springer International Publishing AG 2017
T. Yoshino et al. (Eds.): CollabTech 2017, LNCS 10397, pp. 153–167, 2017.
DOI: 10.1007/978-3-319-63088-5_14

or not in a multiple device scenario, which enhances analysis. Our system records children's behavior with accelerometers and Bluetooth Low Energy; therefore, it has effective battery conservation and can be used both indoors and outdoors. Moreover, the size of the battery and thus the system can be reduced when necessary. In addition, our system does not require special operation by the child.

In the following sections, we first explain the design of our system, which consists of the child's device, the parents' application, and an analysis server. We implemented the system and conducted a preliminary experiment to test its capabilities in terms of detecting friends nearby the user (a child) and activity recognition. After that, we conducted a five-day experiment with four families that are assumed as actual users of our system. We also interviewed the families parents and compared their responses with the analyzed results to investigate the accuracy of the detection and usability of our system. Finally, we present our future work and conclusions.

2   Related Work

Local governments and various companies have worked on the prevention of incidents such as kidnapping. Local governments employ police and volunteers to keep children secure when going to school and returning home. In addition, companies have developed various crime prevention tools, one such major tool being a personal alarm. IoT-based crime-prevention tools have been increasingly used for protecting children; for example, GPS [1], classic Bluetooth [4,17], and other communication channel-based tools have been developed.

Various works have also focused on the location of the user. Zheng et al. [18] proposed an approach based on supervised learning to infer people's motion from their GPS logs. Their method uses common-sense constraints of the real world and typical user behavior in addition to GPS logs. Mizuno et al. [12] presented a system that tracks the user's position, which is considered to be related to the user's activity. Our system uses BLE information rather than the specific position.

In addition to GPS, which is a specialized system for position tracking, Bluetooth has attracted attention as a method of behavior tracking and activity logs; thus, many attempts at using only Bluetooth have also been undertaken. For example, Chang et al. [3] proposed a system that uses Bluetooth tags and beacons to reconstruct the user's route and uses the information to improve the user's experience. Nishide et al. [13] used the detection history of classic Bluetooth devices to analyze a single user's behavior. Katevas et al. [9] presented a system that is able to detect dynamic groups by combining the estimated distance between people using Bluetooth data with motion activity classification. In particular, this method can estimate the stationary versus moving status of each user to detect the group's state.

Many studies in this field have been conducted using BLE, a new standard of Bluetooth with the feature of high battery conservation, in contrast to classic Bluetooth with its high energy consumption. In crowd-sensing applications, using smartphones as the main source of sensor data is difficult because of the need for downloading and installing applications, and the added burden of energy consumption. Jamil et al. [7] proposed a novel hybrid participatory sensing approach to capture large group dynamics by distributing a large number of BLE tags and smartphones to the group members. They performed a large experimental deployment with 600 tags and 10 smartphones, which was conducted during the Hajj, to prove that the approach was effective. Our approach makes use of BLE for the detection history of Bluetooth devices and their social relation, in order to analyze the child's and his/her friends' behavior.

There are various research works on behavior and relation recognition of children. Imaki et al. [6] automatically extracted children's friendship relationship by using RFIDs and accelerometers. They placed RFIDs in each area of a kindergarten, and observed the friendship relationship of each child by analyzing the RFID logs and acceleration logs. In addition, Kousaka et al. [10] classified group behaviors by attaching accelerometers to children and analyzing the logs. These studies mainly support activities in kindergartens, and focus on group activities and relationships in a specific place. Our system can also estimate group relationships and even estimate the behavior of children in any place.

Activity recognition systems based on sensors and vision are being studied recently [8,15]. Series of sensors such as camera, microphone, accelerometer, gyroscope, barometer, digital compass, GPS, are used. In particular, smartphone-based activity recognition systems [2,11] are popular, because a smartphone has many sensors embedded and widely used. These systems can recognize activities with high accuracy. However, we focus on primary school children, while most societies do not encourage the use of smartphones at such an early age. Thus, we adopt alternative means of activity tracking. We focus on less complex devices which can be more easily carried/worn by children. The work in [5,16] presented methods using only accelerometers and these methods can also recognize activities to some extent. Therefore, we decided to use the accelerometer as the primary sensor to recognize the activity of the children.

3 System Description

Our system, as shown in Fig. 1, consists of small BLE devices for children (child's device), a smartphone application for the parents (parent's application), and an analysis server.

3.1 Child's Device

The child's device (Fig. 2) continuously reads and sends IDs via BLE. We designed the device in such a way that a child is able to carry it in his or her bag. It consists of a microcontroller (Switch Science mbed TY51822r3), an SD card as internal storage, a 3 dimensional accelerometer (Analog Devices ADXL345), and an LED. The size of the device is $4.8 \times 4.5 \times 1.4$ cm and it weighs approximately 24 g, without the battery. Various batteries can be connected to the

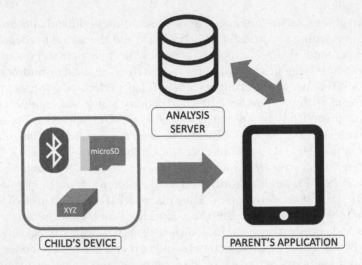

Fig. 1. System components

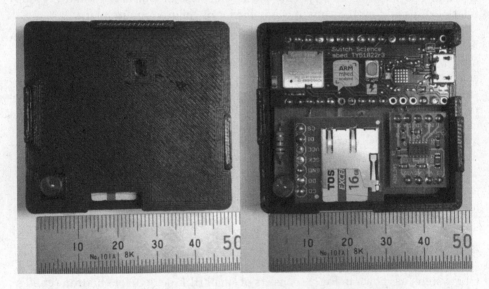

Fig. 2. Child's device (left) and inside of child's device (right)

child's device (we used two AA batteries in our experiments). The case of the device is printed using a fused deposition modeling 3D printer. The device reads IDs sent by other Bluetooth devices, including those of the child's friends. The IDs and acceleration are stored as a log in the internal storage of the device. The device also sends out its own ID to be received by other children's devices. The IDs and relationships are registered to our system's server beforehand, and the values obtained are saved to the internal storage. The LED is used for indicating the operation status of the device.

3.2   Parent's Application

When a child returns home with his/her child device, his/her parents connect the SD card of the device to their smartphone or tablet, and transfer the saved log to the parent's application. The parent's application has functions for visualizing the periods when the child was alone (alone periods), and for communication with the analysis server for the visualization.

In order to reduce the operational burden of checking the child's alone period, we implemented two functions in the application. The first function, namely the glance screen, displays the alone period in a simple manner (Fig. 3), where the user can check the alone period in hourly units. The purpose of this screen is to enable the parent to easily understand the alone period and reduce the burden of the parent's operation. The second function, namely the detail screen, displays the number of friends nearby in detail (Fig. 4). In each function, the user can select the item of the date they wish to view from the date column.

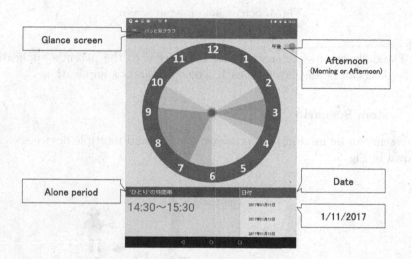

Fig. 3. Screenshot of glance screen

3.3   Analysis Server

The analysis server processes the received log and returns the total number of nearby friends per time unit time to the parent's application. The server process operates as a daemon on CentOS, and we use SFTP as the transferring protocol. The following data processing is implemented in Python. Because the child's device does not have a hardware clock, it cannot record the global time when the device detects other children's devices. Therefore, the device records the time starting with the moment when the device is activated. When the server receives the data, it converts the data recorded by the child's device into global time. Thereafter, only the log with the registered IDs in the friend list is extracted as data from the log, and the total number of friends is collected for each time

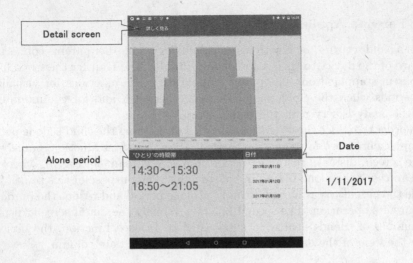

Fig. 4. Screenshot of detail screen

unit. The daily results are created and transferred to the parent's application, and the data can be displayed on each screen of parent's application.

3.4   System Scenario

Our system can be used in two scenarios: a single and multiple device scenario, as shown in Fig. 5.

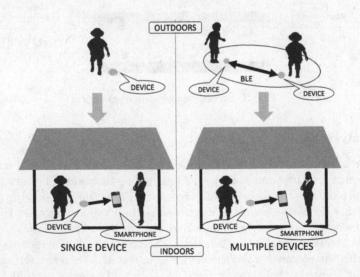

Fig. 5. Single device scenario (left) and multiple device scenario (right)

- In the single device scenario, where there are no child's friends' devices in proximity, the system uses the child's movement, as analyzed by the accelerometer log, to estimate whether the child was walking or not. From these logs, the parents can determine that the child was alone, and walking or staying in one place.
- In the multiple device scenario, where there are one or more of the child's friends' devices, the system uses the IDs to estimate whether the child was near his/her friends, and also uses the child's movement to estimate whether the child was walking or staying still.

By using the system, parents can identify opportunities to provide crime prevention behavior education to their children.

4   Preliminary Experiment

We conducted a three-day preliminary experiment using our system to test its capabilities in terms of detecting friends nearby the user (a child) and activity recognition. The participants in this experiment were four male graduate students (P0–P3), 22 to 25 years old. We explained informed consent (based on the ethical guidelines of our university) to all subjects and obtained their consent. They all carried a child's device which is described in Sect. 3.1 during the experiment and went about their usual daily life. Since these participants were in the same research group, they spent most of their time together. After returning home, they checked the results with the parent's application. Furthermore, during the experiment, each participant recorded the names of all their friends (participants in the experiment) who were nearby in their notes every time the number of friends changed.

As an example of the results, Fig. 6 shows the number of friends nearby P0, which includes the number as determined by the analysis server and that recorded by the participant himself. As shown in the graph, these numbers agree. This result suggests that the system can correctly detect the period when the user is with friends or alone.

Figure 7 shows a graph representing the average acceleration per minute of P0. The graph also shows the number of friends collected by the system (the same data as shown in Fig. 6). We found three characteristic sections (1, 2, and 3) in Fig. 7, and interviewed P0 regarding his activities on the given day to examine the three findings.

1. P0 was alone between 10:50 and 11:30. However, during this period, the acceleration changed rapidly; therefore, we estimated that he was walking or running alone. P0's comments support this, as he stated that he was walking alone during this time.
2. P0 was not alone between 16:30 and 17:30. We can see there is no significant movement; therefore, we estimated that P0 was not moving. P0 confirmed this by stating that he was working at a desk with his friends during this time.

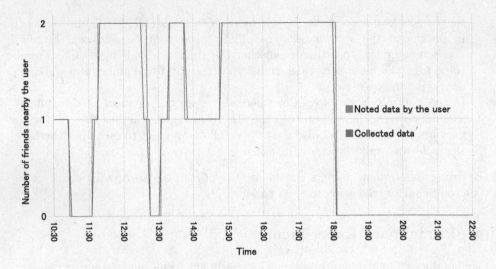

Fig. 6. Friends nearby P0 in a day

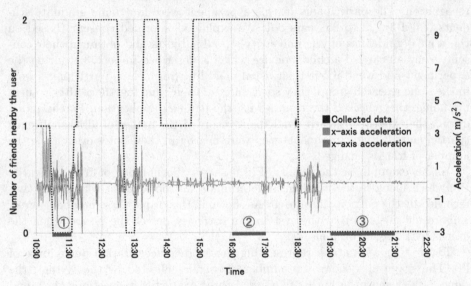

Fig. 7. Graph of the number of friends nearby and average acceleration per minute

3. P0 was alone between 19:30 and 21:30. We can see that there is no significant change in the recorded acceleration; therefore, we estimated that P0 was not moving. P0 stated that he was studying alone.

We observe that we can estimate the type of activity the user was involved in by using the Bluetooth IDs and accelerometer logs. Moreover, if we simultaneously log the activity of the accelerometer, we can estimate the user's activity more precisely.

5   Experiment

In this section, we describe the five-day experiment with four families that are assumed as actual users of our system. The purpose of this experiment was to investigate the detection accuracy of the BLE signals and usability of our system.

5.1   Participants

The participants were five elementary school students (four male participants A, B, C, and D; one female participant E who is the younger sister of D) and four mothers of them. Two of the mothers are stay-at-home mother, while the other two are part-time workers. All five participants go to the same elementary school, and A, B, C, and D are in the same class. In addition, participants who live close by go to the school together: C, D, and E go to the school using the same route every morning, while A and B go to the school via a different route However, since E is in a different grade, there are cases where E goes back home alone. When returning home, A, B, C, and D leave the school at the same time, but they separate one by one on the way home. Also, A, D, and E take the same lesson after school. Based on the ethical guidelines of our university, we obtained the parents' consent to participate in the experiment. We paid them monetary rewards for participating in the experiment.

5.2   Procedure

Firstly, the mother inserts a new battery in the child's device and puts it inside the child's bag. The mother takes notes of the time when the child left the house, and the time when the child came home manually. Throughout the experiment, the child goes on with his/her normal daily routine. After the child comes home, the mother uses the parent's device to see the result. Finally, the mother answers a questionnaire and ends the experiment of the day. The above sequence is repeated for five days.

5.3   Results and Discussion

Fig. 8 shows a graph representing the average acceleration per minute of A, and the number of friends collected by the system on day three. We found three characteristic sections (1, 2, and 3) in Fig. 8, and interviewed A's mother regarding A's activities on the given day to examine the findings.

1. A was alone from 7:45 and then eventually the number of friends around him increased to three. Also, the acceleration is changing rapidly; therefore we estimated that he was going to the school. The record of this day supports this: 7:45 was the time when A left his home. After increasing to three, the number of friends does not change for several hours, and there is no rapid change of acceleration during this period. Therefore, we can estimate that A was in the school.

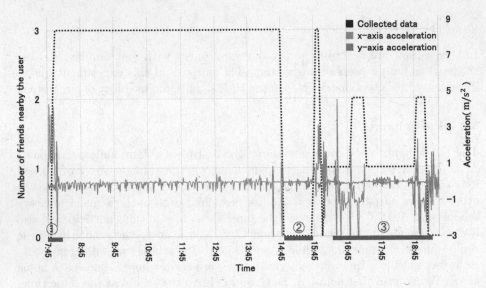

Fig. 8. Graph of the number of friends nearby and average acceleration per minute of A in day three

2. There is little change of acceleration and the number of friends is zero between 14:50 to 15:40. We can estimate that the participants separated during this period. According to an interview of A's mother, A, B, C, and D had classes in separate rooms during this period. Therefore, although A was not with the other participants, there was no significant change in the acceleration.
3. Between 16:00 and 19:05, we can estimate that A went somewhere with a friend. As explained above, on this day, A, D, and E went to the same lesson after school.

Figure 9 shows a graph representing the average acceleration per minute of E, and the number of friend collected by the system on day five. We found four characteristics section (1, 2, 3, and 4) in Fig. 9, and interviewed E's mother (who is also D's mother) regarding E's activities on the given day.

1. We can see that until 7:50 there are two friends nearby and E becomes alone from 7:55. During the 7:35 to 7:55 period, the acceleration is changing rapidly. We estimate that E was going to the school. E's mother's comments support this estimation, as she stated that E left the house with her brother (D) at 7:35. After 7:55, E is alone, and the acceleration does not change for a long time. This is because only E was in a different class from the other participants (A, B, C, and D).
2. From 14:45 to 15:25 the acceleration is changing rapidly. Therefore we can estimate that this was a period when the school ended and the children went home. E's report of the day supports this estimation: the time of returning home was 15:23.

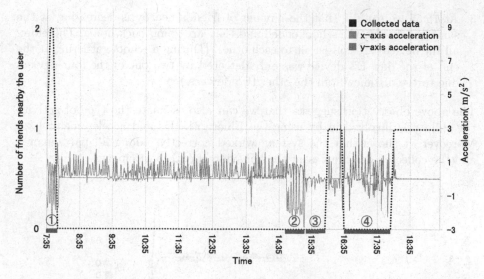

Fig. 9. Graph of the collected data and average acceleration per minute of E in day five

3. Between 15:25 and 16:00, when we can assume that E is in her house because there is no rapid change in acceleration, the number of friends increases at 16:05. We can estimate that her brother, participant D, has returned home at the time. Participant D's report of the day support this estimation: the time of returning home was 16:07.

4. After E was at home with her brother until 16:30, she becomes alone and the acceleration changes rapidly between 16:35 and 18:00. We can estimate that she moved somewhere, and came home at 18:05. E's mother's comments support this estimation: she went to her friend's house during this time with her device.

Figure 10 shows a graph representing the average acceleration per minute of participant A, B, C, and D, and the number of friends collected by the system on day four. We found three characteristic sections (1, 2, and 3) in Fig. 10, which shows that the system is working correctly among all the participants at the same time.

1. The number of friends nearby increases at the same time. We can see that three of the participants were in the classroom. However there is no change in C's data. Therefore, we can assume that C is not in the school or in a different place. After the experiment, we interviewed C's mother and found that C went to the school late.

2. From the graph, we can understand that the number of friends nearby increased by one at 11:35. Also, in C's report, it is recorded that 11:35 was the time C arrived the school.

3. At 15:55 we can see that the number of friends nearby is decreasing at the same time; thus, the school ended and they are going back home. Therefore, all the devices are consistent to each other. (During a school gathering at the end of the day, E's device was only detected by two out of the four devices due to the distance from the other two devices.)

The above observation suggests that we can also estimate the type of activity the child was involved in by using the Bluetooth IDs and accelerometer logs. Moreover, it shows that the system worked correctly among all participants, and the collected data represent the behavior of each participant.

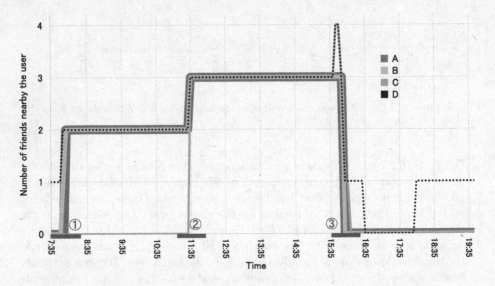

Fig. 10. Graph of the number of friends nearby of A, B, C, and D in day four

We also interviewed all the mothers regarding how they felt using our system. As a result, the detail screen was highly rated. One mother stated "It was fun looking at my son's daily life by the number of friends nearby." However, two of the opposing comments were also collected, depending on the working situation of the mother. Among the families with a stay-at-home mother, they already knew the situation of their children, and thus they could not feel the usefulness of the glance screen. In the case where both parents work, one mother stated "It was very good that I could actually see the activity logs of my child." In these families, knowing the child's movements is very helpful for the parents.

6   Future Work

We observed several problems during the experiments. In our current implementation, the parents have to remove the SD card from the child's device each time they wish to transfer the saved log from the device to the parent's application, which is time consuming and troublesome. In the future, we plan to enable the system to transfer data wirelessly. Moreover, our implementation of the child's device was not small enough to be worn by children. Therefore, the device had to be put in the bag for safety reasons. Therefore, we could only distinguish whether the child was moving between school and house or not. As our future goal, we plan to downsize our system so children can wear the device so that we can collect much more data.

Furthermore, since we only performed simple analysis of acceleration in this research, we will use various analytical methods [5,16] in the future to present more accurate behavior to the parent.

7   Conclusions

In this paper, we have presented a system employing BLE and an accelerometer to estimate the social behavior of children. The results of our preliminary experiment show that using BLE logs and accelerometer logs enable us to estimate the behavioral history with the participant's friends accurately. Furthermore, the system could detect periods when the participant was with friends or alone and estimate multiple activities in both the single device and multiple device scenario. We had four families, that are assumed as actual users of our system, to conduct an experiment, and verified the preciseness of the system from estimation from collected data and hearing surveys. As a result, our system was working correctly among all participants. Based on the result of the interview to the participants, we also found that the working-mother thinks our system is useful while the stay-at-home mothers do not feel the usefulness since they already knew the situation of their children very well.

In the future, we plan to enable the system transfer data wirelessly. In addition, we plan to downsize our system so that children can wear the device, and we can collect much more data. Furthermore, since we only performed simple analysis of acceleration in this research, we will identify variations of activities in a high accuracy by performing various evaluations.

Acknowledgement. This work was supported in part by JSPS KAKENHI, grant numbers 16K00265 (Grant-in-Aid for Scientific Research (C)) and 16H02853 (Grant-in-Aid for Scientific Research (B)).

References

1. Amber Alert: Amber Alert GPS Locator. http://www.amberalertgps.com/. Accessed 21 Oct 2016
2. Bedogni, L., Di Felice, M., Bononi, L.: By train or by car? detecting the user's motion type through smartphone sensors data. In: Wireless Days (WD), 2012 IFIP, pp. 1–6. IEEE (2012)

3. Chang, C.M., Li, S.C., Huang, Y.: Crowdsensing route reconstruction using portable bluetooth beacon-based two-way network. In: Proceedings of the 2016 ACM International Joint Conference on Pervasive and Ubiquitous Computing: Adjunct, UbiComp 2016 Adjunct, pp. 265–268. ACM, New York (2016). http://doi.acm.org/10.1145/2968219.2971361

4. Chen, Z., Chen, Y., Hu, L., Wang, S., Jiang, X., Ma, X., Lane, N.D., Campbell, A.T.: ContextSense: unobtrusive discovery of incremental social context using dynamic Bluetooth data. In: Proceedings of the 2014 ACM International Joint Conference on Pervasive and Ubiquitous Computing: Adjunct Publication, UbiComp 2014, Adjunct, pp. 23–26. ACM, New York (2014). http://doi.acm.org/10.1145/2638728.2638801

5. Das, S., Green, L., Perez, B., Murphy, M., Perring, A.: Detecting user activities using the accelerometer on android smartphones. In: TRUST REU The Team for Research in Ubiquitous Secure Technology, vol. 29 (2010)

6. Imaki, K., Kousaka, K., Shibata, M., Haga, H., Kaneda, S.: Automatic extraction of children's friendship relation from the integration of RFID and accelerometer. In: Proceedings of the Annual Conference of JSAI. Japanese Society of Artificial Intelligence, May 2009

7. Jamil, S., Basalamah, A., Lbath, A., Youssef, M.: Hybrid participatory sensing for analyzing group dynamics in the largest annual religious gathering. In: Proceedings of the 2015 ACM International Joint Conference on Pervasive and Ubiquitous Computing, UbiComp 2015, pp. 547–558. ACM, New York (2015). http://doi.acm.org/10.1145/2750858.2807548

8. Sunny, J.T., Gellar, S.M., Kizhakkethottam, J.J.: Applications and challenges of human activity recognition using sensors in a smart environment. Int. J. Innovative Res. Sci. Technol. 2(4), 50–57. http://www.ijirst.org/articles/IJIRSTV2I4024.pdf

9. Katevas, K., Haddadi, H., Tokarchuk, L., Clegg, R.G.: Detecting group formations using iBeacon technology. In: Proceedings of the 2016 ACM International Joint Conference on Pervasive and Ubiquitous Computing: Adjunct, UbiComp 2016, pp. 742–752. ACM, New York (2016). http://doi.acm.org/10.1145/2968219.2968281

10. Kousaka, K., Imaki, K., Shibata, M., Haga, H., Kaneda, S.: Classification of children's group activity from acceleration data by using wavelet transformation. UBI 13, 1–8 (2009). http://ci.nii.ac.jp/naid/110007995126/

11. Mafrur, R., Nugraha, I.G.D., Choi, D.: Modeling and discovering human behavior from smartphone sensing life-log data for identification purpose. Hum.-Centric Comput. Inf. Sci. 5(1), 31 (2015)

12. Mizuno, H., Sasaki, K., Hosaka, H.: Indoor-outdoor positioning and lifelog experiment with mobile phones. In: Proceedings of the 2007 Workshop on Multimodal Interfaces in Semantic Interaction, WMISI 2007, pp. 55–57. ACM, New York (2007). http://doi.acm.org/10.1145/1330572.1330582

13. Nishide, R., Ushiokoshi, T., Nakamura, S., Kono, Y.: Detecting social contexts from bluetooth device logs. In: Supplemental Proceedings of Ubicomp, pp. 228–230 (2009)

14. Saitama Prefectural Police: Approaching Incidents to Children by Suspicious Person (2016). https://www.police.pref.saitama.lg.jp/, https://www.police.pref.saitama.lg.jp/c0020/kurashi/documents/koekakeh27cyu.pdf. Accessed 28 Oct 2016, (in Japanese)

15. Shoaib, M., Bosch, S., Incel, O.D., Scholten, H., Havinga, P.J.: A survey of online activity recognition using mobile phones. Sensors 15(1), 2059–2085 (2015)

16. Wang, X., Kim, H.: Detecting user activities with the accelerometer on android smartphones

17. Zhang, Y., Martikainen, O., Pulli, P., Naumov, V.: Real-time process data acquisition with bluetooth. In: Proceedings of the 4th International Symposium on Applied Sciences in Biomedical and Communication Technologies, ISABEL 2011, pp. 21:1–21:5. ACM, New York (2011). http://doi.acm.org/10.1145/2093698.2093719

18. Zheng, Y., Li, Q., Chen, Y., Xie, X., Ma, W.Y.: Understanding mobility based on GPS data. In: Proceedings of the 10th International Conference on Ubiquitous Computing, UbiComp 2008, pp. 312–321. ACM, New York (2008). http://doi.acm.org/10.1145/1409635.1409677

Extension of Smartphone by Wearable Input/Output Interface with Floor Projection

Nobuchika Sakata[1(✉)], Fumihiro Sato[1], Tomu Tominaga[1], and Yoshinori Hijikata[2]

[1] Division of Systems Science and Applied Informatics, Graduate School of Engineering Science,
Osaka University, 1-3 Machikaneyama, Toyonaka, Japan
{sakata,sato,tominaga}@hlab.sys.es.osaka-u.ac.jp
[2] School of Business Administration, Kwansei Gakuin University, Uegahara, Nishinomiya, Japan
hijikata@hlab.sys.es.osaka-u.ac.jp

Abstract. In this paper, we propose an extension of smartphones with a wearable input/output interface with floor projection (WIIFP). WIIFP has advantages in comparison with smartphones. First, WIIFP allows the user to access information without retrieving the device. Thus, information access is quick and easy in comparison with typical smartphone. Second, floor projection is large and public. Therefore, WIIFP performs well at pasting temporal information on floor and sharing information with other users. Thus, we propose interaction between WIIFP and smartphones to take advantages of WIIFP and comfort mobile computing. Then, we illustrate utilization of WIIFP, which extends the function of smartphones describing a specific scenario. We studied the usability of the extension of smartphones by WIIFP. We obtained feedback of using the smartphone and WIIFP. The combination of the smartphone and WIIFP was found to be suitable for multi-tasking and multi-users.

Keywords: Augmented reality · Mobile interaction · Floor interaction · Floor projection

1 Introduction

The widespread use of mobile terminals such as smartphones enables us to access information services both indoors and outdoors, even while walking. For example, we use information services to find a route, check e-mails and use a social network service (SNS). These information services are used frequently and briefly. Furthermore, most of them can be used by a simple operation. However, such mobile terminals have several limitations. First, presentation of information by the mobile terminal is limited by the display size. Second, it is difficult for users to pay attention to their surroundings while watching the display screen in their hands. Third, the mobile terminal needs to be retrieved from a pocket or bag. Fourth, the user has to hold the device itself with at least one hand, even while only viewing. Therefore, it is difficult to use the mobile terminal when both hands are occupied.

Thus, we focus on a type of projection system that can compensate for these limitations and provide a more efficient way of viewing information [1, 2]. Some studies

© Springer International Publishing AG 2017
T. Yoshino et al. (Eds.): CollabTech 2017, LNCS 10397, pp. 168–181, 2017.
DOI: 10.1007/978-3-319-63088-5_15

focused on a wearable projection system that enables the user to access information via a large screen without retrieving the device [3, 4]. Additionally, Matsuda proposed a wearable input/output interface with floor projection (WIIFP) composed of a mobile projector, depth sensor, and gyro sensor, which are equipped on the user's chest [5, 6]. WIIFP allows the user to perform "select" and "drag" operations by controlling the projected image on the floor using fingertips and feet (Fig. 1). In this paper, we propose the utilization of WIIFP to extend the visual output and motion input of smartphones. Then, we describe a scenario that illustrates the rich and innovative mobile computing achieved by collaboration between WIIFP and the smartphone. We conducted a user study to research the usability of the combination of WIIFP and the smartphone.

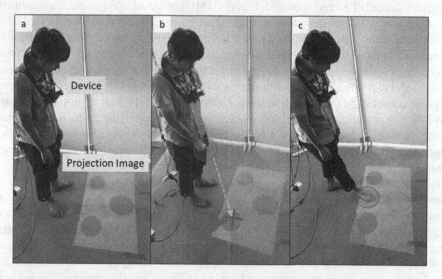

Fig. 1. a. Wearable input/output interface (WIIFP) with floor projection; b. Hand input; c. Toe input; d. Transferring map data to floor; e. Aiming a red point in floor surface and the information of the red point is opened on the smartphone. (Color figure online)

2   Related Work

Our working group have conducted some VR and AR researches that are not using general HMD. Actually, we have focused to non-head mounted wearable computers [26–28].

2.1   Input to GUI

Standard GUIs are operated using a pointer on the screen with pointing devices, such as a mouse and a trackball. However, the operability worsened as the device was downsized for portability. There was a trade-off between portability and operability. Mobile terminals also restrict the use of one hand, and these devices need to be taken out of a pocket or a bag. Related works have investigated hands-free input with wearable computing devices. For example, an input system using pointing by the fingers, such as hand mouse [7], and an input system based on line of sight [8] were proposed. These systems burden the user because the devices are equipped on the head. These systems also occupy the hands and eyes. This makes it difficult to conduct other tasks because these are the most frequently used parts of a user's body.

2.2 Accessing Information Using Projector

Accessing information via a projector has been studied for many years [9]. Technology that combines reality with wearable computers has been developed. The use of a projector instead of a head-mounted display (HMD) offers advantages such as mobility, accurate display in a certain location, and reduction in the burden on users in studies of augmented reality. Studies on augmented reality have used projectors such as the tele-direction interface [10]. These studies have demonstrated the effectiveness of displaying annotations in the real world by using a projector. Karitsuka superimposed a movie or annotated a real world surface with graphics or characters [11]. However, the system required a marker on the projection surface, which made it difficult to project the image anywhere. Yamamoto projected information on a palm-top using a projector attached to the shoulder, which provided a stable display [12]. However, this system was not hands-free and the display was not large for accessing information. Mistry projected information onto a wall or real objects using a head-mounted or neck-strap-mounted projector, where inputs using finger gestures were recognized by an RGB camera [13]. However, this system required image processing because the system often failed to recognize the finger with different ambient light and background colors. OmniTouch, which was developed by Chris [14], uses a depth sensor to detect fingers and touch everywhere. Those studies show that using hands and fingers as an input interface is an applicable and efficient way in wearable projection system. However, these studies required the users to raise their arms, which led to strain, and the system occupied both of the user's hands.

2.3 Multi-device Interaction

In recent years, information terminals have become diversified and widespread. Use of multiple devices, such as desktop computers, tablet computers and smartphones, has become popular. Accordingly, multi-device interaction has been a subject of extensive research. Chen explored joint interactions on a smartphone and smartwatch [15], and, Kane combined laptop and tabletop interaction [16]. Baur explored optical projection as a metaphor for interaction between a handheld device and stable display [17]. AMP-D [25] project ambient information with wearable projector. They also address concept and design to combine ambient floor display and private hand display with hand gesture. This study unveils effectiveness to collaborate data among hand display, public ambient display and a smartphone with some hand gestures. ReflectoSlates [24] combine tabletops and projector and camera system to allow for bringing personal contents to public tabletop display and carrying away information on the tabletop display. Gravi-tySpace [21] are composed of touch-sensitive furniture, pressure sensing floor and projector deployed under the floor. It realize kind of smart room and allow to track users and recognize their activities. In this research, floor back projection can provide enough information to user with embodiment. These studies show that multi-device interaction makes information processing rich and comfortable.

It is necessary to transfer objects smoothly among multi-devices. Rekimoto proposed a direct manipulation technique for a multiple computer environment, Pick-and-Drop [18]. Yatani proposed techniques for transfer from a mobile device to a remote device using toss motion.

3 Wiifp and the Smartphone

WIIFP has advantages in comparison with smartphones. First, WIIFP allows user to access information without retrieving the device. Even user attach arm strap or some holder to his/her own body, both hands occupy slightly. For example, it is slightly hard to drink water from bottle grasped by own single hand while controlling some information terminal. Thus, information access is quick and easy in comparison with typical smartphone. Second, floor projection is large and public. Therefore, WIIFP performs well at sharing information with other users, if user can find adequate place such as flat surface, appropriate surface color and public situation.

WIIFP also has several disadvantages in comparison with smartphones. First, it is more burdensome to input using hands and feet than to input using smartphones, which requires using only fingers. Second, input by WIIFP is not accurate, as shown in [5], because the operating point is farther than the smartphone and the user cannot touch the contents directly by hands. Third, the floor projection may be seen by people around the user.

Considering the above, WIIFP is suitable for applications that request simple operations and watched frequently such as map navigation. In contrast, input by WIIFP is not suitable for applications that request many operations such as e-mail and SNS. On the other hand, smartphones are not suitable for applications that request simple operations such as checking annotations, because of the necessity to retrieve the device from a pocket or bag. In addition, at least one hand is restrained to holding the smartphone even while confirming the information.

In addition, some relevant researches proof and assist above features. ShoeSense [22] focuses gestural interaction when standing. Shoe-mounted depth sensor can recognize three-gesture sets to enable unobtrusive always-available input without some body strains. Jason [23] focus to Foot-based gesture. They explored the mapping of foot-based gestures to mobile device commands and interaction gestures. Multitoe [20] realize floors based on high-resolution multi-touch input to deploy FTIR, Front-DI and touch panel.

Thus, we propose interaction between WIIFP and smartphones to take advantages of WIIFP and comfort mobile computing. Figure 2 shows the conceptual diagram of the extension of a smartphone with WIIFP. The user can lay out some applications such as maps, news readers and web browsers in WIIFP.

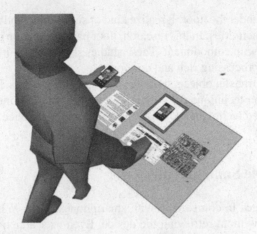

Fig. 2. Conceptual diagram of extension of smartphone with WIIFP.

4 System

4.1 System Configuration

We implemented WIIFP as shown in Fig. 3. The system consists of an RGB-D sensor, a mobile projector, and a gyro sensor. All the components are mounted on the user's chest. We used a Seeser M1 (ESplus Korea) laser micro projector to project visual feedback onto the floor. Furthermore, we used an InertiaCube4 (InterSense, Inc.) to measure the orientation of the system and to fix the projected image on the floor. This prevented the projected image from moving because of the user's motion when stepping on the floor. We used a DS325 (SoftKinetic) as an RGB-D sensor. The position and the motion of hands and toes were detected by the depth sensor in the same way of [5]. The DS325 is robust against changes in background color and ambient light. The physical burden on the user is light, and the chest mounting is more socially acceptable than mounting on the user's head because the user wears only one device on the chest. All image processing and control of input/output are managed on a desktop computer (Core i7-3770 K 3.50 GHz, RAM: 16.0 GB). The desktop computer placed on a desk is wired to the depth sensor, projector, and gyro sensor. WIIFP enables the user to input to the contents in the floor projection by using hands and feet as described in [5]. In contrast, in this study, we focused on the combination hand input of WIIFP and the smartphone and explored the potential of this combination. The smartphone used was Nexus 5 (LG Electronics, Inc.: 2.26 GHz, RAM: 2.0 GB). The smartphone and WIIFP were connected via wireless LAN (IEEE 801.11a).

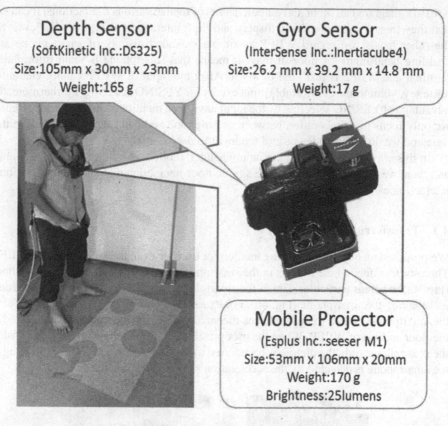

Depth Sensor
(SoftKinetic Inc.:DS325)
Size:105mm x 30mm x 23mm
Weight:165 g

Gyro Sensor
(InterSense Inc.:Inertiacube4)
Size:26.2 mm x 39.2 mm x 14.8 mm
Weight:17 g

Mobile Projector
(Esplus Inc.:seeser M1)
Size:53mm x 106mm x 20mm
Weight:170 g
Brightness:25lumens

Fig. 3. WIIFP configuration

4.2 Design Criteria

We designed the combination of WIIFP and the smartphone with several design criteria. First, great changes in the smartphone GUI bewilder the user because smartphones are widespread and popular for mobile computing. Therefore, the existing smartphone GUI is adopted for the smartphone GUI in the proposed system. We also set WIIFP as an assist and extension of the smartphone. It means that our proposed interaction is smartphone oriented. It is major difference of AMP-D [25]. Second, WIIFP and the smartphone can be operated independently because the user can access information anywhere and anytime. This study focused on the joint interaction of WIIFP and the smartphone. Third, WIIFP GUI is designed to be similar to the smartphone GUI not bewilder the user. AMP-D [25] implement some hand gestures, private display on hand and ambient display on floor. It allows to move data between hand display, public floor display and smart phone display with some multiple gestures. They make a complex prototype and contribute interaction concept. Our system and scenario are quite similar to AMP-D at a glance. However, note that, our proposed system is smartphone oriented because WIIFP is not suitable for applications that request many operations. On the other hand,

AMP-D integrated all input and outputchannel to realize various interactions. It can say that they treat smartphone, hand display and floor interaction as equivalents level. On the other hands, we regard WIIFP as simple extended display of smart phone and enabling hand input for floor display. It means that smartphone is main information terminal and WIIFP is just kind of assist. Also, toe input of WIIFP cannot guarantee accuracy, volume and comfortable input except for YES/NO selecting. Furthermore, the advantage of YES/NO selecting by toe input have been mentioned in [5] already. Hence, we only focus to collaboration between smart phone and hand input of WIIFP in this time and we do not includea task of toe input to user study.

In this way, we try to keep the input channel, motion and data attribute as simple, and then, we examined that even the simple floor interaction and simple data attribute interaction can enhance usability.

4.3   Transferring Technique

We proposed an object transferring method for transfer from the smartphone to WIIFP. The user transfers whole objects in the smartphone simply by shaking the smartphone (Fig. 4a), whereas particular data in the smartphone is transferred by pressing the data and shaking the smartphone (Fig. 4b). For example, the user browses web pages using the smartphone. When the user shakes the smartphone, the web page is transferred to the floor surface of WIIFP. When the user presses a picture in the web page and shakes the smartphone, only the picture is transferred to the floor surface of WIIFP. Shaking of the smartphone is detected by the acceleration sensor in the smartphone.

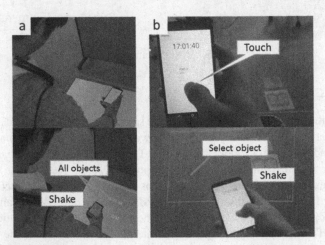

Fig. 4. Motion for transferring from smartphone to WIIFP; a. Transferring all objects; b. Transferring selected object

On the other hand, transfer of data from WIIFP to the smartphone is performed by holding the smartphone over the data in WIIFP (Fig. 5left). In this way, the user can transfer data simply by using one hand to hold the smartphone. The user can transfer not only data such pictures but also perform functions such as using application shortcuts and switching on the silent mode of smartphone. For example, when the user holds the smartphone over the application shortcut of a map, the map application is started in the smartphone (Fig. 5right). Also note that, when the user selects the application shortcut using WIIFP, the map application is started in WIIFP. The aiming point on the display of WIIFP is fixed by the position of the smartphone. The position of the smartphone is detected by tracking the color marker on the smartphone by the RGB camera of WIIFP.

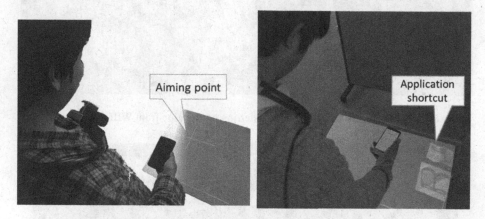

Fig. 5. Motion for transferring from WIIFP to smartphone (Left) and application shortcut (Right).

5 Scenario

In this section, we describe a scenario that illustrates the rich and innovative mobile computing achieved by collaboration between the smartphone and WIIFP. We then described the features and advantages of this interaction.

(1) A college student equips this system on the body and walks downtown. An email is received. The notice of the emailis displayed on WIIFP (Fig. 6a). He understands that it was an e-mail from his friend. Therefore, he takes a smartphone out of a pocket and holds it over the notice to confirm the e-mail contents (Fig. 6bc).

(2) He exchanges emails and promises to meet the friend in a park. He opens a map application to confirm the route to the park by using the smartphone. Then, a map is displayed automatically on WIIFP. The map of WIIFP displays a range that is wider than the map of the smartphone. Thus, he can see the outskirts of the map displayed on the smartphone (Fig. 7a). He starts navigation to the park by using the smartphone, as WIIFP shows navigation at the same time. He puts the smartphone away in the pocket and, walks to the park with hands-free use of just WIIFP.

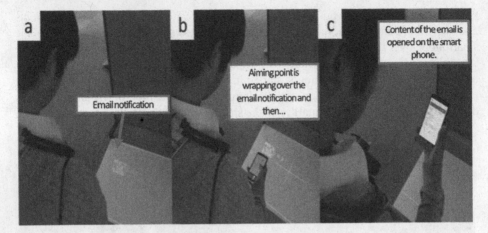

Fig. 6. a. Notification on WIIFP: bc. Transferring notification from WIIFP to smartphone

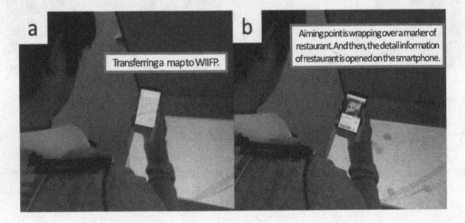

Fig. 7. Map application

(3) He meets the friend and searches for neighboring restaurants for a lunch by using the web browser via the smartphone. He finds a restaurant and transfers the web page of the restaurant to WIIFP by shaking the smartphone. This allows him to share the web page with the friend and to keep it for comparison with the web pages of other restaurants. Furthermore, he can confirm the route to the restaurant by using WIIFP while reading the web pages of the restaurant (Fig. 7b). The web page on WIIFP can be transferred to the smartphone of the friend by holding the smartphone of the friend over WIIFP.

The features and advantages of interaction in events (1)–(3) in the scenario above are described below.

(1) The user can check the notification visually without taking the smartphone out from a pocket. If the notifications are not private and request a simple operation such as

schedule reminders and news, the user can perform it just using WIIFP. Otherwise, the user can transfer information from WIIFP to the smartphone quickly by holding the smartphone over it.

(2) WIIFP helps the user grasp necessary information efficiently by displaying information that supports display by the smartphone. In addition, if the application does not need much operation, the user can put the smartphone in the pocket and use WIIFP. In consequence, the user need not hold the device and do not deed to watch the hand closely.

(3) The user can share information with other people smoothly and easily by transferring it from the smartphone to WIIFP. In addition, because of the extension of display and input area, the user can multi-task.

6 User Study

We conducted a user study to gather feedback on the extension of the smartphone with WIIFP. The participants performed five tasks regarding the transfer of information between the smartphone and WIIFP. The participants performed transfer of all objects and selected objects from the smartphone to WIIFP. In particular, the participants transferred clock and notepad widgets on the home screen of smartphone (Fig. 4). In addition, they performed transfer from WIIFP to the smartphone. The participants transferred the e-mail notification (Fig. 6) and operated application shortcut (Fig. 5) by holding the smartphone over WIIFP. As a more specific task, the participants used the map application and searched for a restaurant (Fig. 7). The participants confirmed the route to the restaurant by using WIIFP at the same time as they checked the web page of the restaurant by using the smartphone, that is, they multi-tasked.

The study took approximately 30 min. Subsequently, we interviewed the participants and sent questionnaires. The questionnaire items were "Do you feel easy?", "Do you feel burdened?", "Do you find it useful?" and "Do you want to use it?" The participants were 15 males, with age in the range of 23 to 25. All of them use smartphones every day.

7 Result and Discussion

The results of questionnaire are shown in Fig. 8. We extracted the participants' responses and present them here. The multi-tasking ability was appreciated by almost all participants. For example, two of the responses were "This task is aptly composed of a large display of WIIFP and dexterous operation by the smartphone." and "It is efficient to confirm the route of the restaurant while reading the information about the restaurant." Furthermore, some participants liked the behavior of WIIFP by which information can be shared with other people. They wanted to share information such as "pictures," "web pages," and "maps" with other people. In regard to the e-mail notification, two of the responses were "It is useful to check the visual notification without taking the smartphone out from a pocket" and "The motion of transferring from WIIFP to the smartphone felt easy." However, holding the smartphone over the notification was burdensome

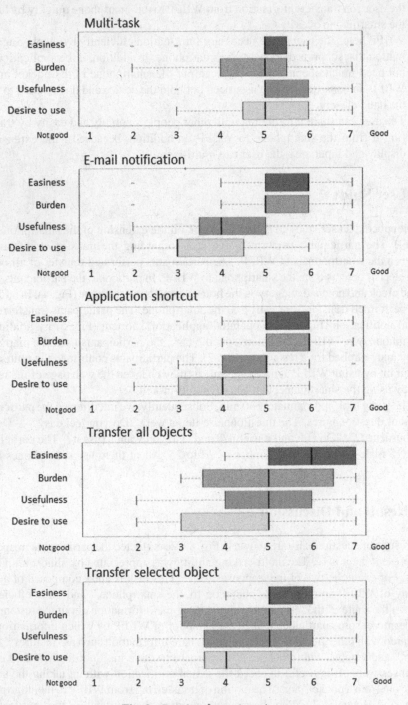

Fig. 8. Results of questionnaires

because the smartphone can make transition to a mail application with a few operations by the fingers. Generally, the participants did not want to use WIIFP because of "burden of wear," "appearance of user," and "projected image seen around the user."

Almost all of the participants were able to use the smartphone and WIIFP without difficulties or problems. In contrast, some subjects reported issues of occlusion when they held up the smartphone over WIIFP to transfer data from WIIFP to the smartphone. For a few participants, WIIFP sometimes recognized the normal use of the smartphone as holding the smartphone over the display of WIIFP. However, when they became familiar with the operation, this problem did not recur.

According to the results, we found out that WIIFP as an extension of the smartphone is suitable for Multi-task and multi-users. Therefore, we will focus on these utilization features of WIIFP.

Recently, some people put small smartphone in own pocket and big large tablet in a bag. They use both devices selectively based on adequate situation such as sitting, standing in train and walking. In the case of realizing same situation by those multiple devices, we assume that it causes some burden to user due to using devices selectively.

8   Conclusion

We proposed an interaction between hand input of WIIFP and smartphones. Also, we described an efficient method and typical scenario of using this interaction. We studied the usability of this interaction and obtained feedback on using the smartphone and WIIFP together. The results showed that the combination of the smartphone and WIIFP is suitable for multi-tasking and multi-users.

References

1. Pinhanez, C.S.: The everywhere displays projector; a device to create ubiquitous graphical interfaces. In: Ubiquitous Computing 2001 (Ubicomp 2001), pp. 12–17 (2001)
2. Wilson, A.D.: Play anywhere; a compact interactive tabletop projection-vision system. In: UIST 2005 Proceedings of the 18th Annual ACM Symposium on User Interface Software and Technology (2005)
3. Konishi, T., Tajimi, K., Sakata, N., Nishida, S.: Projection stabilizing method for palm-top display with wearable projector. In: 13th IEEE International Symposium on Wearable Computers Advances in Wearable Computing 2009, pp. 13–20, September 2009
4. Tajimi, K., Uemura, K., Kajiwara, Y., Sakata, N., Nishida, S.: Stabilization method for floor projection with a hip-mounted projector. In: Proceedings of the ICAT2010, pp. 77–83, December 2010
5. Matsuda, D., Sakata, N., Nishida, S.: Wearable input/output interface for floor projection using hands and a toe. In: ICAT, pp. 122–128
6. Matsuda, D., Uemura, K., Sakata, N., Nishida, S.: Toe input using mobile projector and kinect sensor. In: 16th International Symposium on Wearable Computers (ISWC 2012), pp. 48–51 (2012)
7. Kurata, T., Okuma, T., Kourogi, M., Sakaue, K.: The hand mouse: GMM hand color classification and mean shift tracking. In: Proceedings of the 2nd International Workshop on Recognition, Analysis and Tracking of Faces and Gestures in Realtime Systems, pp. 119–124

8. Ono, T., Mukawa, N: An eye tracking system based on eye ball model. In: Toward Realization of Gaze Controlled Input Device. Information Processing Research Report 2001-HI-93, pp. 47–54 (2001)

9. Wellner, P.: Interacting with paper on the DigitalDesk. Commun. ACM **36**(7), 87–96 (1993)

10. Tojo, K., Hiura, S., Inokuchi, S.: 3-D tele-direction interface using video projector. In: Trans. Virt. Real. Soc. Jpn. **7**(2), June 2002

11. Karitsuka, T., Sato, K.: A wearable mixed reality with an on-board projector. In: ISMAR 2003 Proceedings of the 2nd IEEE/ACM International Symposium on Mixed and Augmented Reality

12. Yamamoto, G., Sato, K.: PALMbit: a PALM interface with projector-camera system. In: UbiComp 2007 Adjunct Proceedings of 9th International Conference on Ubiquitous Computing, Innsbruck, Austria, pp. 276–279 (2007)

13. Mistry, P., Maes, P., Chang, L.: Wuw - wear ur world - a wearable gestural interface. In: Proceedings of the 27th International Conference Extended Abstracts on Human Factors in Computing Systems, pp. 4111–4116

14. Harrison, C., Benko, H., Wilson, A.D.: OmniTouch wearable multitouch interaction everywhere. In: Proceedings of the 24th Annual ACM Symposium on User Interface Software and Technology, UIST 2011 (2011)

15. Chen, X.A., Grossman, T., Wigdor, D., Fitzmaurice, G.: Duet: exploring joint interactions on a smart phone and a smart watch. In: Proceedings of ACM CHI 2014 (2014)

16. Kane, S., Avrahami, D., Wobbrock, J., Harrison, B., Rea, A., Philipose, M., LaMarca, A.: Bonfire: A nomadic system for hybrid laptop-tabletop interaction. In: Proceedings of the UIST 2009, pp. 129–138 (2009)

17. Baur, D., Boring, S., Feiner, S.: Virtual projection: exploring optical projection as a metaphor for multi-device interaction. In: Proceedings of ACM CHI 2012 (2012)

18. Jun, R.: Pick-and-Drop: a direct manipulation technique for multiple computer environments. In: Proceedings of UIST 1997, pp. 31–39 (1997)

19. Yatani, K., Tamura, K., Hiroki, K., Sugimoto, M., Hasizume, H.: Toss-it: intuitive information transfer techniques for mobile devices. In: Extended Abstracts of the ACM CHI Conference on Human Factors in Computing Systems, pp. 1881–1884 (2005)

20. Augsten, T., Kaefer, K., Meusel, R., Fetzer, C., Kanitz, D., Stoff, T., Becker, T., Holz, C., Baudisch, P.: Multitoe: high-precision interaction with back-projected floors based on high-resolution multi-touch input. In: Proceedings of the 23nd Annual ACM Symposium on User Interface Software and Technology (UIST 2010), pp. 209–218. ACM, New York (2010)

21. Branzel, A., Holz, C., Hoffmann, D., Schmidt, D., Knaust, M., Lühne, P., Meusel, R., Richter, S., Baudisch, P.: GravitySpace: tracking users and their poses in a smartroom using a pressure-sensing floor. In: Proceedings of the SIGCHI Conference on Human Factors in Computing Systems (CHI 2013), pp. 725–734. ACM, New York (2013)

22. Bailly, G., Müller, J., Rohs, M., Wigdor, D., Kratz, S.: ShoeSense: a new perspective on gestural interaction and wearable applications. In: Proceedings of the SIGCHI Conference on Human Factors in Computing Systems (CHI 2012), pp. 1239–1248. ACM, New York (2012)

23. Alexander, J., Han, T., Judd, W., Irani, P., Subramanian, S.: Putting your best foot forward: investigating real-world mappings for foot-based gestures. In: Proceedings of the 30th International Conference on Human Factors in Computing Systems (CHI 2012), April 2012

24. Plasencia, D.M., Knibbe, J., Haslam, D.A., Latimer, J.E., Dennis, B., Lewis, J.G., Whiteley, M., Coyle, D.: ReflectoSlates: personal overlays for tabletops combining camera-projector systems and retroreflective materials. In: CHI 2014 Extended Abstracts on Human Factors in Computing Systems (CHI EA 2014) (2014)

25. Winkler, C., Seifert, J., Dobbelstein, D., Rukzio, E.: Pervasive information through constant personal projection: the ambient mobile pervasive display (AMP-D). In: Proceedings of the SIGCHI Conference on Human Factors in Computing Systems (CHI 2014), pp. 4117–4126. ACM, New York (2014). doi:http://dx.doi.org/10.1145/2556288.2557365
26. Kurata, T., Sakata, N., Kourogi, M., Kuzuoka, H., Billinghurst, M.: The advantages and limitations of a wearable active camera/laser in remote collaboration. In: Conference on Supplement (Interactive Poster) of CSCW (2004)
27. Honda, D., Sakata, N., Nishida, S.: Activity recognition for risk management with installed sensor in smart and cell phone. In: HCI International 2011, pp. 230–239 (2011)
28. Sakata, N., Kurata, T., Kato, T., Kourogi, M., Kuzuoka, H.: WACL: supporting telecommunications using wearable active camera with laser pointer. In: Proceedings of ISWC2003, NY, USA, pp. 53–56 (2003)

Introducing Gamification to Cleaning and Housekeeping Work

Satoshi Ichimura[✉]

Information Design Course, School of Social Information Studies,
Otsuma Women's University, Karakida 2-7-1, Tama, Tokyo 206-8540, Japan
ichimura@otsuma.ac.jp

Abstract. Gamification is the concept that utilizing elements and ideas of video games in non-gaming fields. It aims at improving user experience, user engagement and users' motivation by utilizing elements and mechanisms by which video games entertain many people. In the paper, we explain some basic ideas to let people enjoy housekeeping work, and propose a vacuum cleaner with gamification elements as an example of the ideas. As a result of the experiments, it turned out that our vacuum cleaner with game elements could provide more enjoyable experience to users than usual.

Keywords: Gamification · Cleaning · Housekeeping · Vacuum cleaner

1 Introduction

Although household chores as typified by cleaning must be repeatedly done every day, sustaining the motivation to do them is not easy for many people. Therefore, we thought that it is important to improve the motivation of doing housekeeping, and came up with an idea to introduce gamification elements to housekeeping.

Gamification is the concept of applying game mechanics and game design techniques to fields other than games. It aims at improving user experience, user engagement and users' motivation by utilizing game elements and mechanisms that attract a number of people.

Game elements include mechanisms to visualize the results that the user achieved through the use of ranking, scoring or giving a badge. It becomes easier to understand how hard he/she tried or how much his/her progress is being achieved. Furthermore, merging SNS mechanisms to gamification has a possibility to provide pleasure of collaboration or competition with friends having the same purpose, so that it could increase users' motivation more.

In this paper, we propose a vacuum cleaner with gamification elements. The vacuum cleaner has an acceleration sensor, and is capable of detecting the movement of cleaning behavior. As a result of the experiments, it turned out that our vacuum cleaner with game mechanisms could provide more enjoyable experience to users than usual.

© Springer International Publishing AG 2017
T. Yoshino et al. (Eds.): CollabTech 2017, LNCS 10397, pp. 182–190, 2017.
DOI: 10.1007/978-3-319-63088-5_16

2   Backgrounds

During recent years "gamification" has gained significant attention. It is an idea to apply elements and ideas, that attract many gamers, of video games to non-gaming fields. Gamification is also said to be good at maintaining motivation and preventing getting bored.

As elements to improve motivation, Scientific American [10] claimed the following three points:

1. Autonomy: People can strive if they feel that "they are responsible and actively doing things, not being forced to do them".
2. Value: Motivation is improved if people can find value in goals. If they can recognize that the goal is important, they are likely to make effort.
3. Competence: The more you improve, the more your motivation increases.

Kishimoto [7] claimed the following points are important to design attactive computer games.

1. Immediate feedback: It is important in game design to immediately return the responses to user actions. If the reaction is slow, the user can not enjoy the game itself.
2. Growth visualization: Indicates the growth of the character self-projected by the user. The user gets into the game when he/she wants to see their growth.
3. Achievable goal: If a difficult goal is imposed in the early stages, the user stops the game before feeling fun. Give users a small sense of accomplishment frequently.

Many games have elements that improve users' motivation as mentioned above. Gamification aims to utilize these elements to revitalize the behavior of daily life.

3   Related Work

Here we describe examples of gamification where the game is applied to solve problems that happens in daily life.

Nike + Running [4] is a smartphone application that calculates mileage and calorie consumption. GPS in the smartphone is used. The level is judged according to the running distance, and the level is visualized by color. The color level starts from yellow, goes through orange, green, blue and goes black. When the running situation is published to Facebook, and "Like" arrives from a friend, cheering voice is emitted during running.

Foursquare [1] is a smartphone application that automatically records shops and facilities visited by users. GPS in the smartphone is used. Users can earn points by "checking in" to the places, and earn badges such as Mayor (mayor) of that place when checking more than predetermined number of times. Users can compete with their friends.

Ingress [2] is also a smartphone application that makes walking activity a funny game. A user can acquire a base (portal) that is located all over the world by vising the location, and get the area as his/her territory. The portal is often located near famous historical sites or art work, so that a user can enjoy regional sightseeing at the same time.

Studyplus [5] is a learning management SNS integrated with gaming mechanisms to promote continuation of learning. When the user inputs the progress of the day into the site, the progress is visualized as a graph. In addition, users can compete with a number of anonymous friends having the same goal.

Microsoft [6] introduced gamification called "language quality game" to the development process of Windows multilingual version. During localization, correcting misunderstanding of languages requires a tremendous amount of work, so it was a problem that the motivation of debugging staffs gradually declined. In the language quality game, Microsoft employees around the world were asked to find suspicious word. Every time they find a suspicious word, they get a point. Based on that point, ranking was announced to maintain motivation. It was reported that more than 7000 suspicious word had been discovered.

Hashiguchi et al. [8] proposes an application with a gamification mechanism to correct irregular sleeping time in college life. As a result of comparing the application with and without gamification function, it turned out that users of the application with gamification function had been able to use the application longer.

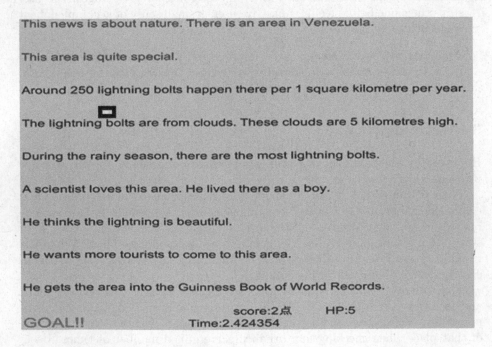

Fig. 1. English reading game.

We have conducted research on how to utilize the effect of gamification since several years ago, and we developed a PC game called "English reading game" (Fig. 1). The application constantly monitors the movement of the user's eye using an eye tracker Tobii EyeX Controller [9]. The color of letters that a user has seen changes. A high score is given when the eye moves in the order in which the English sentences are written, and a low score is given when the user read the same sentence more than once. Various badges are given depending on the score, and also the level is determined by the score.

In order to examine the usefulness of gamification function, we conducted an experiment to compare different versions with and without the gamification mechanism mentioned above. As a result of the evaluation, the motivation of reading the English sentence was higher in the version with the gamification element.

4   System Design and Implementation

4.1   System Design

We conducted research on how to utilize the effect of gamification since several years ago. In this paper, we propose a vacuum cleaner that can make cleaning work fun. A typical user might be a person who thinks cleaning is troublesome, or who cannot maintain his/her motivation for cleaning.

There is no vacuum cleaner equipped with the gamification function in the market so far. Development of Conventional vacuum cleaners has been aiming only for performance improvement such as suction power, silence, power saving, etc. As far as we know, vacuum cleaners have not been developed from the viewpoint of making housework fun. We think it is necessary to support housekeeping work from such a new viewpoint.

Our a vacuum cleaner has following unique functions:

1. Score acquisition: The device detects the motion of the vacuum cleaner and calculates its score, whereas score is high when the speed of the movement is appropriate. Score is determined from 1 point to 5 point according to the movement.
2. Game sound generation: Different sound is generated depending on the acquired score. A user can know how good the movement of the vacuum cleaner was by listening to the sound.
3. Twitter submission: When a user starts cleaning, the system submits a tweet to Twitter, and lets his/her friends know he/she starts cleaning. In addition, if the tweet is retweeted or replied by someone, a cheering message is displayed in the user's PC screen and a funny sound is generated.

A device capable of measuring triaxle acceleration is attached to the vacuum cleaner (Fig. 2). The device attached to the vacuum cleaner transmits the detected motion to a PC for processing via XBee wireless [11], and the PC analyzes the motion.

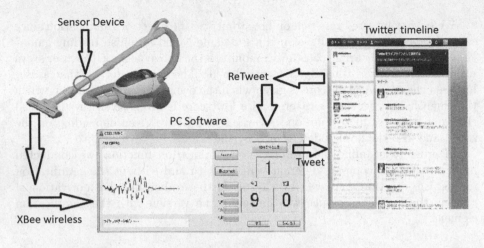

Fig. 2. System architecture.

Fig. 3. PC software.

When a user starts cleaning, he/she presses the "Declaration of Start" button and logs in to Twitter account, then a tweet like "Cleaning started on January 30th at 17:03! The yesterday's score was 120 points # Cleaning Gamification" is posted in the Twitter timeline. When "End" button is pressed, today's score is recorded (See Fig. 3).

4.2 System Implementation

This system consists of a device attached to the vacuum cleaner (Fig. 4) and PC software (Fig. 3) running on the PC. The device attached to the vacuum cleaner detects the reciprocating motion of the vacuum cleaner with built-in

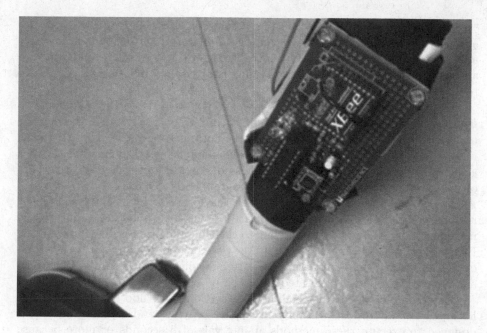

Fig. 4. Sensor device.

acceleration sensor and transmits the motion value to the PC. The software on the PC analyzes the reciprocating motion transmitted from the device, calculates game score.

Device Attached to the Vacuum Cleaner. Three axis acceleration sensor, KXM 52-1050 of KYONIX Corporation, to acquire reciprocating motion is built in the device. This sensor is capable of measuring XYZ-axes acceleration in a range of ±2G. An 8-bit microprocessor PIC16LF88, which is often used in small built-in computer systems due to features such as low power consumption, is embedded in the sensor.

Figure 4 shows how the sensor device attached to the vacuum cleaner. The program that controls the device attached to the vacuum cleaner is written in assembler. Through this program, the 3-axis acceleration data are transmitted to the PC. For wireless communication between the PC and the device, XBee module [11] is used. XBee's wireless reaches about 30 m indoors.

PC Software. Software running on the PC processes reciprocating motion data transmitted from the device attached to the vacuum cleaner via XBee, and calculates game score, etc. Software is mostly implemented in C++, and Twitter linkage part is written using Java Twitter4J library [12].

Software has functions to display the waveform of 3-axis acceleration data from the sensor device, calculate game score and also post tweets to Twitter when a user starts cleaning or tweet is retweeted or replied by someone.

The usage of software is explained using Fig. 3.

By pressing the "Connect" button, a communication between PC software and the device attached to the vacuum cleaner starts, and the waveform of 3-axis acceleration data is displayed in the left figure. At the same time, software automatically posts a tweet, like "Cleaning started on January 30th at 17:03", to Twitter.

The numbers under the text "Today" and "Yesterday" in the middle of the figure are today's high score and last high score, respectively. Also, the number under the text "Declaration of Start" is the current total score. The bar to the right of "1 point" to "5 points" indicates the number of each point that the user acquired. When the "End" button is pressed, the score of today and the score of yesterday are recorded and software program ends.

The score is designed to be high when the speed of the cleaning movement is appropriate. Score is determined from 1 point to 5 point according to the movement, and a sound corresponding to the acquired score is emitted from the PC speaker. Also, during cleaning, if the tweet posted by software is retweeted or replied by someone, a cheering message is displayed in the user's PC screen and a cheering sound is generated.

The updateStatus method and getRetweetCount method of the Twitter 4 J library are used to post a tweet and acquire retweets and replies. Software is designed to execute these methods at intervals of 5 seconds or more because Twitter API does not allow applications to issue more than 180 requests per 15 min.

5 Evaluations

We conducted experiments in order to verify the effectiveness of the proposed system.

5.1 Experiment 1

The subjects, eight males and two females in the early twenties, were asked to clean rooms for five minutes through the use of a vacuum cleaner with gamification device, and were required to answer some questionnaire. To the question "Was it fun to clean a room?", the subjects answered in 5 grades of 5:strongly yes, 4:yes, 3:yes/no, 2:no, 1:strongly no.

As the result, the average score was 4.5, indicating that the satisfaction level was high.

We also conducted experiments to compare our system and Twitter standard client. The same subjects, eight males and two females in the early twenties, were asked to use Twitter official client and enter some comments when they start and end cleaning. To the question "Was it fun to clean a room?", the subjects answered in 5 grades of 5:strongly yes, 4:yes, 3:yes/no, 2:no, 1:strongly no.

As the result, the average score was 2.1. This result indicates our system appears to get a higher satisfaction than Twitter client.

5.2   Experiment 2

Next two experiments were conducted to compare whether each function provided by this system was valid or not.

First, the function to generate game sound was tested. Our device detects the motion of the vacuum cleaner and calculates its score, and game sound is generated depending on the acquired score. To the question "Was it fun to clean a room?", the subjects answered in 5 grades of 5:strongly yes, 4:yes, 3:yes/no, 2:no, 1:strongly no. Subjects were the same eight males and two females.

As the result, the average score was 4.3 when the sound generation function was used, and 3.4 when the sound generation function was not used.

Second, Twitter submission function was tested. When a user starts cleaning, the system submits a tweet to Twitter, and if the tweet is retweeted or replied by someone, a cheering message is displayed in the user's PC screen and a funny sound is generated. To the question "Was it fun to clean a room?", the subjects answered in 5 grades of 5:strongly yes, 4:yes, 3:yes/no, 2:no, 1:strongly no. Subjects were the same eight males and two females.

As the result, the average score was 3.5 when the Twitter submission function was used, and 2.8 when the Twitter submission was not used.

Above results indicate certain effects are recognized for both the sound generation function and Twitter submission function. Both functions indicated that cleaning became fun by adding gaming elements. It turned out that the purpose of this research was achieved.

6   Conclusions

In this paper, we explained the outline of gamification, and also described our sample application to gamify household chores.

We would like to build a mechanism on the SNS that encourages competition compared with others and a mechanism to give pleasure that everyone is enjoying it. In addition, if a location sensor that detects the cleaning place can be installed to the device, for example, an enjoyable treasure hunting game may be implemented.

We would also like to support not only cleaning but also other tasks, like gardening, toothbrushing, make-up and other activities at home.

This work was supported by JSPS KAKENHI Number 16K00506.

References

1. Foursquare (2017). https://foursquare.com/
2. Ingress (2017). https://www.ingress.com/
3. Mailbox (2015). http://www.mailboxapp.com/
4. Nike+ Running (2017). http://www.nike.com/us/en_us/c/nike-plus
5. Studyplus, Studyplus SNS, in Japanese (2017). http://studyplus.jp/
6. language-quality-game, Microsoft (2012). https://social.technet.microsoft.com/wiki/contents/articles/9299.language-quality-game.aspx

7. Kishimoto, Education using Game Design, in Japanese (2013). http://hrdm.jp/2013/04/post-129.html
8. Hashiguchi, Correcting irregular sleeping time by gamification, Graduation thesis, in Japanese (2015). http://www.net.c.dendai.ac.jp/hashiguchi/11nc038.html
9. Tobii EyeX Controller (2017). http://www.tobiipro.com/
10. Yuhas, D.: Three Critical Elements Sustain Motivation, Scientific American (2014). http://www.scientificamerican.com/article/three-critical-elements-sustain-motivation/
11. XBee (2017). http://www.zigbee.org/
12. Twitter 4J (2017). https://github.com/yusuke/twitter4j

Author Index

Printed in the United States
By Bookmasters